Online Communication in a Second Language

SECOND LANGUAGE ACQUISITION
Series Editor: Professor David Singleton, *Trinity College, Dublin, Ireland*

This series brings together titles dealing with a variety of aspects of language acquisition and processing in situations where a language or languages other than the native language is involved. Second language is thus interpreted in its broadest possible sense. The volumes included in the series all offer in their different ways, on the one hand, exposition and discussion of empirical findings and, on the other, some degree of theoretical reflection. In this latter connection, no particular theoretical stance is privileged in the series; nor is any relevant perspective – sociolinguistic, psycholinguistic, neurolinguistic, etc. – deemed out of place. The intended readership of the series includes final-year undergraduates working on second language acquisition projects, postgraduate students involved in second language acquisition research, and researchers and teachers in general whose interests include a second language acquisition component.

Full details of all the books in this series and of all our other publications can be found on http://www.multilingual-matters.com, or by writing to Multilingual Matters, St Nicholas House, 31–34 High Street, Bristol BS1 2AW, UK.

Online Communication in a Second Language

Social Interaction, Language Use, and Learning Japanese

Sarah E. Pasfield-Neofitou

MULTILINGUAL MATTERS
Bristol • Buffalo • Toronto

Library of Congress Cataloging in Publication Data
Pasfield-Neofitou, Sarah E.
Online Communication in a Second Language: Social Interaction, Language Use, and
Learning Japanese/ Sarah E. Pasfield-Neofitou.
Second Language Acquisition: 66
Includes bibliographical references and index.
1. Japanese language—Study and teaching—Foreign speakers. 2. Japanese language-
-Computer-assisted instruction for foreign speakers. 3. Japanese language—Social
aspects. 4. Web-based instruction—Social aspects. 5. Online social networks. 6. Internet
in education. I. Title.
PL519.P37 2012 495.6'8007–dc23 2012022013

British Library Cataloguing in Publication Data
A catalogue entry for this book is available from the British Library.

ISBN-13: 978-1-84769-825-4 (hbk)
ISBN-13: 978-1-84769-824-7 (pbk)

Multilingual Matters
UK: St Nicholas House, 31–34 High Street, Bristol BS1 2AW, UK.
USA: UTP, 2250 Military Road, Tonawanda, NY 14150, USA.
Canada: UTP, 5201 Dufferin Street, North York, Ontario M3H 5T8, Canada.

The policy of Multilingual Matters/Channel View Publications is to use papers that are
natural, renewable and recyclable products, made from wood grown in sustainable
forests. In the manufacturing process of our books, and to further support our policy,
preference is given to printers that have FSC and PEFC Chain of Custody certification.
The FSC and/or PEFC logos will appear on those books where full certification has been
granted to the printer concerned.

Typeset by Techset Composition Ltd., Salisbury, UK.

Contents

Tables and Figures

Tables

Figures

Acknowledgements

I have been very fortunate to have the support of numerous people and institutions in the production of this book, and first and foremost, would like to express my sincere appreciation of the 18 Japanese and 12 Australian volunteers whose generous participation made this research possible, and whose enthusiasm increased my own. My special gratitude goes to A/Prof. Helen Marriott and Dr Robyn Spence-Brown, who mentored me throughout this research. Helen has provided me with constant support and encouragement, sharing her knowledge of the field while allowing me to grow as a researcher. Robyn has also provided me with valuable guidance, in the form of her passion for teaching, and knowledge in the area of second language acquisition. A number of other staff at Monash University also provided me with valuable support, including Prof. Farzad Sharifian, Prof. Ross Mouer, and the late Prof. Michael Clyne. I thank them sincerely for the interest they showed in my research. Dr Hiroko Hashimoto and Mari Morofushi kindly proofread the Japanese version of the interview questions for this project and I am grateful for their support.

I am particularly grateful to my wonderful editors who have made possible the publication of this book, everyone at Multilingual Matters who worked on the production side so efficiently, and the anonymous reviewer who provided valuable suggestions to the manuscript. I was also fortunate to receive feedback on earlier versions of my work from Prof. Tony Liddicoat and Dr Glenn Stockwell, whom I thank warmly for their kindness and advice.

My trip to Japan to complete fieldwork for the current project was greatly facilitated by my friends the Terada and Otsuka families, whom I thank for their hospitality. I also thank Prof. Satoshi Miyazaki and Dr Ji-Hyun Yoon for the use of facilities at Waseda University during my stay.

As always, I owe a large debt to those I love, and am grateful for the support of my friends and family. My brothers, Simon and Mark Pasfield, helped to proofread sections of this text relating to software terminology and World of Warcraft respectively. My parents, Jenny and Alan Pasfield, have given me support and encouragement when I needed it most. Finally, I am indebted to the very first reader of this book, my husband Simon Neofitou, for his unwavering belief in me, and his constant support, care and love. This volume is dedicated to the memory of my grandparents, Irene and Victor Pasfield, and Alison and George English.

1 Introduction

Second language (L2) use and acquisition in Computer Mediated Communication (CMC), such as blogs, social networking, email, and chat, is an increasingly important field. One often-cited yet underexplored benefit of tools such as these is that CMC may provide a vehicle for students to not only have contact with native speakers (NSs) of their target language, but to also learn language outside of the classroom. In particular, little research has been completed on the use of languages other than English in authentic intercultural online settings, outside of teacher- or researcher-led activity.

This book describes a multi-method, longitudinal study of L2 learners' social CMC use, in which over 2000 instances of Australian learners' naturally occurring interaction with their Japanese contacts via blogs, email, video, chat, mobile phone, video games, and social networking were collected, in addition to in-depth interviews with the learners and their informal online contacts. Although the main languages under consideration are Japanese and English, the findings presented should be applicable more widely to other language contexts.

Throughout, the book aims to not only increase our understanding of CMC interaction in an L2, but the nature of language in CMC in general. The volume serves to challenge traditional categorisations of 'synchronous' and 'asynchronous' CMC mediums, assumptions about the 'placelessness' of online domains, and previous characterisations of online conversations as 'haphazard' and 'unstructured', providing an alternate, sophisticated view of CMC interaction which highlights identity, the skilful management of communication, and user agency in interaction with technology.

Online Social Interaction, Language Use, and Language Learning

This book has two interlinked goals. Firstly, from a sociolinguistic standpoint, despite the well-established importance of interaction in the target

1

language (Krashen, 1982; Long, 1983, 1996; Swain, 1985) it appears that there have been very few studies of CMC examining naturally occurring 'authentic interaction'. The present study therefore aims to increase our understanding of intercultural social interaction in L2 CMC, in terms of what language learners do, how, and why, and also to explore the nature of language and communication in CMC in general, and in intercultural CMC in particular.

Secondly, from a pedagogic viewpoint, an understanding of the types of interaction learners take part in outside of the classroom will necessarily have educational implications. As Coulthard (1985) states, a detailed description of the skills of the 'competent non-native speaker' is vital for the effective teaching and learning of additional languages. While Knobel and Lankshear (2004) rightly claim that simply because a practice like blogging is widely engaged in outside of the class does not mean that it should be addressed within class, Matsumoto-Sturt (2003) and Stockwell and Levy (2001) argue that teachers cannot afford to ignore providing students with the basic skills and strategies they will need to deal with Internet use outside of the classroom.

Although these two foci are obviously linked, there has been very little convergence between sociolinguistic and Second Language Acquisition (SLA) approaches to the study of CMC. The present study endeavours to examine how learners utilise CMC socially in their L2, and related opportunities for language learning, within a social realist framework (Sealey & Carter, 2004) by addressing the following questions:

(1) How do learners establish and maintain relationships in which they use a second language online?
(2) What is the nature of learners' CMC, and in what combinations are they using CMC in their second language?
(3) How does the use of CMC in conjunction with other resources provide opportunities for second language acquisition?

Before exploring these issues in detail, this chapter will provide an introduction to the 'language of CMC' and previous research in the area from both a sociolinguistic and SLA perspective. Informed by this state-of-the-art review, the theoretical framework employed in the present volume, Sealey and Carter's (2004) social realist approach, and the methodology of the study, will be introduced.

The 'Language of CMC'

In the introduction to *Computer Mediated Discourse*, Herring (1996b) identifies three key areas for research: the 'language of CMC'; the interplay of technological, social, and contextual factors; and, the role of linguistic variability. Throughout the 'Internet era' of the 1990s and beyond, much research on online communication focused on describing the 'language of CMC', much of which has been criticised as technologically deterministic, in the sense that it viewed online language use as largely determined by the CMC medium utilised.

A large body of work on CMC has drawn a sharp distinction between synchronous and asynchronous communication, and makes comparisons between individual CMC tools and with 'traditional' spoken and written language (Baron, 1998, 2000, 2001; Bordia, 1997; Callot & Belmore, 1996; Crystal, 2001a, 2001b, 2004b; Dimmick *et al.*, 2000; du Bartell, 1995; Ferrara *et al.*, 1991; Lantz, 2001; Mar, 2000; Neuage, 2004; O'Neil & Martin, 2003; Yates, 1996). In this tradition, online Bulletin Board Systems (BBS) were likened to 'pin-up boards' and chat and Instant Messengers (IM) described as 'conversations in writing'.

Many researchers assert that CMC has features that are distinct from either spoken or written communication, and various labels to describe the 'language of CMC' have been coined, including 'Interactive Written Discourse' (Ferrara *et al.*, 1991), 'Electronic Language' (Callot & Belmore, 1996), and of course, Crystal's 'Netspeak' (2001b). More recently, Crystal (2011) has noted the emergence of terms such as 'Electronically Mediated Communication' and 'Digitally Mediated Communication' to incorporate mobile phone and other forms of CMC which do not require a traditional computer.

Some common features of digital writing in English and Japanese include multiple punctuation and eccentric spelling (読みたいですぅ〜〜〜！！！, I want to read iit 〜 〜〜 !!!), capitalization (I'M REALLY ANGRY), emphasis (I'm really *angry*), written-out laughter (ふふふ, hahaha), descriptions of actions ((笑), <laughs>), emoticons (^_^, :-)), abbreviations (lol), rebus writing (4649, CU), and non-linguistic symbols (見ようと思ってます♪, I'm thinking of looking at it♪) (Y. Nishimura, 2007: 169). These features fulfil two main functions: to express prosody or emotion, such as the use of capital letters to add emphatic force or music notes to decorate/denote tone of voice, or to shorten messages, such as the rebus writing CU (see you) or 4649 (*yo-ro-shi-ku*, pleased to meet you, based on the phonetic values of the numbers in Japanese), which originated in pager or cell phone use (Miyake, 2001). Some well-known varieties include '1337' ('leet' or 'elite')-speak, a numbers or symbols for letters substitution system based on English, used mainly by online gamers (Carooso, 2004), and '*gyaru moji*' ('girl-characters'), a Japanese symbol substitution system created by young girls using mobile phones (Hada, 2006).

Reports on CMC language in the popular media link such features of 'CMC language' to 'declining standards' of language, 'poor academic achievement', and 'social breakdown' (Onishi, 2008; Ōtawa, 2007; Strong, 2007; E. Takahashi, 2007). Murray (2000) also summarises previous research as having found that CMC exhibits 'simplified' registers. However, Herring poses the question that if CMC is 'fragmented, agrammatical, and internally disjointed' (1999: 1), why does its popularity continue to grow? Androutsopoulos too challenges the exoticism of language on the Internet, calling it 'the netspeak myth' (2006a: 420) after Dürscheid (2004). Furthermore, not all CMC users make use of the supposedly 'unique' features of 'netspeak' to the same extent – in fact, Dwyer (2007) found that some students reported a dislike for abbreviated forms.

In attempting to describe the 'language of CMC', many researchers have made use of technological categorisations as a starting point. Variables include: 'message size' (Cherney, 1995), 'communication commands available' (Cherney, 1995), 'degree of anonymity' (Selfe & Meyer, 1991), and 'text versus non-text' (Yates & Graddol, 1996), cited in Herring (2003). Yet Androutsopoulos (2006a) characterises the 'first wave' of linguistic CMC studies as overwhelmingly using the distinction between synchronous and asynchronous forms of communication as the pivotal point for linguistic description.

Spoken vs written and synchronous vs asynchronous

Asynchronous forms of CMC typically have greater delays between sending and replying than synchronous forms, as they do not require both users to be logged in simultaneously. Past research has found that asynchronous communication may afford language learners some benefits; for example, by removing some of the pressure associated with face-to-face communication or synchronous CMC (Inagaki, 2006; Itakura & Nakajima, 2001). Synchronous communication tools, on the other hand, typically require both users to be logged in at the same time. One important benefit associated with synchronous technology is an increase in language production, both in terms of complexity and length (Darhower, 2002; Kern, 1995).

Despite the prevalence of the synchronous-asynchronous model, the present study takes the view that technology cannot be neatly separated. Even 'synchronous' tools such as chat programs do not operate on 'real time'. Unlike analogue communication (for example, analogue telephones, radio, etc.) both 'synchronous' and 'asynchronous' CMC tools do not receive a constant stream of input; rather, the program 'samples' at regular intervals to see if any new messages have been sent. In this way, technically, there is no difference between, for example, email, generally thought of as asynchronous, and 'instant' messaging, generally thought of as synchronous. This is especially true when one considers that email clients can be set to automatically check for incoming mail just as frequently as chat applications check for new messages. So-called 'asynchronous' web email applications like Yahoo, Hotmail, or Google Mail (Gmail), and even social networking sites (SNSs) and BBSs also display whether or not a recipient is online, in the same way that 'synchronous' programs do. 'Synchronous' tools like IM allow the sending of 'offline' messages, and hybrid tools like Google Wave and Facebook further blur any distinction. This argument is further expanded upon in Chapter 4, while the example of email, one of the most familiar modes of CMC, is used below to illustrate the inherent tensions in categorisation.

What's an email?

Homer: What's an e-mail?
Lenny: It's a computer thing, like, er, an electric letter.
Carl: Or a quiet phone call.
('The computer war menace shoes', *The Simpsons* ep.12A6, cited in Crystal, 2006: 130)

The quote above, although from a cartoon, bears a striking semblance to many academic descriptions of email, which, for the most part, have translated CMC through previous media (Leung, 2005). Crystal (2006) cites a range of linguistic descriptions, similar to the quote above, including Hale and Scanlon's characterisation of email as 'a cross between a conversation and a letter' (1999: 3). Yet it is not only studies from the 'Internet era' of the 1990s that define email by drawing comparisons with other modes of communication. Morris *et al.* (2002) compare speech and email, while Bertacco and Deponte (2005) later described email as similar to letters. In this way, the 'simple' distinction between spoken-like versus written-like is highly contended. Of the two, email, as a form of 'asynchronous' CMC, is generally claimed as 'written-like' (Baron, 2000; Bertacco & Deponte, 2005; Crystal, 2001b; Danet & Herring, 2007; Herring, 2003, 2004; Ko, 1996; Werry, 1996; Yates, 1996), as Lenny describes in the Simpsons quote above. Crystal even states 'We "write" emails, not "speak" them' (2006: 32), although some conflicting perceptions are presented in Chapter 4. Despite these claims, a number of researchers agree with Carl in the quote above, and make note of the more spoken-like qualities of email.

In an important study of Finnish learners of English and their NS partners, Tella (1992) suggests that email should be characterised as spoken language. However, Tella's own results show that students drafted their emails via a word processor before compiling their final emails, despite their teacher's leniency towards spelling mistakes and similar errors in the electronic medium. Obviously, this type of strategy is unavailable in spontaneous speech. Tella shows that as a result of the drafting process, the non-native speakers (NNSs) used more business-like writing than their NS peers, yet by the end of the project, had been influenced by the spoken-like style of their counterparts. However, rather than showing anything about the definitive nature of email communication, this suggests that how learners and their interlocutors frame the activity (as a form of assessment or as correspondence with a friend) greatly influences the form their communication takes. A difference in CMC genre selection has been suggested as one way to account for participants' differences in thinking about the same activity.

CMC genre selection

Drawing on genre studies, de Nooy and Hanna (2009) explain how cultural differences may be manifested in CMC use in the way that participants view their communication as belonging to one genre or another. When confronted with new communication modes, users tend to model their communication on an existing genre. In a survey of Japanese university students, Tanaka (2001) found that letter/postcard was the most popular model for both mobile/cell phone (38.7%) and personal computer (PC) (61.1%) emails; however, the second most popular model for PC emails was fax (22.2%). Fax use was extremely prevalent in Japan until relatively recently, due to the slow development of computer-based typing in Japanese, and it is unlikely that fax messages would be such a common model for emails in countries where fax usage was largely limited to business use in the 1990s.

Tella's (1992) study cited above is also an early demonstration that the genre of language produced using a single CMC tool is not fixed, but may vary according to user and over time. In a separate study, Orlikowski and Yates (1994) found that a group of users had at least four distinct email styles. Murray (1991) also states that users may select speech- or writing-oriented genres based on what they deem appropriate at the time.

Conceptualising 'the language of CMC'

As researchers like Tella realised that email, and indeed other forms of CMC (cf. Ko, 1996; Taylor, 1992), comprised features commonly associated with 'traditional' spoken and written language, new ways for conceptualising the language of CMC were needed. Some researchers (e.g. T. Hashimoto, 2006) have suggested that CMC fits no traditional categorisation, but is instead a wholly new form of language. For example, Crystal (2006) and Ōta (2001) contend that email is neither spoken nor written, but a hybrid form. The terms 'hybrid' and 'continuum' appear to be used interchangeably by some authors, although a distinction may be drawn: hybrid referring to predictable variation across a fixed set of variables, and continuum referring to a fluid position between two poles. One of the first models for understanding 'asynchronous' CMC, in particular email, as positioned on a continuum, was proposed by Baron (1998). Baron's model locates email on a continuum anchored by 'writing' and 'speaking' at each end, in contrast to early assertions that it was one or the other (spoken-like versus written-like) or constituted predictable elements from both (hybrid), allowing researchers to consider online communication without declaring any one form as being spoken or written. However, while valuable, this model is inadequate to account for variation across time, interlocutors, and a number of other factors, which will be addressed at the end of this section.

In order to examine the complex interplay of technological, social, and contextual factors identified by Herring (1996b) and Androutsopoulos (2006a) and highlighted in the first research question, it is crucial to adopt a framework that avoids classification on the basis of asynchronous-versus-synchronous or spoken-versus-written alone. While the continuum model may be initially attractive, it is also crucial to recognise that while CMC is influenced by both traditional spoken and written communication, it is also subject to the influence of technological factors alien to either of these modes. Sealey and Carter's (2004) model, which accounts for these factors, will be introduced towards the end of this chapter.

'The Internet' vs 'the internet'

de Nooy and Hanna (2009) note that the drive to classify and describe the 'language of CMC' has led to the segregation of online tools in research, as investigators strive to omit unwanted variables in attempting to define the effects of technology on language learning and use. Isolating CMC tools and examining them removed from context, including surrounding practices, does not take into account the numerous influences from other tools that are used by multi-taskers, where the majority of CMC users make use of multiple tools at a time. I propose that the subject of analysis instead be an individual's personal 'internet', as defined by Miller and Slater (2000), who state that '*the* Internet' does not exist. Just as no one culture should be considered a monolithic entity (Sugimoto & Levin, 2000), neither should 'the Internet'. Rather, the various tools and technical possibilities users assemble constitute '*their* internet' (Miller & Slater, 2000). In accordance with this distinction, the present volume will utilise an initial capital for 'the Internet' only when it is used to refer to the imagined monolithic entity.

L1 Perspectives

While a large body of work has examined L1 workplace-based uses of CMC (Handel & Herbsleb, 2002; Herbsleb *et al.*, 2002; Issacs *et al.*, 2002; Lantz, 2001) the sociolinguistic studies most relevant to the present investigation are those conducted on social use. This section will outline some of the main characteristics of social L1 CMC, prefaced by a background to each of English- and Japanese-based CMC. Possible implications for L2 use will be noted where relevant.

English-based CMC

More research has been completed on English-based CMC than any other language. Some of this research focuses on social uses of CMC, in particular by teenagers and those in their early 20s. A body of work on young people's use of CMC for social purposes in English has been carried out by boyd and others (boyd, 2007b; boyd & Ellison, 2007; boyd & Heer, 2006), who found that participation online is increasingly seen as an essential part of teenage social lives. Participation, however, is influenced by physical location and (offline) social relationships. Students who live with roommates or alone are more likely to engage in SNS use than those who live with their parents (Hargittai, 2007), and those with net-ready computers in their bedrooms use CMC for social communication far more than for study purposes or academic exchange (Crook & Light, 2002). Kraut *et al.* (1999) state that 87% of Internet users use CMC, such as blogs, for keeping in touch with friends and family. The typical blog, according to Drezner and Farrell (2004), is written by a teenage girl, posting on average twice a month in order to update her friends and classmates on what is happening in her life. A longitudinal analysis of blogs by Herring *et al.* (2007a) also showed that the most popular form of blog was a personal journal. Blood (2002) argues that writing a blog and gaining an authentic audience helps to build better writers, who are self-aware critical thinkers, a potential benefit for L2 users also.

In their research on social CMC use, Greenfield and Subrahmanyam (2003) found that young chat users generally discuss several topics simultaneously, often resulting in the dislocated adjacency pairs and turn-taking sequences also found in my previous research on L2 CMC use (Pasfield-Neofitou, 2006). Investigating high school and college teens' use of IM,

Grinter and Palen (2002) found that peer pressure, socialisation, and group membership are the major factors influencing out-of-classroom use of CMC. Therefore, it is vital to conduct research on L2 learners' use of CMC outside the classroom, and not form assumptions about young people's whole use of CMC on the basis of class and laboratory results alone.

Japanese-based CMC

Japanese young people's use of CMC is characterised by T. Takahashi (2008) as involving constant and complex interaction, mostly via mobile phone. In contrast with the research on English CMC, most studies of Japanese CMC have involved mobile Internet use, which is more popular than PC Internet in Japan. In fact, Japan has one of the world's largest Internet mobile phone markets (McVeigh, 2003), and its main users of mobile phones are 15–24 years old (Y. Hashimoto, 2001).

A host of studies report that mobile Internet is mostly used for email in Japan – bored young people messaging friends about everyday things (Kawaura, 2001; Kimura, 2001; Miyake, 2001; Nojima, 2001). Most Japanese university students in McVeigh's (2003) study used mobile email primarily to contact their friends or boy/girlfriends, and the majority of their messages were about recent events and arranging social activities. Murase and Inoue (2003) discovered similar findings in their survey of eight university students in Japan. Furthermore, Sawa (2000) reports that 83% of Japanese university students use mobiles to covertly send emails to one another during class time. In one opinion piece, a teacher reported noticing students checking their Mixi SNS pages in class (Dias, 2007), indicating the extent to which the use of CMC tools has become a part of everyday life, an influence Ogino (1996) noted over a decade prior.

Self and identity in CMC use

'ASL?' (Age/Sex/Location) is a common question online for ascertaining basic information about an unknown interlocutor's identity. Gee (2000) states that despite a need for a more dynamic approach to identity, a similar static trio (Race/Class/Gender) has been commonly used in research. One major distinction has been made between experienced users and 'newbies', with the younger generation labelled 'digital natives' (Prensky, 2001). However, in addition to age and experience, other factors such as culture or nationality, and gender have also been reported to influence CMC use. Faiola and Matei (2005) and Sugimoto and Levin (2000) claim that cultural identity clearly influences Internet use. Yet Leung (2005), in the introduction to *Virtual*

Ethnicity, states that gender and technology has been the primary focus of cybercultural studies to date. de Bakker *et al.* (2007), Herring (1996a), and Nowak and Rauh (2005) have all considered the influence of identity online. However, it is important to note that some caution is warranted when interpreting such findings, as, in many studies, these categories are assigned by researchers with little regard for participants' own identification as a certain age or gender, or with a certain ethnic group or skill level. In the present volume, Sealey and Carter's (2004) concept of the psychobiography is drawn upon, which they define as an individual's biography grounded in their personal feelings and attitudes, influenced by their own unique history.

The performance/construction of online identities

Both online and offline, identity is constructed through a variety of linguistic and visual means. Online, linguistic means include SNS profiles or quizzes, forum and email signatures, not to mention the language of communication itself, while visual means include in-game, three-dimensional (3D) avatars, IM display photos, emoticons, and so on. In this way, users employ both text and images to describe who they are, what they like, and what they do (S. Jones *et al.*, 2008). In the introduction to her influential book, *Life on the Screen*, Turkle (1995) defined identity in CMC as multiple, fluid, and constituted in interaction via technology. Yet a decade later, Hewling (2005) argued that CMC research continues to take a nationality-based view of culture, and suggested instead that identities be viewed as a site of ongoing negotiation.

There is a famous cartoon from *The New Yorker* with the caption 'On the Internet, nobody knows you're a dog' (Steiner, 1993: 61). A similar sentiment is echoed by one CMC user who said 'You can be whoever you want to be. You can completely redefine yourself if you want. You can be the opposite sex. You can be more talkative. You can be less talkative. Whatever' (cited in Turkle, 1995: 184). Indeed, so long as language competencies do not indicate otherwise, the signalling of 'race', ethnicity, 'sex', gender, or indeed any other aspect of identity online, appears to be at the participant's discretion (Burkhalter, 1999; Herring, 2003), although users may choose not to make use of this potential, as seen in Chapter 3.

It is widely acknowledged that identity online is both influenced by and constructed via CMC discourse (Köszegi *et al.*, 2004; Lam, 2000; W-N. Lee & Choi, 2005). One of the major benefits of online communication for L2 learners and users, according to Murray (2005), is a chance to form their own identities through the hybrid use of language(s). Sundén (2003) argues that online we write ourselves into being.

Part of life online, boyd (2007a) claims, is learning how to accessorise our 'digital bodies', just as one chooses what to wear to university, the workplace, or a social function. Yet it is not only one's own profile that projects one's identity. In an article subtitled 'are we known by the company we keep?' Walther *et al.* (2008) state that the display photos of friends one links to also affect perceptions of the profile owner. Similarly, Utz (2010) examined impression formation on SNSs and found that information generated by others about a user had an impact on perceived social attraction. An in-depth analysis of Japanese young people's use of mobile phones and SNSs also revealed that users create their profiles and lists of friends for 'impression management' (T. Takahashi, 2008).

Group identities online

One important way of constructing identity online is via the simple act of joining or selecting a certain CMC medium. Most teens learn about the various types of SNSs available through their friends, joining in response to peer pressure (boyd, 2007b). Selection is also related to one's interests, according to Ellison *et al.* (2007). They note that SNSs may be oriented towards work-related (e.g. LinkedIn), romantic (e.g. RSVP), musical (e.g. MySpace), or collegial (e.g. Facebook) networking. Other kinds of interests are also represented in online groups, a particularly strong example being online gamers (Kock, 2008). Toshima (1998) states that in-game characters may be thought of as 'another self' that humans perform during day-to-day life.

Donath and boyd (2004) claim that a public display of links to friends' profiles is another implicit way of both constructing and verifying identity. If you have linked to someone you know, and they have accepted you as a 'friend', this should demonstrate some form of acceptance of the authenticity or representativeness of your profile. In a study of digital relationships on MySpace, Dwyer found one student who blocked a girl because 'she was fatter in person' (2007: 5) than her profile photo showed.

Although, as Donath and boyd (2004) point out, users have many other reasons for 'friending' and accepting 'friends', including friend collecting, one common theme throughout the previous research is that young people are more interested in communication with people they already know personally than with strangers. Teenagers, according to boyd (2007b), mainly focus on socialising online with friends they have already established relationships with offline. For this reason, the present study aims to examine the ways in which language learners use CMC to cement or maintain existing relationships in addition to new relationships they may form via the Internet.

Language Learning Opportunities in Instructed L2 CMC

While the main focus of studies on CMC in general has been the nature of language used, many studies of L2 CMC have highlighted learning opportunities (Gray & Stockwell, 1998; Itakura & Nakajima, 2001). A number of features, including provision of an authentic audience, flexibility, records of communication, opportunities for independent learning, negotiation of meaning, amending stereotypes, and exposure to language variation, are summarised below.

Situated interaction and language learning

Natural communication in the target language via CMC provides opportunities for authentic social interaction, the importance of which is emphasised in all major theories of SLA (Ohm, 2007), including the Interaction Hypothesis, Sociocultural Theory, and Depth of Processing Theory. Although interpersonal interaction has often been defined as 'the activity that arises during *face-to-face* communication' (Ellis, 1999, emphasis added), Baralt (2008: 167) cites a number of studies, including de la Fuente (2003), Smith (2003, 2004), Shekary and Taririan (2006), and Sachs and Suh (2007), which demonstrate that CMC affords many of the same benefits, providing an enjoyable way to make use of one's L2 as a means of communication, as noted by Yoshinari (1998).

Stockwell and Levy's (2001) study of 48 learners of Japanese and their email interactions with NSs found evidence to suggest that those who produced higher numbers of messages were more likely to show improvement in their L2 output. However, despite many studies linking NS–NNS email interactions and increases in L2 proficiency (Aitsiselmi, 1999; Florez-Estrada, 1995; Ioannou-Georgiou, 1999; Stockwell, 2003), Stockwell (2004) observes, that while there are benefits for learners, there are problems also, including communication breakdown, which learners attempted to deal with in just 13 of the 36 cases observed.

One of the most important benefits of CMC for learners is the opportunity to improve linguistic and grammatical competence. Kitade's (2000) study of Japanese learners' chat and Torii-Williams' (2004) research on emailing in Japanese demonstrate numerous opportunities for vocabulary and grammar learning, peer editing, character learning, and noticing gaps, as students realise what they can and cannot express in Japanese.

Interactionist approaches posit that SLA is facilitated by the opportunity to negotiate for meaning (Long, 1996). Relating their findings to an interactionist account of L2 development, Stockwell and Harrington (2003) found that learners of Japanese involved in a five-week email project with NSs made consistent improvements. The authors point to a number of benefits of emailing with NSs, including the fulfilment of the conditions of Long's Interaction Hypothesis, identifying task conditions that provide an opportunity to engage in meaningful and authentic interaction, and psycholinguistic conditions that facilitate learner uptake and input processing.

Interaction allows learners to receive feedback in the form of recasts, explicit grammatical questioning, and confirmation checks (Baralt, 2008: 168). Swain (1985, 2000) argues that negotiating for meaning also provides learners with the opportunity to produce language and test hypotheses, which may enhance fluency. Many researchers have claimed that online communication affords learners such opportunities (T. Hashimoto, 2006; Jepson, 2005; Smith, 2003, 2004). Herring (2003) argues that CMC allows users to choose words with greater care and reveal less doubts and insecurities, which is very important for language learners. Kano (2004), however, takes a somewhat different approach, stating that it can be good preparation for students to experience the frustration of trying to negotiate meaning.

One study of the effects of CMC on L2 vocabulary acquisition by de la Fuente (2003) researched the occurrence of negotiation of meaning, and found that both face-to-face and computer-mediated interaction appeared equally effective in promoting acquisition via the negotiation of meaning. Baralt (2008) also examined negotiation of meaning in CMC and found that chat served as a tool for language learning and reflection via negotiation.

In an examination of Persian students' English chat sessions, Shekary and Tahririan (2006) show that language-related episodes and the negation of meaning occurred astonishingly frequently. However, while Shekary and Tahririan's study is described as 'naturalistic', the researchers selected participants based on their computer proficiency, set specific tasks for the sessions, and used a pre-treatment session in which participants were instructed to negotiate for meaning. Students in Coniam and Wong's (2004) examination of chat as a tool for English as a Second Language (ESL) development were similarly instructed to concentrate on a specific element of grammar. Thus, further research on the occurrence of negotiation of meaning in naturalistic settings appears necessary.

Although most studies concentrate on NNS–NNS communication in instructed settings, students' desire to communicate with NSs of the target language is highlighted by Tudini (2003), whose students emphasised that they enjoyed being able to interact with 'real' Italians. According to Tudini (2007) and Stockwell and Stockwell (2003), CMC with NSs provides opportunities for learners to develop their intercultural communicative competence through negotiation sequences, sometimes triggered by pragmatic and culture-specific content. Yet, O'Dowd (2007) argues that it remains for the most part unclear how CMC contact contributes to intercultural learning. This is particularly true in out-of-class, informal communication, such as that under investigation in the present study.

Instructed CMC as a resource beyond the classroom

In a cautionary tale for all who might be tempted to overemphasise the benefits of CMC for language learners, Hanna and de Nooy (2003) analyse the threads of four Anglophone students of French and their NS interlocutors on the online forum of a French newspaper. Two of the students framed the activity primarily as a language learning exercise and eventually gave up, while the other two, engaged in passionate debate from the outset, learned about French culture (even if they got distracted from 'studying' French). The researchers make the sobering claim that while language learning can be achieved online, it is certainly not guaranteed. Furthermore, it was found that 'language practise' was not a useful way to frame online activities; rather, forum participation must be viewed as a social, communicative behaviour if students are to be successfully accepted. This highlights the focus of the present study on authentic social communication as a vehicle for opportunities for L2 use and acquisition.

Intercultural and L2 Uses of CMC in Social Settings

As research on intercultural CMC in social settings has been relatively rare to date, this section will be necessarily brief, drawing on studies that deal with the intersection between social and L2 uses of CMC. One study dealing with intercultural and L2 uses of CMC in a non-institutional environment is my own previous research (Pasfield-Neofitou, 2006) on Japanese–English IM use, which showed that while IM may provide many opportunities for language learning, learning outcomes are often more dependent on the participants' investment in their social relationships, than on their desire to learn the language of their partner. Pairs with established friendships were also more likely to ask one another questions and seek feedback on their language use. The present study aims to go beyond the focus on IM to examine the interplay of various technological and social factors.

One study in which a participant's psychobiography was found to affect (and in turn, be affected by) CMC use is found in the case study by Lam (2000) examining a Chinese immigrant to the US. This teenager's communication with his transnational Internet peer group figured in his identity formation and literacy development in English. In a later study, Lam (2006) found that two young immigrants engaged in chat and *anime*-related multimedia use underwent new learning experiences as a result of their participation in situated CMC. This led to an increase in their competence, and changes in their language and literacy practices. Importantly, CMC participation allowed these users to redefine themselves as competent learners, people, and workers, within their digitally mediated social settings, and to draw on contextual resources in order to construct global identities as English speakers.

Kurata's (2008) study of opportunities for language acquisition and use in the informal bilingual social networks of learners of Japanese in an Australian university also provides a valuable glimpse of students' informal CMC use. The research shows that CMC channels were often a more significant part of learners' communication with NSs than face-to-face speech, suggesting that deeper analysis of learners' CMC is warranted.

While an example of bilingual but not intercultural CMC, Huang's (2004) examination of a network of NSs of Chinese living in Taiwan, who use both Chinese and English to communicate with one another via computer, is an important study on the occurrence of code-switching and language use in emails. As Huang points out, while bilingualism has become one of the most researched areas of linguistics, most studies in this area have concentrated on spoken language, and most research on CMC use has concentrated on monolingual communities. Huang's (2004) data exhibits two types of code-switching, namely single word (or intra-clausal) and inter-clausal. Importantly, Huang points out that unlike code-switching in speech, which is often claimed to be subconscious, switching between Chinese and English in CMC entails a physical switch of the input method. The same is true for the language pair of Japanese and English most relevant to the current study. Thus, Huang argues, code-switching in CMC should be thought of as a conscious choice.

An important preliminary review of opportunities for interaction in social L2 CMC was undertaken by Thorne *et al.* (2009), with a particular focus on interest communities and online gaming. They suggest that the social settings of fan communities provide rich opportunities for exploring forms of L2 engagement, development, and socialisation, and those communities centred on Japanese media such as *anime* cartoons and *manga* comics provide compelling examples of the hybrid and participatory nature of online language and literacy practices. Thorne (2008) mentions the case of an American gamer who became interested in studying Russian, in part to improve his gaming with Russian speakers. In-game guilds appear important in such environments, as they often provide explicit instructions to newcomers, and strategy-focused discussion (Thorne *et al.*, 2009). Furthermore, participation in massively multiplayer online (MMO) games may lead to language socialisation, as Pe'na and Hancock (2006) found significantly more socioemotional talk than purely task-associated communication in their analysis of online video game communication. Experienced players were also found to use more specialised 'gaming' language, including variants of the types of language described in the outset of this chapter, having undergone a process of language socialisation as they ascended in rank.

While there is much talk of opportunities for language learning in the literature relating to CMC, much of the speculation is still based on L1 use, and it is unclear how frequently these opportunities actually occur in naturalistic L2 settings, or what factors may influence them. Furthermore, O'Dowd (2003) argues that while intercultural learning is assumed to be an automatic benefit of much computer-mediated intercultural collaboration, there is little research that examines whether learners' understandings are developed. The present study aims to examine these factors under the third research question, which addresses the influence of CMC participation on opportunities for language acquisition. The following section explores the social realist framework that will be employed to investigate these questions.

A Social Realist Approach

As described above, research on digital communication has been carried out by researchers from diverse fields, utilising a varied set of theoretical approaches (boyd & Heer, 2006). The present study may be broadly situated within the fields of applied linguistics and sociolinguistics. In their book *Applied Linguistics as a Social Science*, Sealey and Carter (2004) make use of a broad definition of applied linguistics which encompasses not only the teaching and learning of additional languages, but other aspects of language in use, including CMC. As Davies (2005) has observed, this conception of applied linguistics overlaps to a large extent with what is traditionally considered the domain of sociolinguistics. Sealey and Carter themselves state that some of the issues they discuss within their social realist approach might equally be considered sociolinguistic (2004: 30). Following Halliday (1978: 111), Sealey and Carter have developed a case for a close collaboration between linguistics and sociology over a number of publications (Carter & Sealey, 2000, 2004, 2009; Sealey, 2007; Sealey & Carter, 2001, 2004), a view that fits neatly with the focus of the present study.

In an investigation of telecollaborative email, chat, and website construction, Belz (2002) provides a useful summary of the realist position from both a theoretical and methodological perspective. *Theoretically*, the approach views the empirical world as highly complex and multifaceted, where social action is shaped by the interplay of macro (structure) and micro (agency) level phenomena, embedded within history (Belz, 2002: 61). *Methodologically*, social realism reflects the complex and layered nature of the empirical world, relying on an exploratory, multi-strategy approach. Layder summarises the central aim of realism as 'an attempt to preserve a "scientific" attitude towards social analysis at the same time as recognising the importance of actors' meanings' (1993: 16).

As the following sections will elaborate, Sealey and Carter's (2004) social realist perspective views the social world as stratified, comprising structure, agency, and culture, and with language as a cultural emergent property. As those elements associated with structure are more abstract, and further removed from direct experience, than those associated with agency, the social realist view requires acknowledgement of the limits of the empirical, and places emphasis on *discovering* rather than *revealing*. In contrast with many approaches which rest on the assumption that the social world is already constituted and can be revealed via the research process, the social realist approach argues for the centrality of theory in research, and accords some relevance to the role of theory in constituting the social world. Finally, the approach entails a relational view of the world, where epistemological considerations (as will be explored in the following section) play a critical role.

Epistemological considerations

In line with their belief that the social world may not simply be *revealed*, Sealey and Carter (2004) favour an approach which acknowledges some relevance of the role of theory. Thus, while a modest form of objectivity is desirable, a level of reflexivity is also required, recognising that the researcher too is a factor in the inquiry. As Linker (2001) maintains, proposing that knowledge may be relativised to individuals and social groups does not entail that there are no 'facts of the matter'. As the social world itself is, at least in part, symbolically constituted, and theoretical representations of it are of course fallible, there cannot be a direct appeal to 'neutral' observation in order to prove or disprove a given theory (Sealey & Carter, 2004: 185). However, as Schegloff (1997) states, this does not entail that all theories are equally warranted, legitimate, or entitled to identical uptake and weight.

Another epistemological issue relevant to the present research is the problem of generalisability and variables. Sealey and Carter (2004) maintain a distinction between people and things, in that phenomena in the natural world are indifferent to how they are labelled, yet human and social phenomena may be affected by the labels they are given, as pointed out by Hacking (1997). Sometimes discrepancies occur between how researchers and the researched understand categories. The distinction that has been made between 'Native' and 'Non-Native' speakers, as if these were given, absolute categories (Firth & Wagner, 1997), has long been problematised. Pawson (1989) and Sealey and Carter (2004), too, have highlighted the danger of 'selective measurement', whereby the researcher makes use of a preconceived concept, such as 'NNS', already infused with theoretical notions. While labelling an individual as a 'NNS' may be adequate for 'everyday' purposes, the authors warn that the process of research is compromised by the deployment of such categories as variables without specifying the theoretical basis on which they rest. The utilisation of such categorisations need not always be problematic, however, if done with due caution and an awareness of these connotations (Ellis, 2007; Long, 2007).

Sealey and Carter (2001) outline their social realist approach to social categories, following Greenwood's (1994) distinction between 'social aggregates', constituted by involuntaristic characteristics, and 'social collectives', characterised by a degree of choice on the part of their members. Much research in sociolinguistics and applied linguistics, including research on CMC (cf. Androutsopoulos, 2006b; Baron, 2004; Basharina, 2007; Boyd, 2007b; Chung et al., 2006; Dowdall, 2006; Greenfield & Subrahmanyam, 2003; R. Jones et al., 2001; Leander & McKim, 2003) has focused on members of the aggregate category, 'adolescents'. Sealey and Carter (2001) state that research of this type often starts with the researcher identifying as salient the property of falling within a given age range. Then, sociolinguistic variables are identified, analysed, and correlations are established between membership and use. While these findings often point to significant patterns, the authors maintain that they remain *descriptions* as opposed to *explanations*. To explain such patterns, we need to introduce a strong notion of agency (Sealey & Carter, 2001). This requires the utilisation of categories that recognise the relevance of individuals' own understandings.

In a critique of Carter and Sealey's (2000) earliest publication on social realism, Potter (2000) argues that a coherent analysis of participants' discourse requires a stance of methodological relativism, and that anything else runs the risk of inadvertently siding with some participants rather than others: 'Who is to judge what is actually relevant?' (Potter, 2000: 22). Sealey and Carter (2001) address this point, noting that because such decisions involve a degree of choice, actors' understandings must be a central component in the theoretical description of social collectives. However, Sealey and

Carter remain wary of drawing solely on participants' own formulations as a source for categorisation. They point out that there are limits to people's discursive penetration of the social world, and, therefore, asking informants about their attitudes, for example, regarding their social networks (e.g. online contacts), or language varieties (e.g. 'netspeak' use), may not reveal the complex actors operating to link membership of a particular social category with particular patterns of language use (Carter & Sealey, 2004).

Ontological considerations

One of the major themes of sociological debate is 'do people make society, or does society make people?' (Sealey & Carter, 2004: 6). Many of the traditional approaches to L2 studies are characterised by an emphasis on the agency of the individual, while many of the approaches associated with the 'social' or 'linguistic' turn place a greater emphasis on the role of structure. Both structure- and agency-focused approaches have been represented in studies of CMC. Some, such as Johnson and Brine (1999), Thorne (2000), Donath and boyd (2004), and boyd and Heer (2006), have to a greater or lesser degree emphasised the role of society and social structures in influencing online communication and language acquisition, while others, like Baron (1998), Orita (1999), Grinter and Palen (2002), Freiermuth and Jarrel (2006), Ohm (2007), and Beißwenger (2008), have concentrated to a greater or lesser extent on the role played by individuals. However, strong structuralist approaches are often unable to convincingly account for social change, as an emphasis on structure often entails a diminished view of agency. At the same time, interactionist accounts may find explaining social persistence and stability equally problematic (Sealey & Carter, 2004). Sealey and Carter demonstrate that, in social theory, doubts about the value of the above formulations have given rise to some fresh approaches, including the realist account of structure and agency. According to social realism, it is people, not structures (such as a given society) or properties (like language) that make history, because of the cardinal power of agency – to maintain or modify the world. Distinguishing *properties* and *powers* of agency include self-consciousness, reflexivity, intentionality, cognition, and emotionality.

For social structures, distinctive *properties* include their anteriority, in that they are often already features of the world into which we are born, and endurance. Amongst the *powers* possessed by social structures are enablement and constraint. One example of a constraint is access to linguistic resources (Sealey & Carter, 2004). Although an individual may seek to become fluent in a language not widely used in their locality, they may be constrained by social structures. In addition to practical difficulties of gaining access to other speakers, adopting the speech style of members of a different social category may be seen as a form of 'crossing' (Rampton, 1997), which may lead to social censure. However, Sealey and Carter (2004: 119) point out that such deviations from 'norms' do occur, because language itself has properties which make it potentially available to any human speaker. As previously noted, CMC may facilitate language use in certain ways, such as providing access to other speakers in the example above, and constrain it in other ways. However, these probabilities should be seen primarily as conditioning not determining forces (Sealey & Carter, 2001). This is of particular importance in the area of CMC under investigation, where issues of technological and social determinism have been prevalent in prior research.

Culture, language, and electronic discourse

According to Archer (2000: 136), language is characterised as a 'cultural emergent property'. Carter and Sealey define 'emergence' as 'the generation of new entities or phenomena from the combination of other entities or phenomena' (2004: 118). Languages are viewed as emergent products of the engagement of human practice with the material world, and cannot be reduced to any of their constituents (in the sense that they are not merely what human beings say, nor merely an internal relationship between linguistic signs, nor merely a grammar which is grasped intuitively). They have partial autonomy from both human beings and the material world (in the sense that we learn a language that pre-exists us, and through language can create things which have no physical counterpart). Finally, language itself is a practice capable of enabling people to act upon and modify the world, themselves, and others (in the sense that we do things with language, and it allows us to reflect upon, interpret, and make judgements about ourselves and others). Carter and Sealey (2004: 165) argue that language itself may be combined with other elements in the social world to produce second and even third order emergent properties. Written language is one such second order cultural property, emergent from oral language, human practice, and physical resources, distinct from each of these, and capable of acting back on any of them.

One of the strengths of Sealey and Carter's (2004) social realist approach is its specific treatment of electronic discourse, however brief. Sealey and Carter define electronic discourse as a cultural emergent property of speech and writing. In the present research, this is seen as an important way of addressing the tensions raised in recognising the similarities of electronic discourse with speech and writing previously mentioned, while maintaining the ability to describe its differences also, due to the fact that, as an emergent property, electronic discourse is reducible to neither. December (1993), too, argued that the 'emerging discourse culture' of CMC is based not only on text, but also learned technical skills, and, additionally, exhibits many characteristics of oral culture. Yet, while December viewed the oral characteristics of CMC as surprising, considering it based primarily on print and technology, Sealey and Carter (2004: 167) view CMC as influenced by both traditional speaking and writing cultures, as well as technology.

Sealey and Carter (2004) briefly outline an approach to the treatment of CMC, which distinguishes between the properties of the cultural system which electronic discourse comprises (including similarities to, and differences from, the properties of speech and writing from which it is emergent), the constraints and affordances entailed by the structural distribution of material and cultural goods (access to the Internet and 'netspeak' conventions), and the properties and powers of the human agents who actualise what is available online (in terms of choice, intentions, propositional knowledge, and affective communication).

Contrary to research with a technologically deterministic focus, according to the social realist point of view, spoken language, written language, and computer-mediated language do not produce particular kinds of communication. However, social realism emphasises that the contexts that people confront in various societies or modes of communication (e.g. an 'oral society' versus a 'literate society'; an email exchange versus a video conference via Skype) present individuals with different kinds of possibilities for social interaction, which are dependent on human agency.

Various researchers, such as Newmeyer (2002), Halliday (1989), Ong (1982), and Goody (1986), have identified properties of written language that differ from those of speech. Sealey and Carter (2004), following Goody (1986), state that writing enables the construction of texts that can lead to the contemplation of those same texts, and the development of thoughts about thoughts by freeing language from its immediate dependence on human interlocution. They argue that while orality can facilitate thought and philosophising, it is unable to produce a library of texts. The properties of writing enlarge the possibilities for 'context-free' language, make memories more durable, and enable texts to have critics. As will be explored in the following chapters, CMC too, in part emergent from writing and technology, can facilitate the production of a library of L2 texts for the user to draw on in future communication. However, it is important to remember in the case of electronic discourse that it is not the *written* nature of written language that Sealey and Carter (2004) refer to that facilitates such a record. Rather, it is the property of *durability* that facilitates the production of a library. Thus, I argue that other durable modes of communication, including audio- and video-based communication such as podcasts and YouTube videos have similar properties to what Sealey and Carter describe as properties of written language.

The social world as stratified

The social realist model, drawing on Layder's (1997) Domain Theory, views the world as stratified, comprising agency, structure, and culture, with language viewed as a cultural emergent property. Layder's model comprises four interlinked, interdependent social domains, two of which are associated primarily with agency ('psychobiography' and 'situated activity'), and two that are associated primarily with structure ('social settings' and 'contextual resources'), which all move through history, and are depicted in Figure 1.1.

Psychobiography refers to the development of the self along a series of evolutionary transitions. All people develop unique biographies grounded in personal feelings and attitudes, which contribute to a continuing selfhood. This is the most distinctive of Layder's domains, as it runs contrary to some of the current claims from postmodernism about selfhood. Although our existence is constantly changing and shaped by forces separate to us, social realism maintains that we each have not only a physical identity, but also a continuous sense of self. *Situated activity* also focuses on human agency. In spite of the uniqueness of each person's psychobiography, people are primarily social actors. In the case of the present study, online interaction forms the situated activity under investigation. At this level, language is the principal resource available for the purposes of communicating information, conveying a sense of identity, and positioning others in relation to ourselves

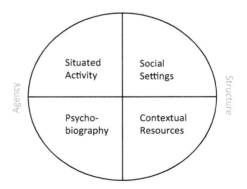

Figure 1.1 Social domains
Based on Carter and Sealey (2000), adapted from Layder (1997: 78).

(Carter & Sealey, 2000). Shifting the focus from structure to agency, *social settings* are where situated activity is embedded. Within the social setting, contextual resources of the cultural system are drawn on as individuals interpret contexts; however, as discussed above, the practices in which they engage are not fully determined by the typical or dominant beliefs of that society. Finally, *contextual resources* refers to material and cultural capital, and constitutes the fourth and final domain in Layder's (1997) model. In the present study, language, or linguistic capital, certain hardware and software, and objects such as dictionaries and textbooks form relevant contextual resources. Language is pre-eminent among cultural resources, as it is not only a resource in its own right, but is also a means of accessing other resources (Sealey & Carter, 2001).

Although Sealey and Carter (2004) do not claim that we experience these domains in a stratified manner, they maintain that our lives are constantly shaped by all four of them, and the relations between them. According to Sealey and Carter (2004: 184), it is only natural that the applied linguistic researcher will be concerned with situated activity; for example, the online interaction examined in the present study. However, they emphasise the importance of recognising other factors while cautioning that it is crucial not to oversimplify these complex issues, as is highlighted in the following section.

Methodology

The social realist approach also offers an investigative methodology through which to examine and interpret complex social action, such as L2 use in CMC (Belz & Müller-Hartmann, 2003). As a relatively new area of enquiry, specialised data collection and analysis methods in studies of online language use and acquisition are still emerging. While much has been made of the ease with which researchers can gather electronic data (cf. Mann & Steward, 2000), Chapelle (2003) states that the investigation of language learning through CMC cannot be limited to 'process data', such as chat logs and email messages alone, in order to explain the complex and dynamic nature of CMC use (Warschauer & Kern, 2000). Employing Sealey and Carter's (2004) approach, the present study draws on Androutsopoulos' (2008) concept of 'ethnographically enhanced research'. Ethnographic approaches to data collection, including the use of interviews, qualitative surveys, and focus-groups, have proven very useful in the context of CMC research, in addition to collecting empirical evidence of participants' online communication (cf. Kitade, 2000; Toyoda & Harrison, 2002).

The data for this study was collected in four stages, in accordance with the social realist approach of Sealey and Carter (2004) outlined above, and the process of theoretical sampling advocated by Glaser and Strauss (1967), whereby an analyst jointly collects, codes, and analyses data, using the data to decide what to collect next. As Belz (2004) argues, the investigation of intercultural CMC should involve research methodologies that take into account social as well as linguistic and cognitive factors. Accordingly, the present study employs a longitudinal, multiple case study approach, triangulating the use of both qualitative and quantitative data sources and methods of analysis.

Participant recruitment

Students studying Japanese at an Australian university with one or more online contacts whom they considered a NS of Japanese were invited to participate in the present research via posters, a website, and class visits. Twelve students and 18 of their Japanese contacts volunteered to participate. Although the Australian participants listed a total of 100 Japanese contacts between them, they did not feel comfortable inviting many, especially those they had fallen out of contact with, to participate in the research. In this sense, the present study is limited to focusing largely on relationships in which CMC use was still ongoing at the time of data collection. Participant backgrounds are described in Chapter 2.

Background interviews

While the interview technique has been widely used in applied linguistics (Nunan, 1992), its potential to uncover underlying motivations and awareness has been unfortunately neglected in the majority of studies on L2 CMC. The current study employed two interviews. The first, semi-structured historical interview consisted of general questions regarding the participants' relationships with their online contacts, Japanese study and use, and history with computers and CMC. In accordance with the principles of grounded theory (GT), where necessary, additional information was gained through chat conversations and emails. As with any form of data collection, there are some issues with the use of interviews, such as the constraints noted by Block (1995). Taking these issues into consideration, the present study employs a triangulation of methods, comparing interview data with that obtained via other methods, and will discuss these constraints where appropriate throughout the volume.

For Japanese participants, the background questions formed the basis of an 'email interview' (Mann & Steward, 2000), similar in format to an open-ended questionnaire, which 12 participants opted to complete. The interview questions were accordingly rewritten as questionnaire items, consistent with Brown and Rodgers' (2002) guidelines. Communication with all participants was conducted in their native language, as recommended by Gass and Mackey (2000).

Participant observation and collection of online profiles

In order to experience using the relevant tools and platforms, the researcher joined the SNSs and played the online games that participants reported using. Furthermore, the importance of collecting data from profiles as well as communication, in order to gain further insight into participants' negotiation of 'self' online, is highlighted by boyd and Heer (2006). Facebook, Mixi, and MySpace all have privacy options which restrict profile access to members on a 'friends' list. In order for the researcher to view participants' profiles, it was necessary to create a profile and then request 'friendship' with each of the participants. Participants were asked to give the researcher their blog address (in the case of Ameba) or username (in the case of SNSs), and were aware of the collection of this data. Profiles (or avatars) from World of Warcraft (WoW) were publicly accessible on http://www.wowarmory.com/ (Blizzard Entertainment), and Noah's character profile was sourced from this website.

In producing profiles for each site, the researcher filled out the minimal required information (truthfully, as to maintain transparency and build rapport with participants) and ensured that details such as profile picture did not differ across platforms. The researcher's profiles on these sites were used only as a technical means to access participants' profiles at the end of the data collection period, and as a way for the researcher to become familiar with the tools participants made use of. As participants did not change their profiles in any way after seeing the researcher's, it can be safely assumed that the researcher's profile did not influence the creation and maintenance of participants' online identities.

CMC data collection

In total, 777 CMC data files (chat conversations, emails, etc.) were collected, comprising a corpus of 2460 naturally occurring instances of communication (where an instance is defined as a single electronic turn). The Australian participants were asked to keep a record of their online communication, simply by saving a copy of their messages using 'Save Draft' in email, or 'Message History' in chat, or a similar function in other tools. All participants reported already using these functions for their own purposes. Just prior to the final interview, participants sent a copy of these 'log files' to the researcher via email.

Participants were asked to give the researcher access to any archived communication they may already have saved, providing they felt comfortable in doing so. Such archived messages are useful in examining the participants' relationships over time, as well as helping to identify any patterns or changes in the participants' social and language learning experiences. Furthermore, access to archived material may also help gauge whether or how much participants are affected by any observer effect (cf. Labov, 1997). Overall, the corpus collected from participants spanned four years, although not all participants had such extensive archived communication. Table 1.1 shows the period of time for which data was available for each Australian participant and the number and types of files collected.

Participants were allowed to censor any material in their communication of a sensitive or personal nature that they did not wish the researcher to see or did not feel comfortable with the publication of. This measure was piloted in my previous study (Pasfield-Neofitou, 2006), and appeared successful in reducing obtrusiveness. In the present study, no participant made use of this option to censor specific segments of text; however, in the case of Scott, whose communications were with his girlfriend, only a limited subset of data was made available to the researcher.

Almost all of the data collected is text-based communication. Although voice-based communication was not precluded from analysis, only Scott and his girlfriend used voice-based online communication (Skype), and, due to the romantic nature of their conversations, opted not to record it for analysis. The only other example of voice-based language use encountered in the data collection was Kaylene's creation of an instructional yoga video in English, which she posted on Mixi.

In addition to the naturally occurring instances of CMC use recorded and collected, a number of participants also provided or allowed for the collection of various supplementary data sources. These data sources include email attachments, screenshots, photographs of computers or other tools, university assignments, and websites. While screen capture or keylog software, which require installation, or video recordings, which require equipment, can reveal important findings, due to the emphasis on observing naturalistic communication in the present study it was decided to rely on participants' screenshots and interview data rather than utilising these more obtrusive methods.

Table 1.1 Data collected for each Australian participant

Participants & years of CMC data collected (N = 12)	Alisha 2006–2008	Cindy 2005–2008	Ellise 2007–2008	Genna 2008–2009	Hyacinth 2008	Jacob 2007	Kaylene 2006–2008	Lucas 2006–2008	Noah 2008	Oscar 2007–2008	Scott 2007–2008	Zac 2008	Totals
Ameba blogs		42		30	6								78
Ameba profiles		1		1	1								3
Emails	98	21		24		12	101	38			17	3	314
Email attachments								4					4
Facebook messages	27						11						38
Facebook wall	5		4					28					37
Facebook albums	2	13											15
Facebook apps	9									1			10
Facebook profiles	1		1				1	1		1			5
Mixi blogs	5	10					17		1	6		4	43
Mixi messages	1									15			16
Mixi videos							2						2
Mixi comments	4						42		1	6		2	55
Mixi profiles	1		1				1		1	1		1	6
MSN conversations	1			3			4	22					30
MySpace comments				2									2
MySpace profiles			1					1					2
Phone emails							114						114
Mind map data		1											1
WoW profiles									1				1
Websites							1						4
TOTALS	154	65	29	61	7	12	294	94	4	30	17	10	777

Notes: The figures in the above table do not reflect rate of use at any one time, but rather the amount of data collected for the present research.

Follow-up interviews and fieldwork focus-groups

Follow-up or stimulated recall interviews were conducted as soon as possible after a pair's most recent communication towards the end of the data collection period, as recommended, for example, by Neustupný (1990), Neustupný and Miyazaki (2002), and Gass and Mackey (2000). Introspective methods such as the follow-up interview are an important methodology in applied linguistics as they give greater access to underlying cognitive processes of language performance (Dörnyei, 2007). However, as Seliger (1983) points out, introspection cannot reveal unconscious language processing and acquisition. Other methodologies and data must be employed in combination with the follow-up interview, as is the case in the present research.

It was up to the individual participants to decide the length of data collection. Once a pair decided they wanted to complete their participation in the study, they would save a copy of their CMC communication, including their most recent conversation, send it to the researcher, and arrange for an interview as soon as possible – usually conducted the next day, giving the researcher the opportunity to formulate questions prior to the interview. Thus, the interview centred on the participants' most recent communication, while it was freshest in their memory. Participants were shown this conversation, which they could then refer to while describing their thought processes at the time of the activity (as per Gass & Mackey, 2000; Mackey et al., 2000), prompted by interview questions based on Neustupný (1990, 2002) and Fan (2002). In order to capture aspects of participants' non-verbal behaviour (for example, pointing towards a specific word in their typed communication) the follow-up interviews were video recorded. Once again, the Japanese participants were sent the follow-up interview in Japanese via email, with excerpts from their communication copied-and-pasted into the questionnaire. Of the 12 Japanese participants who completed the first interview, six completed the second, a response rate fairly typical of social research surveys (Babbie, 2004).

Further data was collected during a period of fieldwork in Japan. After four Australian participants (one-third of the sample) left for various exchange trips to Japan during the data-collection period, it was decided to conduct interviews in Japan where possible, in order to follow their in-country patterns of internet and mobile phone communication. Furthermore, this created an opportunity for the researcher to collect information on technology use in Japan, meet some of the Japanese contacts taking part in the study, and conduct small focus-group sessions in which both the Australian and Japanese participants could take part. Two Australian participants (Kaylene and Jacob) participated in further interviews in Japan, and two

Japanese participants (Watako and Ruriko) joined focus-group sessions, conducted in the same way as the follow-up interviews, except that both participants were able to give their interpretation of a portion of discourse and respond to each other's views. Interview schedules were prepared in both Japanese and English, and all participants employed code-switching.

Transcription

Background, follow-up, and focus-group interview data was transcribed using a method adapted from du Bois (1991) immediately after the completion of each interview. As Conversation Analysis (CA) and Discourse Analysis (DA) conventions do not usually take into account body movements, these were noted in the form of transcriber comments ((in double parentheses)). Each turn was numbered in an interview – original numbers will be preserved in extracts to retain the context of participant comments. Where a response was uttered in Japanese the author's translation will be given.

Analysis

Once collection and transcription were complete, the qualitative data analysis software NVivo was used to organise and analyse the data. A research journal in NVivo was also used to keep track of field notes and emerging themes in the data, in accordance with the guidelines set out by Bazeley (2007) and Richards (2005), and further informed by Agar (1996), Atkinson et al. (2003), and Lofland et al. (2006). The primary use of NVivo, however, was the qualitative coding and annotation of data, which is described in detail below.

Comparative analysis of interviews and questionnaires

Richards, co-developer of the NVivo application and author of *Handling Qualitative Data* (2005), and Bazeley, author of *Qualitative Data Analysis with NVivo* (2007), both advocate coding data for conceptual categories and their properties, and then developing hypotheses or generalised relations among these categories, with a view to generating theory. Over the past two decades, Computer Assisted Qualitative Data Analysis has not only greatly contributed to researchers' archiving and structuring of data, but also assisted in further systematising the kind of qualitative coding advocated in GT (Corbin & Strauss, 2008; Kelle, 2004), which in turn is relevant to Sealey and Carter's (2004) social realist approach.

Three types of coding, as described by Richards (2005), were employed in the analysis:

(1) Descriptive Coding – The identification of attributes such as a participant's age, average hours of computer use daily, and so on which describe a case.
(2) Topic Coding – The organization of passages of text by topic, for example, allocating a section of an interview that describes chat usage to a node named 'chat'.
    (a) Auto Coding – The use of software (such as NVivo) to identify key concepts via a crude analysis of specific words in a text, or by grouping the answers to the same question across a variety of participants to the same node. Only the latter has been employed in the present research.
(3) Analytical Coding – Coding that results from interpretation and reflection on meaning.
    (a) *In Vivo* Coding – A term from GT which refers to categories named by words the participants themselves use. (Richards, 2005: 90–95)

The email interviews were firstly auto-coded, grouping all participants' responses to a particular question into a single category. Due to the semi-structured nature of the face-to-face interviews, this type of analysis was not appropriate, so these interviews were instead coded manually by topic. On second and subsequent passes, descriptive and analytical coding, including *in vivo* coding, were used to generate an extensive list of nodes (a collection of references about a specific theme, to which references may be coded) and organise nodes into hierarchies, in accordance with Glaser and Strauss' (1967) guidelines.

Comparative analysis of the cases was undertaken both at the within-case and cross-case level. Within-case analysis, looking at the interviews with, and language use of, a particular participant or pair, allows for a deeper understanding of that particular case (Bazeley, 2007) through the comparison of a participant's interview comments with their actual use, and the comparison of one interaction (with a particular interlocutor, at a particular time, using a particular medium) with one or many others. Cross-case or multi-case analysis has dual goals according to Miles and Huberman (1994). The first is to increase generalisability and to test whether the processes observed in one case are idiosyncratic or more universal. Secondly, at a deeper level, is to see processes and outcomes across many cases, understand how they are qualified by local conditions, and, from these observations, develop more sophisticated descriptions and theories. Numerical information from the descriptive coding (such as number of years of Japanese study, number of hours of computer use daily) was compiled for basic quantitative analysis, the use of which is outlined in the following subsection.

Corpus analysis of CMC data

Gee states that 'counting things' in stretches of discourse provides an important guide 'in terms of hypotheses that [one] can investigate through close scrutinising of the actual details and content' of language-in-use (1999: 125, cited in Belz, 2003). In addition to the numerical demographic data collected through coding the interviews, basic data on the corpus of CMC interaction was also entered into spreadsheets for quantitative analysis using Excel.

Data such as subject, sender, language choice, length, attachments, comments, and emoticon use were recorded for each instance of communication. In addition to Japanese and English, Chinese, Korean, and Spanish were also present in participants' communication. Not all of the categories described above were relevant for all forms of data; however, these statistics provide a backdrop for the more detailed analysis of the data described below.

Discourse analysis of CMC data

DA and CA have been widely utilised in the analysis of CMC interaction (cf. Antaki *et al.*, 2005; Pasfield-Neofitou, 2006). In the *Handbook of Discourse Analysis*, Herring states that, for as long as CMC involves any kind of language, 'there will be a need for computer-mediated discourse analysis' (2003: 626). Androutsopoulos (2006a) also claims that sociolinguistic and DA studies are making contributions to the growing body of research on CMC.

Given the emergent nature of CMC, an array of tools are required to analyse the data collected for the present study. DA, which encompasses the analysis of both spoken and written language, can provide such a variety of tools. As previously mentioned, Coulthard (1985) states in an introduction to DA, that detailed descriptions of the skills of the 'competent NNS' are vital for the effective teaching and learning of additional languages. The question 'How do some speakers with limited resources manage to understand and communicate with a great degree of success?' (Coulthard, 1985: 159) is particularly relevant with regard to CMC interaction, and DA provides one way of describing this phenomena. Liddicoat (1997) likewise emphasises the need for a focus on what learners can do with the resources they have available.

As the study of language in context, DA consists of two main schools: British DA, based on Halliday's functional approach to language, and

American DA, which grew out of the ethnomethodological tradition (McCarthy, 1991). British DA places emphasis on the social functions of speech and writing, while American DA emphasises the importance of examining communication in natural settings. It is widely held that what is termed CA in the American tradition can be considered under the general heading of DA (although some, such as Seedhouse (2005) argue that DA is subsumed under CA). Despite these variations, all traditions include structure, function, and context, and a methodology that combines analyses from more than one approach may help in balancing the weakness of one kind of analysis with the strength of another (Georgakopoulou & Goutsos, 2004).

DA has been successfully utilised to investigate language use in CMC in a number of studies, including research in classroom settings on email (Biesenbach-Lucas et al., 2000; Biesenbach-Lucas & Waesenforth, 2001), teleconferencing (Belz, 2003), BBSs (Nguyen & Kellogg, 2005), MOOs (MUD, or Multi-User Dungeon, Object Oriented text-based electronic discussions, as examined by Weininger & Shield (2004)), and chat (Darhower, 2002; Freiermuth & Jarrel, 2006; Kitade, 2000; Lam, 2004), including both text and voice chat (Jepson, 2005), and chat in virtual worlds (Toyoda & Harrison, 2002). Studies of SLA in broader contexts, such as Lam's (2004) examination of L2 socialisation via CMC outside of any classroom, have also utilised a DA approach. Other aspects of culture, language use, and intercultural communication in CMC have been examined using DA; for example, comparisons of CMC with spoken and or written discourse (Condon & Cech, 1996; Ko, 1996), a study of culture, ethnicity, and race in web pages (Brock, 2005), and research on online forums and email (Cassell & Tversky, 2005; Paolillo, 1996). It is precisely this applicability to a broad range of CMC mediums that makes DA appropriate for the present study, which encompasses data from a variety of mediums and patterns of use. However, despite the broad applications of DA, Androutsopoulos and Beißwenger (2008) argue that aside from blogs, Web 2.0 platforms such as SNSs have received very little attention from discourse analysts to date. The current study aims to remedy this gap in the present research.

Under the broader umbrella of DA, CA has also been used to investigate the use of online forums or newsgroups in the workplace (Antaki et al., 2005), and language use in chat (Neuage, 2004). CA was also successfully applied in my previous research, where the key concepts of turn management, sequence management, including adjacency pairs, and repair, proved relevant categories for the analysis of chat between students of Japanese and their NS peers (Pasfield-Neofitou, 2006).

One of the most specific applications of DA to online communication is Herring's (2003) CMDA approach, outlined in Tannen et al.'s (2003)

Handbook of Discourse Analysis. As early as 1996, a special issue of *The Electronic Journal of Communication* entitled 'Computer-Mediated Discourse Analysis', edited by Herring, was published. Yet, despite over a decade of research, Androutsopoulos and Beißwenger (2008) claim that CMDA methodology continues to lag behind other areas of discourse studies, despite drawing methods and key concepts from CA, ethnography, sociolinguistics, genre analysis, and pragmatics. In their special issue of *Language@Internet*, the authors point out that Herring's (2004) CMDA is, however, possibly the most fully articulated framework in the field, and Herring invites other researchers to extend it, which the present study aims to do.

Androutsopoulos and Beißwenger (2008) note that linguists need to align their methodologies with continuously changing technologies, and question whether the same methods can be applied to a variety of discourses produced via different mediums. However, I argue, based on the data presented in Chapter 4, which demonstrates that participants' patterns of use are highly fluid between mediums, that what is required is a holistic approach.

Herring (2003) concentrates on four main areas for analysis – the classification of Computer Mediated Discourse (CMD), linguistic structure, interaction analysis, and social practice. As DA utilises a pre-determined set of categories, Herring describes a number of categories specifically for the analysis of CMD:

(1)   Medium and Channel (CMD is a distinct *medium* from either speaking or writing, and a 'lean' medium compared with speech in terms of the number of *channels*, or 'sources of information' available);
(2)   Medium Variables (*synchronicity*, the availability of simultaneous feedback, i.e. whether message transmission is *one-way* or *two-way*); and
(3)   CMD Modes (emic or 'culturally recognised' categories of CMD. Communication modes are defined and categorised socially as well as technologically). (Herring, 2003)

Herring (2003) argues that the linguistic properties of CMD depend largely on the kind of medium used. However, I contend that these 'Medium Variables' are actually cultural models only loosely based on technological affordances and constraints which CMC participants select from as models for their communication. For example, it is possible for a user to take the cultural model 'chat' (which is based upon the usual technological classification of chat as a one-way, synchronous form of communication) and apply it to the medium of email, using what is classified as an asynchronous medium in a synchronous way. These 'technological classifications' are actually little more than early 'culturally recognised' ways of using CMC tools – there is little or no technological difference between the way a computer sends and receives email and chat messages – only a difference in the way the tools were originally conceived of for use (although patterns of use are constantly changing). As such, these 'variables' are considered in the present study to be most useful not when applied as labels by the researcher on the basis of technology, but when understood as interpretive categories, based on an *in vivo* analysis which codes the exact words participants use in describing their own communication. Thus, for the purposes of this study, only Herring's (2003) category of 'CMD Modes' will be considered. 'Medium and Channel' and 'Medium Variables', although important categories in their own right, will be subsumed under this heading, as both may be considered 'culturally recognised' ways of thinking about and using CMC tools, rather than inherent technological differences.

Drawing on traditional DA (and CA) tools to classify interaction management, Herring (2003) highlights the use of concepts such as adjacency pairs, feedback, and the contrast with Sacks *et al.*'s (1974) spoken conversation ideal of 'no gap, no overlap' presented by CMC. It has been widely noted that in CMC there are often lengthy gaps, and, as described above, while strictly speaking individual transmissions cannot overlap, exchanges regularly become disjointed as two messages are typed or sent concurrently. Herring states that there are two main obstacles to interaction management in CMC caused by the medium:

(1)   Disrupted turn *adjacency*, where responses become dislocated, caused by the fact that messages are posted in the order received by the system, without regard for what they are responding to, and
(2)   Lack of simultaneous *feedback*, or an inability to perceive an interlocutor's reaction immediately, caused by reduced audio-visual cues. (Herring, 1999, cited in Herring 2003)

For these reasons, Beißwenger (2008) critiques the verbatim transfer of CA categories such as turn-taking and turn organisation, which were founded on communicative conditions that allow for mutual real-time perception, to the analysis of CMD. In a study of French learners' use of MOOs, Thorne (1999) also discusses the applicability of Sacks *et al.*'s (1974) observable facts on turn-taking. In my previous research on MSN Messenger, I presented my own comments relevant to the specific constraints of that medium (Pasfield-Neofitou, 2006), which demonstrated that many aspects remain relevant across the board. However, Beißwenger (2008) argues that coordination of communication in chat is an 'individual accomplishment', given that:

(1) Messages are transmitted en bloc, so that message production has to be entirely completed before transmission or 'uttering'.
(2) In oral conversation it is almost impossible physically to ignore the occurrence of an utterance as an acoustic event. In contrast, messages in written discourse are not noticed until the reader directs his or her attention to a specific visual target on which textual information is displayed. (Beißwenger, 2008: 2)

I argue that simply because messages are produced en bloc in chat (and in email, blogs, comments, and many other types of text-based CMC) does not mean that all of the above observations on CA should be considered irrelevant. Oral language also has a smallest unit – the phoneme. Similarly, the smallest linguistic unit possible in CMC would be a message containing a single letter. Chat users frequently split their 'turn' over several messages, as do users of other forms of CMC occasionally, demonstrating that one 'utterance' is not always transmitted en bloc but may be sent in stages. Nevertheless, it is readily apparent from Thorne (1999) and Beißwenger's (2008) discussions that there are some important considerations regarding the use of the term 'turn' to take into account when analysing CMC, as will be addressed below.

Units of analysis

Based on an analysis of the data presented in Chapters 3 and 4, the present study proposes three levels of analysis. They are:

(1) *Conversation* at the macro-level
(2) *Turn* at the meso-level, and
(3) *e-Turn* at the micro-level.

For the analysis of CMC, Thorne (1999) proposes the 'e-turn', which, although based on the 'turn', does not include the notions of linear sequencing and juxtaposition, which Beißwenger (2008) rightly objects to. Instead, the 'e-turn' may be defined as a free-standing communicative unit, taking its form from the way the program receives and orders input, and the form and content of the message, as typed by the user. Thorne (1999) lists the features of the 'e-turn' as being the result of a message typed by a human, and which takes its length, orthographic, grammatical, and stylistic characteristics from the user who typed the message. Furthermore, e-turns which relate to one another are not necessarily adjacent, as e-turns relating to other conversational strands or threads may intervene (Thorne, 1999: 154). However, as Herring (2003) observes, the use of quoting in CMC can create the illusion of adjacency, by incorporating and juxtaposing turns or portions of turns within a single message (or e-turn). Finally, Tudini (2003) defines a turn in chat as ending each time the floor is transferred from one participant to another, regardless of its length. Thus, both Thorne's 'e-turn' and Tudini's 'turn' may be observed in a single 'conversation'. Examples of each are provided in Chapter 4.

Book Outline

As previously outlined, the present study focuses on four research elements, namely self, setting, situated activity, and context. Chapter 2 will outline the participants' self or psychobiographies (Layder, 1993; Sealey & Carter, 2004), with respect to language learning, internet use, and relationships with their Japanese-speaking networks. These descriptions will then be drawn upon in Chapters 3–5, in order to address the research questions previously presented. These three analytic chapters will each focus on one of the remaining domains identified in Sealey and Carter's (2004) framework. Chapter 3 will locate participants' L2 CMC practices within the social setting of their broader CMC use and offline L2 communication. This chapter will address the first research question, which aims to uncover how learners establish and maintain relationships in which they use an L2 online. Chapter 4 will then focus on the situated activity of CMC use in terms of language use, as outlined in the second research question, in order to address how and in what combinations participants are using CMC in their L2. The final analysis chapter, Chapter 5, will focus on the contextual resources learners draw upon in the situated activity of CMC use, and the use of CMC itself as a contextual resource. This chapter will address the third research question, which looks at how CMC, in conjunction with other resources, may provide opportunities for L2 use and acquisition. All four research elements will then be drawn together for consideration as a whole in Chapter 6, which concludes the book.

2 Learner Backgrounds and Online L2 Networks

Despite their many similarities, participants were recruited from a broad range of backgrounds. Both the Australian university student volunteers and their Japanese contacts ranged greatly in terms of age, computer use, languages spoken, level of language proficiency, amount of prior language study, and in-country experience. It is precisely this variety which demonstrates the widespread nature of L2 CMC use. Participants' reports of observing other L2 learners' (both learners of Japanese and other languages) use of CMC in their respective target languages also provides evidence of its popularity.

In order to dispel some common stereotypes described in Chapter 1 about the 'typical' Internet user, two points are vital here. Firstly, a variety of CMC modes were used by participants of all ages represented in the study, not only undergraduates in their teens, suggesting that engagement in electronic discourse is by no means isolated to 'digital natives'. Secondly, learners of a wide range of proficiency levels were found to be engaging in bilingual or L2 communication online.

Following Belz and Reinhardt (2004), this chapter will start by describing the 'psychobiographies' of participants, with respect to their language learning and use, and history with CMC. This chapter will describe the Australian and Japanese participants respectively, drawing on the descriptive coding of participants' attributes from their interview comments, and in the case of the Japanese respondents, the auto-coding of their email interview responses. Greater attention will be paid to the sociocultural backgrounds of the Australian participants, who, as previously mentioned, are the focus of the present study.

Three main avenues for becoming involved in CMC in an L2 were identified, namely via education, international exchange, and established CMC networks in the L1, all of which are linked to participants' psychobiographies, or the development of the self along a series of evolutionary transitions (including key events such as beginning language study, participating in an exchange programme or conversation group, or starting work). Attending a formal Japanese language course was one of the first ways several participants were exposed to L2 use online, often with other NNSs or the teacher, as in the various studies outlined in Chapter 1. Exchanges were found to foster communication with NSs in a number of ways, including via CMC, and also to provide learners with up-to-date information regarding preferred CMC modes. Seeking Japanese contacts through one's established online L1 community was also found to be a valuable strategy.

Finally, this chapter demonstrates that one of the necessary resources for participation in much of the online world is an email address, which may be viewed as a 'passport'. However, as will be explored in the next chapter, email addresses are not the only important resource. Mixi, for example, requires members to provide a Japanese mobile phone email address, some online fan clubs require users to have a physical address in Japan, and subscribing to WoW demands a financial commitment that some may find prohibitive. Yet, in addition to providing access to modes like Ameba, Facebook, Mixi, MySpace, MSN, and WoW, as well as more obviously mobile phone or PC email, swapping email addresses or display names in face-to-face settings was also found to assist in maintaining relationships formed in offline settings in the online realm. The following chapter will build on these descriptions to further explore the first research question presented in Chapter 1, which addresses not only participants' backgrounds with respect to patterns of Internet use, but also their CMC networks, and how they are formed.

The Learners' Linguistic Backgrounds

The 12 Australian participants vary in age between 18 and 28 years (an average age of 20 years). Two are postgraduate coursework students (Kaylene and Jacob) while the remaining 10 are undergraduates, roughly representative of the enrolment at the university under examination. The number of female and male participants is equal (six males and six females). All claim English as their native language, although half of the participants say that Chinese (three Cantonese, three Mandarin) represents a second 'first language'. However, none described themselves as literate in Chinese characters. All participants speak Japanese as an additional or 'second' language. Four speak languages in addition to Japanese and their native language(s), including French (Cindy and Kaylene), Mandarin (Cindy and Scott), Korean (Cindy), Cantonese (Scott), and Vietnamese (Lucas). Of the 12 participants, eight speak more than two languages, the most being six (to varying degrees of proficiency).

The participants range in Japanese level from 1–2 (beginners) to 11–12 (very advanced), representing the spectrum of units available at the university in focus. Students take one 'level' each semester; therefore, for example, level 1–2 represents a one-year course. Completion of Japanese level 3 (lower intermediate) is approximately equivalent to N5 on the Japanese Language Proficiency Test, Japanese level 6 (intermediate) the equivalent of N4, Japanese level 10 (advanced) the equivalent of N3 or N2, and Japanese level 12 (very advanced), the equivalent of N2 or N1.

Participants' length of prior study ranges from 1–17 years, although as can be seen in Table 2.1, longer periods of study do not necessarily equate to

Table 2.1 Japanese background of Australian participants

Participant (N = 12)	Age	First language(s)	Additional language(s)	Japanese level	Years of Japanese study	Number of trips to Japan	Total time in Japan
Cindy	18	English Cantonese	French Mandarin Korean Japanese	1–2	8	0	
Genna	18	English	Japanese	1–2	7 (interrupted)	0	
Scott	22	English	Mandarin Cantonese Japanese	1–2	1	7	6 months
Lucas	19	English Cantonese	Vietnamese Mandarin Japanese	3–4	2	1	2 weeks
Noah	21	English Cantonese	Japanese	5–6	2 (interrupted)	1	1 month
Hyacinth	18	English Mandarin	Japanese	5–6	8 (interrupted)	1	3 weeks
Ellise	24	English	Japanese	7–8	5	2	1 year and 2 weeks
Zac	23	English Mandarin	Japanese	9–10	4	2	5 months and 2 weeks
Jacob	23	English	Japanese	9–10	11	2	6 weeks
Alisha	24	English	Japanese	9–10	17 (interrupted)	2	9 weeks
Oscar	20	English Mandarin	Japanese	11–12	6	1	11 months
Kaylene	28	English	French Japanese	11–12	7	2	13 months

higher levels of proficiency. Part of the reason for this may be a lack of in-country experience in comparison to others, and the fact that some partici-pants, like Genna and Alisha, began study in primary school and had an interrupted education. Most participants have been to Japan, with beginners Cindy and Genna the only two who have not. Fellow beginner Scott has had the most trips to Japan, all of them short visits, mostly to see his girlfriend. The participant with the longest time spent in-country is Kaylene, who has been twice for a total of 13 months, closely followed by Oscar and Ellise, who have been for similar lengths of time. These details are outlined in Table 2.1, ordered by learners' Japanese proficiency.

The Learners' Technological Backgrounds

All participants have a computer at home, and most own a desktop PC. Three participants, Genna, Ellise, and Kaylene, use a laptop as their main computer, while Scott and Hyacinth have both. Hyacinth owns both a PC and a Macintosh (Mac), while Genna is the only participant to have a Mac as her main computer. Total daily computer use ranges from two hours a day to what participants describe as 'constant', with Noah and Hyacinth keeping their computers switched on permanently. Although users obviously needed to sleep and so forth, this use is recorded as constant, owing to the fact that leaving a computer switched on with the sound also on provides the poten-tial for the user to be alerted or even awoken by an incoming message, and for them to respond accordingly. In effect, these users were available via CMC 24 hours a day. Most participants use two or three computers on a regular basis, including one or more at home, and one or more at work or university. These details are summarised in Table 2.2.

It may appear at first glance, particularly given the volunteer nature of participation, that these 12 students represent an abnormally technologi-cally savvy sample of the broader student population. However, a survey of over 100 beginners' (i.e. level 1–2) Japanese students conducted in the same year at the same university shows that this may not be the case (Pasfield-Neofitou et al., 2009). According to this data, 40% of students reported using Japanese in CMC before CMC was even introduced in the classroom, and despite having only studied Japanese for one semester. After the introduc-tion of a blogging project, a further 29% of students went on to try out other forms of CMC in Japanese, bringing the total to 69% of students who used some form of CMC in Japanese outside of class requirements. More frequent levels of use among those in higher levels would appear unsurprising.

Table 2.2 Computer background of Australian participants

Name	Type of computer		Total daily computer use	# Computers often used
Cindy	PC	Desktop	~16 hours/day	2
Genna	Mac	Laptop	3~4 hours/day	2
Scott	PC	Both	5 hours/day	3
Lucas	PC	Desktop	2~3 hours/day+	2
Noah	PC	Both	24 hours/day	2
Ellise	PC	Laptop	12 hours/day	3
Hyacinth	Both	Both	24 hours/day	2
Zac	PC	Desktop	5~6 hours/day	2
Jacob	PC	Desktop	2~3 hours/day +	3
Alisha	PC	Desktop	5 hours/day +	3
Oscar	PC	Desktop	4~5 hours/day	2
Kaylene	PC	Laptop	4~5 hours/day	3

A larger-scale survey of more than 2000 first-year students at a university in the same city as the current project was undertaken by Kennedy *et al.* (2008), found 99.4% of students had unrestricted access to a desktop or laptop computer, or both. Similarly, 96.4% of students had unrestricted access to a mobile phone, and 80% used the Short Message Service (SMS) on a daily basis. Over half of the students had purchased something online, 97.3% of students used email, and 89.6% used IM; however, Kennedy *et al.* noted that at the time, SNS use was in its early stages, and thus appeared nowhere near as prevalent as in the current study. Kennedy *et al.* also noted what they termed a 'significant blog culture', in that 34.9% of students surveyed indicated they had kept their own blog in the past year and yet more reported reading (58.6%) and commenting on (43.9%) other people's blogs. A year later, Oliver and Goerke (2007) undertook a similar survey of almost 300 students at another Australian university, and compared these results to those of Kennedy *et al.* (2008), as well as a survey of over 18,000 college students in the US (Caruso & Kvavik, 2005), and an earlier version of their own survey (Oliver, 2005). Oliver and Goerke concluded that Australian undergraduates are comparable to their North American peers in terms of high levels of access to the Internet off-campus and ownership of mobile devices.

Furthermore, the participants in the present research reported use of the Internet in an additional language among fellow learners not involved in the study. Hyacinth reported using Japanese with a fellow NNS in Taiwan, while Genna talked about her sister's use of the Internet in

Japanese. Oscar was also introduced to language tools on Facebook by a learner of French.

While Kennedy *et al.* (2008) concluded that the majority of students surveyed in their research were indeed 'tech-savvy', they warn that it is an overgeneralisation to label all students as 'digital natives', in Prensky's (2001) parlance. However, these broad results related to students' use of CMC, coupled with the more specific L2 CMC use statistics mentioned above, suggest that the computer access, use, and knowledge of the participants described in detail below is perhaps not unusual at all.

Cindy

Cindy is an 18-year-old Chinese-background, first-year female university student, studying level 1–2 (beginners) Japanese. Born in Australia, Cindy identifies Cantonese and English as her native languages. She previously studied French, and in addition to Japanese, is currently learning Mandarin and Korean.

Cindy was inspired to learn Japanese by her love of Japanese food, as her cousin is a *sushi* chef. She is interested in a variety of aspects of Japanese culture, including Visual Kei (a musical movement involving flamboyant and often androgynous fashion, dramatic makeup and hairstyles) and J-Rock (Japanese Rock) music genres. Cindy often looks at Japanese fashion and music magazines, which she obtains through a specialised importer at a highly inflated price. However, Cindy remarks, 'I can't really read anything . . . I just flick through'. Although Cindy's high school had a school trip to Japan, formal language classes were not offered. Thus, Cindy began her study of Japanese informally, in year seven (her first year of secondary school), mostly by reading books. Upon starting university (in the year of the study) Cindy began formal Japanese learning, and said that the biggest challenge for her was 'the sentence structures'.

While in secondary school, Cindy started exchanging emails with three Japanese students who visited her school on exchange. Even though she had been privately studying Japanese, Cindy did not often try to practise her newly acquired language, emailing mostly in English. After a few years, Cindy lost contact with all three after they changed their email addresses and she began to get error messages when trying to contact them. Cindy reports that the end of the communication made her feel 'sad'. However, after writing a letter to Mei, Cindy was excited to regain contact with her old friend when Mei added her on Facebook.

After missing out on a trip to Japan in secondary school with Lucas, Cindy hopes to go on exchange to a Japanese university in her second year.

Currently, outside of class, Cindy has limited opportunity to practise Japanese, so her use is usually restricted to a few Japanese words from *anime* while talking to (non-Japanese) friends face-to-face and online.

Cindy is a prolific computer user. She has a desktop PC that she switches on in the morning and does not turn off until the end of each day. When not at university, Cindy reports that she uses the computer for the whole day, and while on campus, she uses the university's computers regularly. Cindy plays online games (Massively Multiplayer Online Role-Playing Games or MMORPGs), although not in Japanese. The closest she has come is playing on a Japanese mind map game (http://maker.usoko.net/nounai/).

At the time of the study, Cindy's main use of CMC in Japanese was to email her university Japanese tutors, partially in Japanese, but mostly in English. She also code-switched to Japanese in emails or chat conversations with local friends who were also interested in Japanese language and culture. Two of these friends, Lucas and Hyacinth, are participants in the present study. During the research, Cindy also started blogging in Japanese with her friends and fellow participants, Hyacinth and Genna, after hearing that she would be required to produce blogs later in her Japanese course. Practising Japanese with her NNS friends appears to have been a main motivation for Cindy's use of her L2 online.

Genna

A friend of Cindy, Genna is another 18-year-old female, first-year university student studying Japanese level 1–2. Genna has had what she describes as a 'broken education' in regards to Japanese, having studied it intermittently throughout primary (years three to six) and secondary school (years seven to eight, skipping nine, and then completing ten). Genna describes her progress in class as reasonable 'for level 1 standards', stating that the curriculum is more 'in-depth' than her primary and secondary school lessons. The first five weeks of her university course, according to Genna, covered everything she had learnt in her seven years of previous study. She finds listening the hardest, preferring classes to be taught entirely in Japanese in order to acquire 'an ear' for the language, and reading the easiest, because she can go over it in her own time.

Like Cindy, Genna has never been to Japan, but is deeply interested in Japanese culture. In particular, Genna is interested in comparing Japanese and Western youth culture, including the self-expression of Harajuku girls. Harajuku, an area that lies between Shinjuku and Shibuya, consists of two main shopping districts that cater for youth fashion, including Visual Kei, *anime*, and *manga* styles. This interest was sparked by her younger sister's high school trip to Japan, and Genna hopes to go to Japan herself soon. She enjoys watching Japanese television shows with her sister at home, mostly those aimed at teens.

Aside from talking with her sister occasionally, online interactions are Genna's only opportunity to use Japanese outside the classroom. Genna reports that she comes from a 'very computer-oriented family, so we're always fighting over a computer'. For this reason, she got her own computer, a Macintosh laptop, when she started university. Genna says that she uses her computer 'too much', several hours a day, and more on the weekends.

Genna first started communicating in Japanese online when she began writing to her sister's eldest host sister. She said that although she had Japanese friends before, 'we'd never thought to write in Japanese, because my Japanese wasn't good enough'. Despite encouragement from those friends, at the time of interview, Genna had still not tried using Japanese with them online, having established a routine of writing in English.

Genna's main communication in Japanese is with Tokio, whom she met on MySpace. Tokio was motivated to seek out friendships with Australians after recently moving to Australia, and Genna enjoys learning about the aspects of Japanese culture listed above from him. Even before having ever met face-to-face, Genna and Tokio exchanged very frequent emails, almost every day, and sometimes several times a day.

Scott

Scott is a 22-year-old male in his third year of university, also studying level 1–2 Japanese. In addition to Japanese, and his native language English, Scott speaks Mandarin, despite not having a Chinese home background. He reported that he started learning Mandarin four years ago when his father was posted to Hong Kong for work. Scott also learned Cantonese through listening to songs while in China. After living in Hong Kong for a while, Scott moved to mainland China to begin university, where he met his long-term girlfriend, Kieko, from Japan. Scott also met other Japanese speakers in China, with whom he started communicating over the Internet, mostly in Chinese. However, this communication for the most part dropped off once his friends gained full-time employment. Having moved back to Australia and finishing a major in Chinese, Scott was motivated to pick up Japanese study in the second-to-last year of his degree because of Kieko's encouragement.

At the time of interview, Scott was doing well in class, regularly achieving 100% on the mini-quizzes. He reported that the only thing he was struggling with was pronunciation. Scott's main interests in Japanese culture are more traditional than many other beginning students as his girlfriend's father is an artist, influencing Scott's attraction to Japanese ceramics. Of popular Japanese culture, Scott said 'I have an interest, but I don't go out of my way to look into it'. Also in contrast with many other beginners, Scott has been to Japan seven times, and visited Kieko a further time during the course of this research. His longest period in Japan was three months, when his family moved from Hong Kong during the SARS outbreak, and the other trips were all short visits to meet Kieko, each approximately two weeks in length. During his trips, Scott has met members of Kieko's family, with whom he started communicating in Japanese. Currently, Scott's main use of Japanese outside the classroom is in communication with his girlfriend, and a sprinkling of words with local friends.

Like the other beginners Scott is a regular computer user, stating that his five hours a day of leisure time spent on the computer was embarrassing. His main motivation for using CMC in Japanese is to communicate with his girlfriend. While most of this time is now spent communicating with Kieko, like Cindy, Scott has frequented gaming forums and played MMORPGs in the past.

Lucas

A second-year 19-year-old male university student, Lucas is studying level 3–4 (lower intermediate) Japanese and says that English is his 'main' language, despite speaking Vietnamese with his mother and Cantonese with his father at home. Lucas also studies Mandarin. At the time of interview, Lucas had been studying Japanese for just over a year, having completed level 1–2 in his first year of university. Lucas says that spoken Japanese causes him the most trouble, but reading and writing are 'okay'.

Like Genna, Lucas is interested in aspects of Japanese culture that are different from his own, and says he appreciates the 'politeness'. At first, Lucas was interested in watching the Japanese news on television, but given its early broadcast time, he decided to listen to the radio instead. He also watches music shows that Hyacinth, another participant, downloads and passes on to him. Finally, he used to read *manga* and watch some *anime*, but does not have the time anymore.

Lucas has been to Japan once, for a two-week sister-school exchange trip (the one Cindy missed out on) when he was in his final year of secondary school, without having studied Japanese at school. He still communicates online with one of the students he met while in-country, Hisayo, and their exchanges appear to be his main motivation for communicating in Japanese via CMC. Lucas also expressed an interest in making a Mixi profile, but said that he 'can't really read most of it', as the site's instructions are written entirely in Japanese. Aside from his online communication, which is mostly email, Lucas also tries to teach one of his workmates some basic Japanese outside of the classroom.

Lucas has a desktop PC at home, which he uses for several hours every day, and occasionally shares with his father and brother. Sometimes he uses the university's computers to check his email also. Like Cindy and Scott, Lucas has played MMORPGs including WoW in the past, although he does not anymore.

Noah

Noah is a 21-year-old male undergraduate studying level 5–6 (intermediate) Japanese. Like Cindy, Noah was born in Australia and lists English first among the languages he speaks, although Cantonese was the first language he acquired. He started learning English in kindergarten, and now writes and speaks fluently, while he is unable to write in Cantonese.

After completing eight months' intensive study of Japanese at another university in Australia, which offers the only full-time intensive Japanese course in the area, Noah started studying at his current university for three months before deferring. At the time of the interview he was repeating the same three months of study he had undertaken the previous year. Having learned 'all the grammar before, and most of the vocabulary', Noah said that he finds the course fairly easy, and that the only difficulty for him is Japanese characters (*kanji*).

An aspiring English teacher, Noah is interested in the Japanese education system and other elements of Japanese culture, including festivals. It was his dream of being an English teacher in Japan that inspired Noah to learn Japanese. Noah has been to Japan once, for a two-week study tour. While there he met two Japanese university students who introduced him to Mixi, and he started communicating with them online. Keeping in contact with these students appears to be Noah's main motivation for using CMC in Japanese.

Since he currently has no local Japanese friends as they have all returned to Japan, outside of the classroom Noah says that he uses Japanese 'anywhere basically, even to people who don't understand'. He uses Japanese online, and says he often thinks in Japanese.

Noah has both a desktop and laptop PC, which he normally brings with him to university. Like Cindy, he says, 'whenever I have free time, I'm usually on the computer'. He too plays online games such as WoW, even joining a Japanese guild on WoW at one stage.

Hyacinth

Hyacinth is an 18-year-old female undergraduate who was also enrolled in level 5–6 Japanese at the time of interview. She started studying Japanese in her final year of primary school, eight years before the present research. However, Hyacinth's second year at university was the first year she had studied Japanese at the tertiary level, as she took a break after finishing year 12 Japanese a year early in secondary school. In spite of her hiatus from Japanese classes, Hyacinth says she retained 'an interest in Japanese things', including dramas, stating that everyone who studies Japanese does the same. However, Hyacinth says that she does not pick up vocabulary as quickly as she used to.

Hyacinth's home language is Mandarin, but she is reluctant to call this her first language. Like Noah, she started learning English at four years of age, and says that she considers English her primary language.

Although Hyacinth describes her level of Mandarin as very low she says it does help with reading Japanese characters and understanding the function of some Japanese words, as opposed to trying to find an English equivalent. Hyacinth has similar interests to Cindy and Ellise, as she is interested in Japanese music, mostly pop (and downloads Japanese music shows which she passes on to Lucas). She also likes Japanese comics (*manga*), especially 'the girly ones', like *Hana Yori Dango* (Boys over Flowers), which was adapted into a TV show of which Ellise is also particularly fond, and video games, which she attributes to her brother's influence. Hyacinth plays PlayStation 2 and Nintendo DS, and has played a Role Playing Game (RPG) in Japanese before. This represents a significant amount of time investment and linguistic challenge. She has a small collection of Japanese games and comics that she has purchased over the Internet. Hyacinth says that she often feels that she cannot wait for *manga* to be translated into English, and often she will start off reading a few volumes in translation, and then progress to the later volumes that have not yet been translated. Recently, Hyacinth has started reading series which are entirely untranslated. Some she downloads from websites, some she buys, and others are sent to her by a friend from Taiwan who is also learning Japanese. Hyacinth's main motivation for using her L2 online is to gain access to Japanese popular culture, via shopping, downloading, or other NNS friends.

Hyacinth, like Lucas, has also been to Japan once, for the same two-week sister-school high school exchange trip. Like Genna, she has a Mac laptop and a PC desktop. She keeps the computer on all day, and says that one computer the family had was even destroyed by this practice. Furthermore, like Cindy, Scott, and Lucas, Hyacinth reports that she used to play MMORPGs online, although she does not have time anymore.

Ellise

Ellise, born in England, is a 24-year-old female undergraduate student who left for a year-long exchange to Japan part-way through the data collection period. At the time of the interview, Ellise had been studying Japanese for five years, starting when she lived in Japan for a year teaching English. Afterwards, she began formal study at the same university as Noah, and, subsequent to the intensive course, changed universities again and enrolled in level 5–6 Japanese. During this time, she returned to Japan for a two-week holiday.

After moving to Japan part-way through the data collection, Ellise was placed in the equivalent of level 7–8 (upper intermediate) and 9–10 (advanced) courses in Japan. However, Ellise reported that because of her desire to go to Japan, she had concentrated less on her Japanese class and more on her other units over the previous semester, in order to attain the necessary distinction average. Ellise says that listening is the easiest aspect of Japanese study for her, while speaking and writing pose a challenge because of the difficulty of using the correct particles and learning Japanese characters. However, writing on a computer is not so difficult for Ellise, as she can simply type the required characters, stating that, 'I can recognise a lot more than I can read'.

Ellise has a laptop PC, and uses a computer for work as well. She claims to use a computer every day, and, like Genna and Scott, is embarrassed by her frequent use, generally 12 hours a day.

In terms of culture, Ellise is mostly interested in Japanese music, but 'not the traditional stuff'. She enjoys popular music, fashion, and nightlife, and in fact met one of the friends that she communicates with online most at a bar in Japan. When not in Japan, like Hyacinth and Genna, Ellise downloads Japanese dramas from the Internet, first watching them 'raw' (without subtitles), to which she attributes the improvement in her listening comprehension. Furthermore, like Noah, Ellise also talks to herself in Japanese to practise.

Ellise is very interested in Japanese popular culture, especially media and magazines, although, like Cindy, Ellise says 'I don't really read magazines, I look at the pictures'. Despite finding magazines too difficult to read, as a paid-up member of the Gackt fan club, Ellise looks at fan websites and the Gackt website, even going as far as translating his diaries. Gackt is the stage name of an Okinawan alternative musician and idol, who has performed in French, Cantonese, Mandarin, and Korean, in addition to Japanese. Being a fan club member gives her special access to otherwise restricted sections of the website. However, when not in Japan, it is relatively difficult to arrange fan club subscription. In order to overcome the restrictions on overseas membership, Ellise keeps in contact with a friend in Japan via mobile phone email, whom she uses as a proxy. Ellise gives her friend the money to pay her fees and her friend accepts the deliveries of fan club materials, re-mailing them to Ellise while she is in Australia. Keeping in contact with friends in Japan and remaining in touch with the Japanese fan base of her favourite celebrities motivate Ellise's use of Japanese online.

Zac

A 23-year-old male university student, Zac is enrolled in the level 9–10 (advanced) Japanese sequence. Level 9 focuses on popular culture, while level 10 is a translation and interpreting unit. Born in Brunei, Zac says that Mandarin should be his native language, but, because he has not used it in a long time, he now considers English the language he is most proficient in, which he started to learn at the age of five years, just prior to his arrival in Australia. Japanese is his next most fluent language, which he has been studying for around four years, and he describes Mandarin as his 'third tier' language.

After finishing year 12, Zac went to Japan for the first time, a two-week backpacking trip, 'not knowing a single word of Japanese'. His second trip was for work, spending five months in Hokkaido working for a ski company, still never having formally studied Japanese. He began his study of Japanese by undertaking the same intensive course as Noah and Ellise when he returned to Australia. This was supplemented by a summer course at a private school. Now, Zac says that he is enjoying the level 10 interpreting and translation unit, especially as he is no longer required to formally study grammar or complete the Japanese character tests that he struggled with in other units. He says that speaking is his main strength, while reading is his weakness, unless there is *furigana* above the characters to show their pronunciation.

A volunteer at the university *manga* library where Jacob and Kaylene also worked, Zac is interested in both *anime* and *manga*, and developed an interest in Japanese music through listening to the opening and closing songs of his favourite shows. His interest in *manga* and *anime* was sparked before he started learning Japanese, while still in secondary school.

Outside the classroom, Zac uses Japanese occasionally in his capacity as a *manga* library volunteer, but, more importantly, is a member of a conversation group comprised of Japanese and English NSs, convened online, that regularly meets face-to-face in cafés. In addition, Zac's family also often hosts exchange students from Japan, with whom he speaks in Japanese.

Zac uses two computers mainly, one at university and his desktop PC at home. After his electronic dictionary was stolen, Zac began using his

Nintendo DS handheld game system to look up words and Japanese characters. He enjoys video games, and, like Cindy, Scott, Lucas, and Hyacinth, used to play online games, including the MMORPG Phantasy Star Online, which was popular in Japan. Also similar to Hyacinth, he uses the Internet to download two *anime* episodes per night. Zac's brother recently married a Japanese woman and now lives in Japan. Zac used this point of contact, for example, to help set up a social networking profile on Mixi. His Mixi blog is largely made up of translations that he has produced for class, and posting these translations and obtaining feedback on his language use appears to be Zac's main motivation for his use of Japanese online.

Jacob

Jacob is also a 23-year-old male, but is a postgraduate student, having completed a major in Japanese up to level 10. After finishing his Masters in translation (Japanese to English) partway through the present study, Jacob left for Japan to work as an assistant English teacher, an aspiration shared by Noah. Jacob is a NS of English, and began learning Japanese 10 years ago when he started secondary school, although he describes the curriculum as very slow paced during the first few years. He explains that he never really got the opportunity to practise speaking in either the secondary or tertiary environment, and as a result is not 'comfortable' now speaking or listening. Reading and writing, on the other hand, he reports do not pose much trouble.

An employee of the *manga* library where Zac and Kaylene also volunteered, Jacob is interested in a variety of Japanese popular culture including *anime, manga,* and subversive cinema, for example, *yakuza* films and science fiction. Like Zac and Hyacinth, Jacob downloads *anime*, and has an email subscription to a Japanese YouTube channel.

Jacob has been to Japan twice, both times being three-week trips. The first was a high school exchange, while the second was a mixture of holidaying and Jacob's playing a role in the opening of a *manga* museum. During the data collection period, Jacob left for a two-year Japan Exchange and Teaching (JET) programme placement in Japan. The JET programme provides opportunities for assistant teachers, coordinators for international relations, and sports exchange advisors. Although Jacob applied for a position as coordinator for international relations, he was accepted into the programme as an assistant language teacher instead, and went to Japan to teach English at a rural elementary school for two years.

Like most participants, Jacob has a desktop PC, which he uses for several or more hours a day. Before moving to Japan, Jacob's main use of Japanese online was to communicate with two professors from a Japanese university, whom he met at a symposium at his Australian university. He later worked with them on a *manga*-related project, but they fell out of touch not long after. Previously, Jacob corresponded with Japanese students he met on exchange, but the communication was short-lived.

At the time of interview, Jacob was in charge of the university *manga* library, and used Japanese occasionally in this capacity. He drew on the assistance of researchers from Japan stationed in the building in which the library is located to assist with his Japanese, getting their help proofreading draft emails.

Jacob greatly enjoys translation, and as a personal project in the past has translated Japanese urban legends. He sourced the legends by lurking on Japanese forums, never posting. Jacob's main motivations for using Japanese online appear to be sourcing materials and resources for translations, and work-based communication.

Alisha

A 24-year-old female university student, Alisha started learning Japanese at an early age, in her first year of primary school. At the time of interview, Alisha had been studying Japanese for 17 years, the longest of any participant, and had just finished level 10 Japanese in her third year at university. Alisha is a final year student studying for an Arts/Education degree, undertaking only education units, having finished the arts Japanese language component with a credit. Despite having finished formal Japanese lessons, Alisha still has opportunities to use Japanese as she arranges regular meetings with some Japanese exchange students that she met in her linguistics class, as well as the university language exchange programme (LEP), which Kaylene was also a part of. The LEP is a university-based programme which matches international students with local students for linguistic and cultural exchange, and participants usually meet one hour a week for conversation.

One of Alisha's interests is reading Japanese authors' novels in English, and her goal is to be able to read novels in her L2. At the time of interview, Alisha was reading *The Lion, the Witch and the Wardrobe* in Japanese, stating that she had wanted to start with a children's book that she was already familiar with in English. Alisha says that she is more confident reading and writing in Japanese than listening and speaking.

As a Christian and an aspiring Japanese teacher, Alisha is very interested in family culture in Japan, including religion and education. She has been to Japan twice, the first time for a three-week secondary school trip, and the second for a long holiday during a university vacation.

During the semester, Alisha says that she uses the computer frequently, often for five or more hours at a time. In the holidays, she frequently uses her desktop PC for reading the news, on the *Mainichi Shimbun*'s English website. Like Cindy and Zac, Alisha also enjoys playing Nintendo DS, getting one of her friends in Japan to bring her games in Japanese. Alisha's main motivation for using Japanese online is for communication with her Japanese friends, and some research.

Oscar

Oscar is a 20-year-old male third-year university student completing level 11–12 (very advanced) Japanese, having just returned from a one-year university exchange to Japan. In addition to English, his first/home language, Oscar says that he speaks some Japanese and a bit of Mandarin. Oscar began Mandarin study in secondary school, and completed a first-year stream at university. (He also learned 'some' French and German in primary school, but says he now cannot remember any.) Oscar says that throughout high school learning Japanese and Mandarin at the same time was confusing, as he would mix up the readings for characters, but since starting different levels at university he has found that his Japanese actually helps his Mandarin learning.

Oscar started Japanese in year nine of secondary school, around six years earlier. He studied to year 12 at high school, and continued Japanese study for all three years of university so far, including a one-year exchange. While at the Japanese university, Oscar lived in the dormitories and says that he is comfortable speaking informally, but not in using Japanese honorifics or *keigo*. Since coming back from Japan, one of Oscar's Japanese friends came to visit, and as a result of showing them around, Oscar says he is now 'so behind' in his reading for class. Keeping in touch with the friends he made on exchange appears to be Oscar's main motivation for using his L2 via CMC.

One of Oscar's hobbies is playing Japanese chess or *shōgi*, which he started playing online. Oscar says he learnt to play Western chess in his final year of primary school, and in year 10 of secondary school played *shōgi* online for the first time, learning the rules from a website in English. Now, he sometimes meets a Japanese friend from his Australian church for face-to-face games, and in the past has played online occasionally with Japanese players. Aside from chess, Oscar enjoys healthy Japanese foods, movies, and *anime*, and when he was in Japan Oscar used to play Xbox 360 games online at a friend's house. While playing, he would listen to other players speaking Japanese using microphones in-game.

At home, Oscar has a very old desktop PC, shared with his mother and brother, on which he cannot use Japanese. In order to use Japanese online, he has to use one of the university computers. For this reason, Oscar spends a lot of time at university on Wednesdays, Fridays, and Saturdays when he does not have classes, coming in specifically to use the computers.

Kaylene

Kaylene, a 28-year-old female, is the eldest participant, and a postgraduate student like Jacob, having just finished honours in translation. Kaylene moved to Japan to start a pre-Masters course part-way through the period of the data collection. A volunteer at the *manga* library where Jacob and Zac also worked, Kaylene is very interested in Japanese art, although she attributes this to her love of art in general, not specifically Japanese culture. When asked what elements of Japanese culture she is interested in, Kaylene responded 'I don't know. That's not why I started studying the language'. She retold how, after hating the job she had been doing for two years, she decided to go to France, having studied French in secondary school and art in Technical and Further Education (TAFE). It was while in France that her love of languages was rekindled, and upon her return to Australia, when she found that French courses were not offered at many institutions of higher learning, Kaylene chose Japanese, almost at random.

Kaylene says that she speaks a reasonable amount of Japanese, and a little French, in addition to her native English. Like Noah, Ellise, and Zac, Kaylene started learning Japanese in an intensive course at another university seven years ago, before coming to her current university and completing up to level 12. In her honours year she supplemented this with an Advanced Reading unit.

Drawing on resources such as online dictionaries, Kaylene is fairly confident in both reading and writing Japanese, although she has problems with colloquial language. At the time of the first interview, having been away from Japan for a while, Kaylene remarked that she had lost some confidence in speaking as she did not have many opportunities to practise, but that listening was fine.

Kaylene has been to Japan twice, the first time as an exchange student to a Japanese university for 10 months, and the second time for a three-month trip involving travel and a visit to her yoga and meditation instructor, a Buddhist nun.

In Australia, like Alisha, Kaylene uses the university LEP, and has made a number of friends through that scheme. She has a laptop PC which she uses for around five hours a day, and Kaylene even maintains her own website, including links to Japan-themed pages. Like Jacob, Ellise, Hyacinth, and Cindy,

Kaylene sometimes downloads Japanese television programme episodes, mostly for listening practise. Her main motivations for using Japanese online appear to be a mixture of communicating with friends and work colleagues.

The Learners' Online Contacts

The 18 Japanese participants range in age between 19 and 40 years (an average age of almost 30 years, markedly higher than their Australian contacts). The majority of the Japanese contacts of the Australian participants are female. Of the 18 contacts who signed up to participate in the present research, 14 are female and only four (Tokio, Kō, Yoshio, and Daishi) male. This gender imbalance (78% female versus 22% male) appears unsurprising given the volunteer basis of the study, and the makeup of the Australian participants' wider L2 social circles. Analysis of the interviews, actual communication, and online networking of the 12 Australian participants revealed that they had online contact with a total of 100 Japanese speakers, of whom 72 were female, compared to just 28 males. Therefore, the volunteer sample appears representative of the Australian students' wider L2 circles in this respect. This gender imbalance, as well as the age difference, may also be partially attributed to the number of Japanese teachers who remain in touch with their Australian students online and who are predominantly female.

All Japanese participants claimed Japanese as their native language, and English as their L2. Kieko, Scott's girlfriend, also speaks Mandarin after having completed university study in China, Sae speaks some Swedish, having worked in Sweden, and Hisayo studied Spanish at university.

A number of English proficiency tests are available, and eight Japanese participants provided their scores on these tests for the present research. Five participants, Eri, Ikuko, Noriko, Ruriko, and Watako, had taken the Test of English for International Communication (TOEIC). Eri, Noriko, Ikuko, and Ruriko attained scores within the highest 'Gold' band, while Watako's score placed her in the middle 'Green' band, a similar level to both Hisayo and Chikae, who attained level 2 on the *Eiken* (English Exam), approximately equivalent to a score of 450 in the Test of English as a Foreign Language (TOEFL). Mei was the only participant to undertake the TOEFL exam, gaining a score of 523 (the equivalent of a Grade 2A on the *Eiken*, slightly higher than Hisayo and Chikae, or within the 'Green' band on TOEIC, the same level as Watako). These scores indicate that these participants have an intermediate to advanced level of English competence (ETS, 2011; STEP, 2011; VEC, 2011).

For participants who have not taken a standardised test, their English level is indicated in Table 2.3 by a self assessment (in terms of what they can

Table 2.3 English background of Japanese participants

Contact (N =12)	Name (N =18)	Age	Native language	Additional language(s)	English level	Years of English study	# of trips to ESC	Total time in ESC
Cindy	Mei	19	Japanese	English	TOEFL 523 (Intermediate)	8	1	3 weeks
Genna	Tokio	29	Japanese	English	Living in Australia*	14	3	1 year and 4 months
Scott	Kieko	26	Japanese	English Mandarin	Extremely good**	10+	4	1 year and 3 weeks
Lucas	Hisayo	19	Japanese	English Spanish	Eiken 2 (Intermediate)	10	8	3 months
Ellise	Atsuko	35	Japanese	English	Everyday conversation*	10	20	20 weeks
	Sae	36	Japanese	English Swedish	Living in Australia*	10	6	3 years, 6 months and 3 weeks
Zac	Fumie	27	Japanese	English	Living in Australia*	N/A	N/A	N/A
Jacob and Kaylene	Kō	34	Japanese	English	Little bit**	N/A	N/A	N/A
Alisha and Ellise	Eri	27	Japanese	English	TOEIC 910 (Advanced)	4	3	3 years and 6 months
	Noriko	28	Japanese	English	TOEIC 970 (Advanced)	16	1	2 years and 8 months
Oscar	Yoshio	20	Japanese	English	Business level*	8	1	2 weeks
Kaylene	Chikae	23	Japanese	English	Eiken 2 (Intermediate)	12	3	1 year and 1 week
	Daishi	39	Japanese	English	Little to none*	6+	N/A	N/A
	Ikuko	40	Japanese	English	TOEIC 895 (Advanced)	6+	N/A	N/A
	Junko	40	Japanese	English	Very good**	6+	1+	2 years
	Ruriko	23	Japanese	English	TOEIC 875 (Advanced)	10	2	10 months
	Ukiko	27	Japanese	English	General conversation*	10	3	2 years
	Watako	29	Japanese	English	TOEIC 590 (Intermediate)	6+	5	2 years

Notes: In alphabetical order by Australian contact. ESC = English Speaking Country. * = self assessment (no official test score or interview response available). ** = partner assessment (no official test score or interview response available).

do/feel comfortable with in English), and corroborated by partner assessments, as well as evidence in the online communication collected. Tokio, Sae, and Fumie were all living in Australia at the time of research, and stated that they had enough proficiency in English to get by day to day, as well as to undertake a university degree. According to Scott, Kieko's English is extremely good, having lived in America in the past, and she is now using English in her occupation as a furniture designer for a major international company, as well as communicating with Scott regularly. Likewise, Yoshio rated his English ability as 'business level'. Atsuko and Ukiko appraised their English rather modestly as the level required for everyday or general conversation, and, according to Ellise, Atsuko has the least proficiency in English out of her Japanese contacts. Jacob stated that Kō's English appeared limited, citing his need for an interpreter during a visit to Australia, although he could communicate a little.

Almost all of the 18 Japanese participants were residing in Japan at the time of the study, with the exception of Genna's online friend, Tokio, Ellise's former teacher, Sae, and Zac's acquaintance from the MeetUp group, Fumie. All three were in Australia for study.

Details about length of English study and experience in English-speaking countries (ESC) are available for 14 of the 18 Japanese participants, and are produced in Table 2.3. However, it is assumed that some of the older participants who did not agree to or answer the email interview (Fumie, Kō, Daishi, and Ikuko) would have even more years of English study and use. All of the Japanese respondents had visited an English-speaking country at least once, for between two weeks and over two-and-a-half years. This is markedly longer than the Australian students' experiences in Japan – perhaps because of increased opportunity due to the age difference and the greater number of countries in which English is used. Still, there was great variety in the types of experiences Japanese participants had overseas – some, like Noriko, were on a single lengthy exchange, while others, such as Atusko, took a large number (20) of short trips.

Like the Australian participants, all Japanese respondents reported having access to a computer at home (see Table 2.4). Again, PCs were more common than Macs, with only Kieko (who notably works as a designer, an occupation where Macs are commonly used) and Sae (who also uses a PC) owning a Macintosh. While desktop computers were more prevalent among Australian participants, the Japanese participants owned far more laptop (or 'notebook') computers. Laptop use appears to be the norm in Japan, where home and office space is often limited and there may not be room for a desktop PC.

In general, despite a similar range of one hour per day to leaving the computer always on, the Japanese participants in the present research appear

Table 2.4 Computer background of Japanese participants

Participant	Type of computer		Total daily computer use	# of computers regularly used
Mei	PC	Both	2~3 hours/day	2
Tokio	PC	Both	3 hours/day+	3
Kieko	Mac	Laptop	5 hours/day+	1
Hisayo	PC	Laptop	1 hour/day	1
Atsuko	PC	Desktop	6 hours/day	1
Sae	Both	Both	24 hours/day	2
Eri	PC	Laptop	3 hours/day	1
Noriko	PC	Laptop	2 hours/day+	1
Yoshio	PC	Laptop	2 hours/day	1
Chikae	PC	Both	8 hours/day	2
Ikuko	PC	Desktop	7 hours/day (approx)	2
Ruriko	PC	Both	8 hours/day+	2
Ukiko	PC	Desktop	1.5 hours/day	1
Watako	PC	Desktop	8 hours/day+	2

to use their computers less than the Australian participants do. The average Japanese respondent reported using a computer for approximately six hours a day, a third less time than the average Australian participant (an average of three hours less per day). The only Japanese participant to keep her computer always on during waking hours was Sae, a graduate student. This was a relatively common practice among the Australian students, and it is perhaps telling that Sae too was studying at an Australian university during the period of the research.

Japanese participants in the current study also appear to have had access to fewer computers than the Australians – seven of the Japanese participants reported using only one computer, while all Australian participants used a minimum of two computers regularly. Tokio, the only Japanese participant who used more than two computers on a regular basis (again, not at all uncommon among Australian participants) was also located in Australia during the period of the research. The computer background of the Japanese participants in the present study is summarised in Table 2.4.

Importantly, while mobile phone Internet use was not very common and somewhat costly in Australia at the time of research, it was much more common in Japan. Thus, mobile phones represented a very important port of access to CMC for Japanese participants, with all of those located in Japan who responded to the interview owning an Internet capable mobile phone. By contrast, only one Australian participant, Ellise, was able to access the Internet on her Australian mobile at the time. Oscar had owned a mobile with Internet access while in Japan, and Kaylene and Jacob both bought Internet enabled mobiles when they moved to Japan during the data collection period. The diversity of participants in both groups demonstrates the widespread nature of L2 CMC use, and the relationships of the participants introduced above will be described below.

CMC Networks and Relationships

Although all Australian participants were recruited as volunteers, nine of the 12 Australian participants were found to be linked as 'friends' through the SNSs they use, as seen in Figure 2.1. Despite the fact that they were not deliberately recruited as a 'community', this relationship is unsurprising given that all Australian participants are to some degree members of a larger learning community at the same university, and, more specifically, the Japanese learning community within it. Furthermore, some of the Australian participants were also members of a further sub-community, centred on the university's *manga* library. Jacob, Kaylene, Elli, and Zac, all linked by Facebook, were also all members of the *manga* library and either worked or volunteered there. Friends Hyacinth, Cindy, and Genna also established their own network on the blogging site, Ameba.

Once their Japanese contacts and other forms of communication are taken into consideration, the connectedness of this community becomes

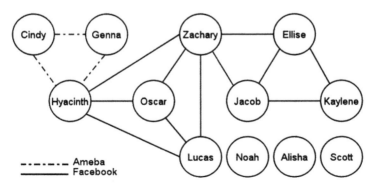

Figure 2.1 Australian participants' social networking

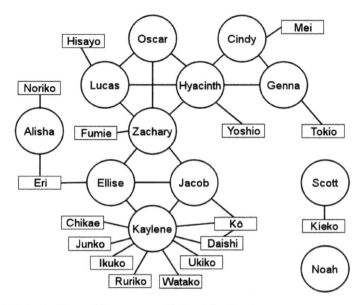

Figure 2.2 Australian and Japanese participants' networks

apparent. Alisha, who was not direct friends with any of the other participants via SNS, is friends with Japanese contacts of other Australians. Only Scott and Noah remain outside this network, which is unsurprising given Scott's very different relationship with Kieko, and the fact that Noah had no contacts participating in the study. This complex array of relationships is displayed in Figure 2.2.

A wide variety of relationships is exemplified in the above diagram, including LEPs, teachers, students, host sisters and brothers, co-workers, employers and employees, classmates, friends of friends, and Internet acquaintances. Participants use numerous means to keep in contact with both their English- and Japanese-speaking contacts. The diagram above only depicts data available for analysis in the present study. Thus, denseness of networking is not representative of participants' entire online networking, and further connections between participants mediated by communication channels not available for analysis in the present study may also exist.

Motivations for CMC use

In addition to the wide variety of types of relationships represented in the present study, participants had various motivations to maintain these relationships via CMC. Although any brief description of participants' relationships is bound to involve oversimplification, it is useful to summarise and acknowledge the ways in which participants defined their own relationships. Table 2.5 provides a list of the Australian participants who had Japanese contacts willing to participate in the present study (Noah and Hyacinth excluded), and the nature of their relationships with their Japanese contacts.

As can be seen from Table 2.5, there are almost as many kinds of relationships (14 broad types) as relationships (20 pairs). Cindy and Mei first met when Mei visited Cindy's high school on exchange, and CMC was the most convenient way for them to remain in contact. Genna and Tokio met via MySpace, and their communication remained primarily via CMC for the data collection period. Scott and Kieko were involved in a long-distance romance, and used CMC to sustain their relationship. Lucas and Hisayo had hosted one another on a school-based exchange, and used CMC to keep in contact. Ellise met Atsuko in a bar in Japan, and they too used CMC to

Table 2.5 Nature of participants' relationships

Australian participant (n = 10)	Japanese contact (n = 18)	Nature of relationship
Cindy	Mei	Former exchange student
Genna	Tokio	MySpace friend
Scott	Kieko	Boyfriend/girlfriend
Lucas	Hisayo	Host brother/sister
Ellise	Atsuko	Friend from a bar
	Sae	Former tutor
Alisha/Ellise	Eri	Friend at Australian university
Alisha	Noriko	Former tutor
Zac	Fumie	MeetUp members
Oscar	Yoshio	Friend at Japanese university
Jacob/Kaylene	Kō	Museum boss
Kaylene	Chikae	Friend at Australian university
	Daishi	Museum boss
	Ikuko	University administration
	Junko	Museum colleague
	Ruriko	Language Exchange Partners
	Ukiko	Unofficial LEP
	Watako	Museum colleague

remain in contact after Ellise returned to Australia. Sae was one of Ellise's former Japanese tutors, whom Ellise added on Mixi so that they could keep in contact after she completed the course Sae taught. Zac and Fumie met via the online group MeetUp, which organises Japanese–English conversation practise sessions, and they used CMC in order to communicate outside of these meetings. Both Alisha and Ellise made friends with Eri, an exchange student at their university, and used CMC to arrange times to meet her when she was in Australia, and to keep in touch after she had returned to Japan.

Alisha and Noriko met when Noriko observed Alisha's Japanese class as part of the university's internship programme. Alisha later employed Noriko as her private tutor. After Noriko returned to Japan they continued to keep in touch via CMC. Oscar and Yoshio met while Oscar was on exchange at a Japanese university, and they used CMC to keep in contact also. Both Jacob and Kaylene used CMC to communicate with Kō, a superior at the *manga* museum. Jacob assisted in one of the museum's research projects from Australia, and Kaylene worked there while in Japan. They both used CMC to communicate work-related information to Kō.

Kaylene also communicated with others at the museum for primarily work purposes, including with Daishi, another superior, and a colleague, Junko. Although she also used CMC to communicate with another colleague, Watako, Kaylene's communication with Watako was primarily social, as the pair engaged in a Japanese–English conversation exchange outside their work setting. Kaylene's other relationships included Chikae, a friend she had met in Japan who then came to Australia on exchange, and used CMC to keep in contact with when Chikae returned to Japan; Ikuko, who worked in administration at the university Kaylene attended in Japan (while working at the museum), and with whom Kaylene communicated about university administrative procedures; Ruriko, who was one of Kaylene's partners in the LEP; and Ukiko, an unofficial language exchange partner. Rather than signing up through the university's official LEP, as Ruriko did, Ukiko advertised for a conversation partner via posters, which Kaylene responded to. While in Australia, Kaylene used CMC with Ruriko and Ukiko to arrange times to meet for language exchange, and after they returned to Japan she used CMC to keep in touch with them.

As can be seen from Table 2.5 and the descriptions, one particularly common motivation for CMC use was to 'keep in touch' after one person returned to their home country. This was the case for Mei, Eri, Noriko, Chikae, Ruriko, and Ukiko, who all visited Australia, met their partners in the current study, and then returned to Japan, and for Scott, Lucas, Ellise, and Oscar, who all visited Japan, met their partners in the current study, and then returned to Australia. Other motivations for CMC use included for work or other professional purposes (mostly Jacob and Kaylene's uses), or to extend communication beyond the institutional setting it started in (as was the case with Zac and Fumie's communication outside of MeetUp, or Ellise and Sae's communication after their course was finished). Genna and Tokio's relationship is unique in that they are the only pair participating in the present study which did not meet for the first time face-to-face, but rather, Tokio approached Genna via MySpace, hoping to make an Australian friend. The initiation of their relationship, and others, is analysed in more detail below.

Initiating CMC in an L2

According to boyd (2007b), CMC participation tends to follow cultural and linguistic lines (see also Hargittai, 2007). Choice of SNS may influence a learner's access to NSs of the target language. This was certainly found to be the case in Herring et al.'s (2007b) investigation of four non-English language networks (Russian, Portuguese, Finnish, and Japanese) on LiveJournal. While English may dominate globally, strong other-language Internet networks do exist, and Herring et al. define the robustness of online language networks according to the number of multilingual or multicultural individuals who create widely accessible content that can bridge linguistic networks. They state that most bilingual 'bridging' blogs are written by expatriates and language learners. Thus, the roles of the participants in the present study as multilingual individuals, language learners, and potential bridge-builders are of great interest.

Despite the general trend for online participation to follow linguistic or cultural lines, the importance of shared interests over linguistic or cultural similarities in online relationships is emphasised by Turkle (1995). The potential for users to become friends online with people they have never met face-to-face was recognised as early as the 1990s (Nojima, 1996). This is crucial in the context of the current study, where investment in a relationship, including shared interests, is very important for successful learning (de Nooy & Hanna, 2009).

Online, users are often forced to articulate relationships in a binary fashion: friend or not (boyd & Heer, 2006). Donath and boyd (2004) state that relationships on SNSs have several important features:

(1) *They are mutual.* Both parties must agree to show each other as 'friends'.

(2) *They are public*. Links are permanently displayed for others to see.
(3) *They are unnuanced*. No distinction in terms of closeness is made.

The final point is intriguing in that users are essentially forced to declare their relationships as either 'friendship' or 'nothing', and may have led to the phenomenon of users 'collecting' friends. In one study, around one-third of university students were found to have over 100 friends on their MSN Messenger buddy lists (de Bakker *et al.*, 2007).

In the present study, three main avenues for initiating CMC in the participants' L2 were identified; namely, through education, international exchange, and established CMC networks, as described below.

Through education

One of the first ways many participants were introduced to L2 use online was through their formal Japanese language education programmes. For example, Alisha started using emails in Japanese for her correspondence language course in high school. She recalls wanting to communicate via MSN with the Japanese students she met when they came to her school on exchange, but at the time, she says 'in Japan, they didn't have Internet in houses, so most of my friends who came over to start off with didn't have email addresses, let alone the Internet'. So, initially, Alisha's main use of her L2 online was with other learners and her teacher.

In other cases, assessment tasks in formal education proved a powerful motivator for out-of-classroom CMC use. Cindy and Genna, classmates in level 1, started their own blogs after hearing that in the second semester they would be required to blog in Japanese on the SNS Bebo for assessment. Genna reported that she and Cindy started blogs in Japanese on the site Ameba in order to practise their Japanese and gain experience for this task. Interestingly, both students continued to maintain their Ameba blogs long after the formally assessed Bebo project concluded. Furthermore, even throughout the duration of their assessed project, Cindy and Genna continued to simultaneously maintain their blogs on Ameba. During the semester-long project, Cindy wrote close to 100 entries on her personal Ameba blog, but only six on Bebo. Additionally, Cindy reported that many of the entries on Bebo that she submitted for assessment were simply copied and pasted from her Ameba blog. This example shows that although students may not always engage in formal assessment tasks above the minimum requirements, the use of formal assessment as a stimulus for encouraging out-of-classroom literacy practices should not be underestimated.

Through exchange

Maintaining contact with Japanese people met through international exchange programmes was the most frequently reported origin of participants' intercultural online interactions. The finding that users are significantly more likely to 'add' or 'friend' people that they know offline than those they do not (Ellison et al., 2007; Lampe et al., 2006) suggests that SNSs are mainly used to maintain existing offline relationships, or to solidify what would otherwise be short-lived, passing acquaintanceships. This is very important for foreign language learners, whose chances to meet NSs may be limited to an overseas exchange, or hosting an exchange student.

For many students, CMC represents a way to maintain relationships with former host family members, exchange students, and classmates (Pasfield-Neofitou, 2006). Similarly, Ellison et al. (2007) and Dwyer (2007) state that by providing an opportunity to connect with former high school classmates, Internet access may help remedy 'friendsickness', the distress that undergraduate students encounter when separated from their high school friends, a relevant concept for former exchange students separated from their friends or homestay families also. Both hosting an exchange student (either in the family home, or as part of a school-wide programme) and going overseas on exchange provided valuable opportunities to not only meet Japanese speakers and swap email addresses, but also to be introduced to other forms of CMC tools.

Meeting people through hosting

Keeping in contact with former exchange students was a motivator for Hyacinth to begin using CMC in her L2. In her background interview, Hyacinth reported that she started using email in Japanese after she hosted some exchange students. Similarly, once Internet access became more widespread in Japan, in 2003 Alisha began communicating via MSN with the students who had visited her school on exchange.

Meeting people through participation in exchanges

Lucas and Hisayo's communication began when Hisayo sent an email introducing herself and her family to Lucas before he stayed with them during a high school exchange. Later, when Lucas started formal study of Japanese, he was able to begin using Japanese in emails as soon as he learned to type, as he already had an established emailing relationship with his former host sister, Hisayo. In fact, the first email Lucas ever sent Hisayo composed directly in Japanese characters was from the classroom while he was learning to type in Japanese (excerpted below).

Extract 2.1 Lucas' first email in Japanese

久代さんへ、

(Dear Hisayo-san)

こんにちは久代さん。おげんきですか。しばらくですね。ぼくはだいじょぶです。

いまはだいがくへ日本語をべんきょします。

(Hello Hisayo-san. How are you? It's been a while. I am okay.
Now I am study Japanese to university)

Hi Hisayo! It's Lucas. I'm am learning how to type Japanese at
university, and せんせい asked me to write a message to you.
　　　　　　　　(the teacher)

ラーカスより

(From Lacas)

Notes: Being his first email in Japanese script, Lucas mistyped his name
in the last line here. This will be further discussed in Chapter 5.

This email shifted their established norm of English as the primary language of interaction. Prior to taking the typing class, all of the emails
between Lucas and Hisayo were written primarily in English (7/20 emails)
or mostly English (13/20 emails), while after the typing class their language
choice changed so that all except one email contained some measure of
Japanese (17/18 emails). In fact, almost half were composed in a mostly
Japanese variety (8/18 emails). In the interview, Lucas stated that the language he most used in email had changed to Japanese because he now tried
to avoid using English as much as possible. Like Alisha and Lucas, Kaylene
learned to type in Japanese as a component of her formal education. However,
at the time, she says, 'I didn't really have anyone to email in Japanese yet'. It
was not until the following year, when Kaylene went on exchange to Japan,
that she began swapping email addresses and communicating with NSs of
Japanese via CMC.

Participation in exchange programmes may also provide indirect benefits
for the family members and acquaintances of exchange students. Having no
experience in Japan herself, Genna utilised the contacts her sister made in Japan
to start an email-based language exchange with her sister's older host sister.

Discovering other forms of CMC tools

Going on exchange or hosting exchange students may provide not only
chances to meet Japanese speakers, but also the opportunity to discover
other forms of CMC tools which are more widely used in the other country.
Mixi, which has limited popularity outside of Japan, but is the most popular

SNS inside the country, is an excellent example. As boyd (2007b) states, most young people learn about SNSs through their friends, joining in response to peer pressure. Trends change, and a medium which had social currency two years ago may not be as popular today. Picking up on these trends is important, as being a member of the most popular medium increases one's chances of finding available interlocutors, or getting a timely response. However, as peers are a major way for people to learn about CMC media, it can be difficult for learners of Japanese as a foreign language to keep up to date with current trends. This highlights the importance of exchange programmes in facilitating socialisation with same-age peers in Japan.

Both Noah and Oscar were introduced to the popular Japanese SNS Mixi while on exchange. In the current study, only participants who had considerable and recent experience in Japan were members of Mixi, suggesting that the selection and use of some CMC modes may be related to in-country experience. Alisha, Ellise, Kaylene, Noah, Oscar, and Zac all used Mixi, and all had over one month's experience in Japan sometime in or after 2006, the year in which Mixi was popularised and membership soared to over eight million members, according to the Mixi Counter (http://s.hamachiya.com/mc/), archived on Wikipedia.

In fact, in-country experience appears to be more closely associated with Mixi membership than language level. While at first glance it may appear that in-country experience may be tied to greater levels of language proficiency, which in turn may facilitate membership of communities that are dominated by NSs, such as Mixi, this does not appear to be the case in the present study. As previously mentioned, Cindy and Genna, two beginner-level students who had never been to Japan, were able to maintain blogs in Japanese on a separate site, Ameba, which, like Mixi, is also maintained and moderated in Japanese. Hyacinth also maintained a blog on Ameba. She was enrolled in the same level of Japanese as Noah, and had actually studied for six more years than he had. Although the length of Hyacinth's experience in Japan was only slightly less than Noah's (Hyacinth was only there for three weeks), her experience was as a high school exchange student back in 2004 when, according to the Mixi Counter, the site only had 10,000 members. Thus, this experience would have been unlikely to give her exposure to Mixi use. However, mixing with Japanese peers in other settings can also be beneficial. Alisha said that she found out about Mixi from some Japanese students on exchange to her university. After hearing Mixi mentioned regularly by this group of students, Alisha says she thought 'what is this Mixi? ... why is everyone talking about this thing called Mixi?'. Alisha stated that this experience gave her the impression that every university student had a Mixi profile, and used Mixi regularly.

In-country experience or interaction with newly arrived exchange students from Japan enabled the participants in the present study to form impressions about the popularity of various tools among their Japanese peers by hearing them casually referred to in face-to-face encounters. Furthermore, learners were able to discover the Japanese equivalents of the tools which have currency in their own cultures. Zac, for example, described Mixi as the 'Japanese version of Facebook', and says that this meant, 'it was a definite guarantee that you would meet Japanese people'. He formed this impression after meeting a number of Japanese people who would ask 'do you have a Mixi?', which Zac likened to the way his peers in Australia would ask 'do you have a Facebook?'. He says that if you said no, 'you're part of the out-group straight away'. While also on exchange, Oscar also found that the Japanese people he met were more likely to check their Mixi profiles for messages than their email accounts, which prompted his joining also, despite the fact that he indicated a personal preference for Hotmail.

Pre-departure uses of CMC

Importantly, some instances of CMC use collected in the present study or described in the interviews by participants originated in pre-departure preparations for exchange programmes. Lucas and Hisayo's email exchange, described above, actually began prior to her visiting Australia on exchange. Hisayo's initial email, written entirely in English, served as a pre-departure self-introduction for her host family. Hyacinth, who had the opposite experience of going to Japan, also swapped emails with her host sister before her departure. In the interview, Hyacinth described the receipt of a fairly typical-sounding information sheet about her host family as a form of pre-departure orientation: 'it also had their email, so the teacher suggested, email them and give them an idea of who you are'.

Although Hyacinth described the experience of writing that first email as daunting, as she did not feel confident in her Japanese, she said that the genre, a self-introduction, was something she felt comfortable in doing, and that it gave her an opportunity to practise something she had already learnt to do in Japanese (describing her likes). Furthermore, Hyacinth said that having introduced herself via the medium of CMC before meeting her hosts face-to-face, she felt much less nervous.

Through established CMC networks

Finally, some participants reported actively seeking out contact with NSs of Japanese, or being sought after as NSs of English, through their established CMC networks. In one example, Noah started playing the online game WoW when it was released in 2004, and when he began studying Japanese in 2006 he started talking to people he described as 'random Japanese'. His excitement at finding a member of a Japanese guild was evident in the interview. Noah said:

> He was speaking awesome Japanese, better than mine, and I thought he was just another student, so I asked him if he was a Japanese student … he was like, I'm from Japan, and I'm like, cool! I wanted to add him as a friend so I can practise my Japanese, and wow, he told me about his guild, and invited me … with all Japanese people! (Noah Interview 1, Line 168)

After this initial encounter, Noah joined the Japanese guild, which was mediated entirely in Japanese, and participated in guild activities on a regular basis.

Conversely, Genna was sought out by Japanese speakers via her established CMC profile on MySpace. In the interview, Genna reported that two of her friends on MySpace had added her because they had been to Australia on exchange before and, although they did not meet Genna at the time, the experience made them interested in 'making friends with Australians'. In both cases, Genna reports that she was 'friended' (a term that has arisen out of the use of SNS, meaning added as a friend, similar in use to 'befriended') because of her status as an Australian and her interest in Japanese culture; in one case, liking the same band. All of this information is displayed on Genna's profile. In addition to listing her nationality, hometown, and ethnicity, Genna's profile was rich in references to Japanese popular culture. Her display photo showed her in a typical peace-sign pose, her personal message was *'*Ashita tenki ni naare*'*, lyrics to a popular Japanese song. Her profile was also embellished further down by videos and music of Japanese bands and lists of her favourite Japanese television shows. One of Genna's friends, and participant in the current study, Tokio, who had recently moved to the same city as Genna, reported that he met her online after looking for Australian contacts using the MySpace search function, to help him 'get used to the culture'.

Email addresses as passports to the online and offline world

In the current study, email addresses were found to function as a passport to both the online world (for relationships that start out in face-to-face settings) and the 'real'-world (for those that start out online). While forms of anonymous CMC do exist, where registration with an email address is unnecessary, all of the interaction data collected in the present study took place via mediums that require an email address for registration. An email address is necessary to register on Ameba, Facebook, Mixi, MySpace, MSN, or WoW, and, obviously, one cannot send emails from a mobile phone or computer without an email address. Furthermore, as will be described in Chapter 3, email communication itself is often used as an organisational tool to facilitate and coordinate the use of other CMC modes.

While some participants like Zac may have felt that they would be social outcasts in face-to-face settings if they were not users of the popular CMC mediums, Genna's case shows that relationships may progress the other way also. That is, online relationships may transform into offline relationships, just as swapping email addresses in a face-to-face situation can facilitate the development of a friendship online. Although Genna and Tokio met online, after making plans on several occasions the pair eventually met face-to-face and developed a friendship offline, in addition to their net-based communication. Genna acknowledged that meeting someone she knew only via online channels for the first time face-to-face, particularly a male 11 years her senior, was potentially dangerous and would make some people nervous. Yet, prior to their meeting, Genna described several safety precautions she planned to take, including informing her mother of her plans, bringing a friend along, and arranging to meet Tokio in a public place.

As the spread and use of the Internet increases, it appears likely that seeking out contacts via established CMC networks will become more common. Previously, students studying an L2 who did not go on exchange appear to have had little opportunity to establish links with native-speaking peers. For Alisha and Jacob, who were 23 and 24 years of age respectively at the time of the interviews, the relatively rare use of the Internet in Japan during their high school years meant that neither had the opportunity to communicate with NSs via CMC until they started university in 2003. Noah and Genna, however, although only slightly younger, at 21 and 18 years of age respectively, were already members of networks that allowed them easy access to an online Japanese community when they began university study.

Discussion

In order to examine participants' psychobiographies, this chapter described the linguistic and technological backgrounds of participants, the makeup of their social networks, motivations for using CMC, and examined the ways in which they began using CMC in their L2. Three main avenues for becoming involved in CMC in an L2 were identified, namely via education, international exchange, and established CMC networks in the L1, all of which are linked to participants' psychobiographies, outlined in the previous section. Key evolutionary transitions in participants' psychobiographies included events such as beginning language study, participating in an exchange programme or conversation group, or starting work. Attending a formal Japanese language course was one of the first ways several partici-pants were exposed to L2 use online, often with other NNSs or the teacher, as in the various studies outlined in Chapter 1. Exchanges were found to foster communication with NSs in a number of ways, including via CMC, and also to provide learners with up-to-date information regarding preferred CMC modes. Seeking Japanese contacts through one's established online L1 community was also found to be a valuable strategy, as was the case for Noah in his WoW participation.

Email addresses were found to function as a 'passport', giving access to participation in much of the online world; although, as the following chapter will demonstrate, for some modes of communication, additional keys are required. Yet, in addition to providing access to a variety of CMC modes, swapping email addresses or display names in face-to-face settings was also found to assist in maintaining relationships formed in offline settings in the online realm.

3 Social Settings of Situated CMC Use[1]

Having outlined participants' psychobiographical trajectories in the previous chapter, in terms of their patterns of computer use, overseas experiences, and language learning histories, the present chapter aims to identify the ways in which these experiences shape CMC use, as outlined in the first research question. Doing so begins to answer Sealey and Carter's (2004) question 'what works for whom in what circumstances?' by addressing the ways in which the participants are differently resourced, in regards to prior language study, linguistic capital, and access to technology. These issues will be expanded upon in Chapters 4 and 5.

Maintaining and managing communication with a vast number of contacts from diverse cultural and language backgrounds, and through a number of different modes, is a complex task, but one performed with considerable skill by the participants in the present study. This section examines the strategies participants employed in their management of communication, identity, and resources, as well as the interpersonal factors that facilitate sustained and successful intercultural communication online, before discussing communication lapse.

Management of Communication

Participants managed their communication with a number of conscious strategies, making use of a variety of tools to manage, sort, and group individuals in their contact lists, arrange conversations, and utilise a multiplicity of CMC modes and supporting tools. All of the interactive CMC mediums utilised in the present study have some sort of function that allows users to create a list of contacts, as mentioned above. Attitudes towards the maintenance of these lists varied between participants. Zac, for example, had a list of approximately 400 contacts in his Gmail address book, and estimated that as few as 5% were 'active' contacts that he regularly communicated with. Jacob took a much more vigorous approach to managing his list, employing a filtering process when he switched mediums. When he moved from Hotmail and MSN (both products of Microsoft) to Gmail and Gtalk (products of Google), Jacob stated that he used this opportunity to 'cull' his contacts down to 'a nice, condensed group that I want to talk to, so I can avoid the MSN crowd'.

Micro-level management of contact lists was also evident in participants' categorisation of their contacts. For example, on many SNSs it is possible to designate certain contacts as 'Top Friends'. Tokio's profile showed his Top 8 Friends, while Genna's showed her Top 20. Each included the other in their Top Friends, with Tokio giving Genna third position, and Genna giving Tokio ninth. This serves not only as a public display of contacts, but also as a set of handy links to one's most frequently visited profiles. A different but somewhat related function in Gmail was utilised by Kaylene to keep track of her 20 most frequently contacted people, which included two of her university Japanese teachers.

The importance of effective management of contacts is exemplified in one of Ellise's experiences. Because so many of her contacts (and in general, the participants in this study) used online names or 'screen names', it can be difficult to identify which alias belongs to whom. Ellise said in her interview that communicating primarily online, she would forget people's 'real' names unless they used a screen name similar to their real name, as the screen names became more familiar. In turn, mistaken identity could lead to misunderstanding or a breakdown in communication. When Ellise received a comment on her Mixi blog announcing her planned trip to Japan from あかっち♡ (*Akacchi*), a handle used by Akane, Ellise thought that the screen name referred to another friend, located in Japan. As the comment invited Ellise to hang out in their city prior to her departure, Ellise interpreted this as a notification that the sender was coming to Australia and replied excitedly, asking when she would arrive. However, the actual sender was already in Australia, and communication breakdown occurred.

As mentioned previously, CMC was also used frequently to organise and coordinate future online and offline communication. A large portion of participants' emails were centred on arranging communication via postal mail, chat, telephone, SNSs, and face-to-face meetings. In one example, Kaylene sent Ruriko an email saying, 「MSNチャットのために、ひまがあったら、言ってね」(Let me know if you have time to chat on MSN). Ruriko responded, 「10日の夜11時、11日の夜、18日の夜、19日の夜の中でkayは平気な日ある!?」(Do you have an okay day out of 11pm on the 10th, the evening of the 11th, the evening of the 18th, and the evening of the 19th kay!と). Likewise, Kaylene used email to share mobile phone details with Ukiko, Hisayo informed Lucas of her membership of MySpace (which he then joined) and Skype via email, and email was commonly used to invite others to SNSs or to find out postal addresses by other participants, demonstrating its important use as a 'passport', as mentioned in the previous chapter.

A final aspect of participants' communication management that required great skill is multi-tasking. In the follow-up interview, when questioned about their most recent communication with a Japanese contact, 10 out of the 12 Australian participants reported multi-tasking during their communication. A list of concurrent activities is given in Table 3.1.

As can be seen from Table 3.1, multi-tasking was quite prevalent amongst participants, both in terms of number of participants engaging in multiple concurrent activities and the number of activities, an average of two or more. Of course, simply because Oscar and Scott did not multi-task at the time of their most recent communication does not mean that they never did so at all.

While many participants simply swapped between separate windows on the one screen, some made use of developments in software designed to facilitate multi-tasking; for example, Kaylene used tabs in her browser Mozilla Firefox, so that she could easily switch between composing an email in Hotmail, looking up words on Jim Breen's website and Eijiro, and checking

Table 3.1 Most recent communication and concurrent activities

Participant (N = 12)	CMC with Japanese contact		Number and type of concurrent activities
Kaylene	Hotmail	5	Gmail, Two online dictionaries, Uni work, Facebook
Lucas	Email	4	Word processor, Uni work, Music player, Chat
Alisha	Facebook	3	Word, Hotmail, University email
Ellise	MSN	2	Other chat window, Website
Genna	MySpace	2	Facebook, Ameba blog
Hyacinth	Email	2	MSN, Online dictionary
Jacob	Email	2	Chat, Website
Noah	Mixi	1	Chat
Zac	Email	1	iTunes
Oscar	Mixi	–	
Scott	Email	–	
	Average	2.2	

Note: Cindy did not communicate with any Japanese friends during the week of the interview.

to see if she had any new messages in Gmail or Facebook in the meantime, in the one instance of the browser. Jacob, on the other hand, employed a rather sophisticated hardware solution:

> My computer set-up at home is two monitors, so usually, if I'm writing an email, I'll have Gmail on one, and I'll have a chat program on the other, or a website that I'm just browsing through, if I'm looking at Wikipedia or that for enjoyment, I'll just read that while I'm waiting for an email to load. (Jacob Interview 2, Line 50)

Even though multi-tasking was frequently engaged in by participants, it may cause some lapses in concentration or communication difficulties, especially when users attempt to manage multiple conversations in multiple languages concurrently. A minor orthographic deviation in one of Kaylene and Ruriko's MSN conversations is one example resulting from multi-tasking. The relevant turn is excerpted below.

Extract 3.1 Kaylene's chat with Ruriko – Orthographic deviation

7. kay says:
ね、ね、奨学金も大学のプレースメントmo絶対もらった。＾＿＾！イエイ！
(Hey, hey, I definitely received my scholarship and my university placement. ^_^ !Yay!)

Kaylene stated in the follow-up interview that she noted the 'typo' in line 7 above – the use of 'mo' in the Roman alphabet rather than in Japanese *hiragana* script (も) – at the time of writing. Kaylene explained 'I must have swapped between the windows partway through ... and accidentally hit the key and then didn't hit it again to get back in, and then accidentally left that bit still in *romaji* (Roman characters)'. Kaylene routinely used the key combination ALT and ~ (tilde) to swap between English and Japanese input methods. In the example in Extract 3.1, the deviation that occurred was a result of forgetting to complete this technical step after switching to converse in English with another interlocutor. Orthographic switching will be examined in more detail in Chapter 4.

Management of Identity

In addition to managing their communication, participants were also concerned with managing their identity and presentation of self online. As Sealey and Carter (2004) state, in addition to one's continuous sense of self, people are constantly changing and shaped by external forces. Accordingly, it was found that participants' identities were constantly and conscientiously maintained over a number of mediums, and several strategies for the management of identity online were apparent in the present study. One important way for users of SNSs to manage their identities was through their profile design, including both visual and linguistic elements, as described in Chapter 1, and group membership. Likewise, participants using email could 'design' their identities using email signatures, such as Kaylene's casual action *hugs*, or simple smile emoticon -love:)kay, appropriate for her mostly informal communication, or Jacob's more formal signature, giving information on his occupation location and website addresses, appropriate for his work-based communication. Such signatures were also very common among the Japanese professionals Kaylene and Jacob communicated with. Even email addresses can be used to signal some part of the owner's identity, such as including the name of a favourite dessert for a 'cute' effect. Users of MSN could also create a username and add a personal message, somewhat akin to Facebook's status updates; for example, Lucas' message「あしたにほんごのテスト」('Tomorrow Japanese test') in addition to selecting a display photo. Gamers also have many options to customise their 3D avatars through personalisation and in-game development.

The primary choice WoW players face when creating their 3D avatar is selecting which faction they wish to fight for: the Alliance or the Horde, each of which consist of numerous 'races'. Choosing a race and faction has an impact on what can be accomplished in the world and who one can communicate with, as members of opposing factions cannot communicate with one another beyond a series of pre-defined emotes (e.g. performing a dance move or an angry pose). Players may also select from nine different classes. According to Corneliussen and Walker Rettberg (2008), classes in WoW are defined rather traditionally; for example, specialisation in different types of combat, magic, or healing (e.g. mage, priest, shaman, or warlock, like Noah's avatar). It is clear that creating and maintaining an avatar is a detailed and ongoing process. Noah's avatar, for example, had 16 different items of clothing/accessories equipped, many of which could then be further customised. Customising one's avatar represents a large time commitment, and is an outward representation of membership of a particular faction, race, and class, and a demonstration of power and individuality.

Participants in the present study were equally attentive to what images of themselves they uploaded. Physical appearance was important for Ellise, who stated that she chose her Facebook profile photo on the basis that she had just gotten a spray-tan when the photo was taken, and said that she would not upload one 'with no makeup, bad hair day, looking like I've eaten a whole tub of ice-cream'. Physical appearance was likewise important to Genna, but in a different way. She reported playing around with some of the functions on her new notebook Mac camera, and posted a photo that she described as 'Emo', or 'emotional hardcore', referring to a particular music fan culture originating in punk rock, because of the predominance of black in the photo and the style of glasses she was wearing at the time.

Of course, as Sealey and Carter (2004) state, people's identities are not static, and neither were participants' displays of identity, either across platforms, or over time. Participants regularly changed their display photos, particularly on Facebook and MySpace, and Lucas even went so far as to change his username on MySpace to 'Rukasu' to make it more 'Japanese-y' when he started studying Japanese. Some participants reported maintaining and updating their SNS profiles by another 'culling' process, in order to eliminate videos and applications that no longer represent their desired projected identity. Genna said of her MySpace profile: 'I go through my culling phase and take out everything that I don't like anymore. Maybe every six months, when I'm bored and have nothing to do.' This would include groups that Genna no longer wished to identify with because they 'weren't all that good or interesting, and don't update very often'. The same phenomenon occurs on Facebook, with Lucas also reporting a need to 'clean up' his profile, which he said mostly consisted of 'useless' applications. Identity performance on other CMC modes was also dynamic, with participants frequently changing their usernames, personal messages, and display photos on MSN, for example.

Although participants' identity performances were neither static across time nor across 'cyberspace', some aspects were consciously retained. One example is Genna's fondness for a particular username which she had been using for over five years, 'everywhere I need to make an account, that's the thing I use', she said. Like many aspects of Internet use, Genna notes that conventions for selecting display names have also changed over time, in that she selected this name before it was widely considered acceptable and reasonably safe to use one's real name online. Despite the recent changes Genna has perceived, she continues to use the same display name, even in 'Japanese domains' – including it in the address of her Ameba blog. Several other participants also retained key aspects of what they perceived as their 'core' online identity across various platforms, regardless of language. The ways in which participants' demonstration of their interests contributed to the maintenance of communication are discussed below.

Maintenance of Interest

While the first section of this chapter discussed technological contributions to the maintenance of communication between participants in the present study, an equal if not greater factor is the interpersonal dynamic of shared interests, and 'psychobiographical' factors that sustain interest. Sealey and Carter (2004: 139) state that each person's life experiences and history mean that they develop unique biographies, with particular personal feelings, attributes, and predispositions. In the present study, shared interests in books, *manga*, music, dramas, *anime*, or art were all influential. Participants' in-game and book-related communication will be taken as main foci in this subsection.

Games

A shared interest or goal appears crucial to sustaining communication and language practise online outside the classroom where there is no encouragement or guidance from a teacher, nor instrumental motivation in the form of assessment. Noah joined a Japanese guild on WoW and found that his in-game communication, with people he had never met, soon outweighed the amount of communication he engaged in on MSN with people he had met on a high school exchange, but shared no significant interests with. The nature of games like WoW is such that communication is central for the efficient movement of the group and achievement of in-game goals. Therefore, Noah and his fellow guild members had a very strong bond forged by their joint in-game objectives, which is evidenced in the modification of their language norms by members of Noah's guild. In order to facilitate his understanding of commands, Noah reports that his guild members refrained from the use of difficult Japanese characters, and utilised *hiragana* instead. This represents a significant deviation from Japanese norms, where such messages would usually involve large numbers of Japanese characters, and demonstrates the extent to which his guild members accommodated Noah's language development and facilitated his participation.

Books

Another example of shared interests manifested online is the Visual Bookshelf application on Facebook, which allows participants to display books (in a variety of languages) that they are currently reading via an Amazon.com search, review books they have finished reading, and recommend books to their friends who are registered. Alisha and Noriko both utilised the Visual Bookshelf application, were connected as 'Book Friends', and frequently exchanged messages about the books they were reading – often translations of the other's favourite novels. Alisha's Visual Bookshelf showed the covers of an English book and a Japanese translation of one of the Narnia books, *The Lion, the Witch and the Wardrobe* by C.S. Lewis.

Although not all of the books she read were reviewed, all of the books Alisha wrote reviews on were related to Japan or originally published in Japanese, and in a review of the novel *Train Man (Densha Otoko)* by Hitori Nakano, which Alisha bills as an Internet love story, she wrote, 'The book is great to see some different ways of typing in smiley faces, though I still don't understand all the different nuances of them all. :) western vs. (^o^) Japanese.' This bestseller in Japan was also quite popular among other participants, incorporating aspects of online and offline life in Japan. One of Genna's blogs was titled 「お。た。く。」 (O-TA-KU), a name that is sometimes used as a badge of honour in English and has its roots in the Japanese word for 'home', denoting an enthusiast, especially of *anime* or video games, who rarely leaves their house. In this blog Genna flaunted her *'otaku'* credentials by posting a photo of the *Train Man* novel she had borrowed from the library, and describing how she wanted to read the latest DeathNote *manga*. Genna and Tokio also exchanged several emails about the 'Train Man' television series, which Tokio saw on television in Japan and Genna watched with her sister on DVD.

In addition to their Visual Bookshelf activities, Alisha and Noriko also emailed each other about the books they were reading and communicated via the Facebook wall, in what Alisha describes as their 'Sōseki discussion' (referencing the famous Japanese author of the Meiji era, Natsume Sōseki, whose books they discussed). In this way, Alisha and Noriko's interest in books spanned not only two modes in Facebook (the Virtual Bookshelf and the wall), but also two mediums (Facebook and email). Lucas and Hisayo also wrote several emails discussing books and video games. Both Alisha and Noriko, and Lucas and Hisayo were frequent emailers.

Showing sustained interest in one's interlocutor was seen as key to successful communication, and something which participants consciously strived to maintain. Although shared interests help, it can be difficult for both sides to maintain interest in a single, unchanging topic for a length of time. For example, Genna said of her most recent communication, 'we're still talking about Train Man, *Densha Otoko*, which has been going for a while now, but that's probably gonna die off soon, I hope! . . . because I don't know what else to say anymore'. She and Tokio had been discussing this topic for their last four emails.

Questions and discussions

Genna stated that her emails with Tokio took the form of 'just conversation, and then you ask a question to keep the conversation going'. This appeared to be an important strategy and, on average, Genna asked one question per email. When more than one question was asked, the second question was likely to be ignored and therefore wasted as a tool to continue the communication. This phenomenon has also been noted by Stockwell (2003) in a formal educational setting, where the inclusion of multiple topics in one email was found to be the most common reason for the premature cessation of a topic thread.

Discussing religious interests also played an important role in maintaining contact for some participants. Alisha's identity as a Christian and her interest in the Bible appeared highly relevant to her online communication in terms of choice of friends and blog topics. This formed an important part of her motivation (for example, Alisha used her online communication with Noriko to aid her in making plans to visit a church in Japan, and to obtain linguistic assistance from Noriko prior to the visit to learn the Lord's Prayer in Japanese), and also provided her with inspiration for blog topics on Mixi (for example, Alisha's blog on religion in Japan). Alisha also decided to maintain an online link with one of her friends' ex-boyfriends, which might otherwise have diminished after their break-up because, in Alisha's words, 'He's Christian, so it's interesting what he has to write about that, although it's difficult to understand'. This contact was aware of Alisha's beliefs also, through her blog discussions.

Non-use, Lapsing, and Lurking

In order to obtain a full picture of learners' CMC use, it is also important to examine non-use as well as maintenance. Of course, despite best intentions, some online communication does end, and eight of the 12 Australians reported that their contact with one or more Japanese NSs they had previously communicated with had lapsed. A further two said that they had stopped maintaining blogs in Japanese (at least for a period), because they were too busy. Only two participants, Genna and Scott, who maintained very small networks, and had only been doing so for a short period of time, did not report any such endings. And yet, as will be evidenced in the latter half of this section, a lapse in communication in Japanese does not entail the cessation of Japanese use, or indeed CMC use, for reading, watching, and listening activities.

Lapsing of CMC

As previously mentioned, the transition from school to university or university to work was a factor contributing to a decrease in communication among some pairs. In some cases, this was seen as the main reason communication ceased altogether. For example, Cindy believed that one of the Japanese boys who visited her school for two weeks as an exchange student stopped chatting with her because he had gotten into university. Around the same time, her messages to two girls from the same group that she had been exchanging emails with also started to 'bounce', or come back as undeliverable. Like other participants who had experienced the same kind of ending, Cindy expressed sadness at this lack of response, saying 'I was sad, because I waited a really long time ... But they never sent me a reply'. Ellise also had a contact whom she had not communicated with in a long time because they had started full-time work, and Noah, too, had several acquaintances he had tried to contact but had no reply from in a long time, which he also attributed to them being 'busy'. Lucas, Oscar, and Zac all reported similar experiences. While it is impossible to know why contact did not continue, as obviously those with whom participants were no longer in contact were not available for comment, Hyacinth and Jacob throw some light on the other side of this issue.

Hyacinth communicated with a Japanese student who studied at her school on a one-year exchange during high school, after the student returned home. However, by the end of their communication most of their messages simply reiterated 'I'm busy too':

> They've got their own lives to worry about, and time does change people. It was great, we were exchanging emails every week, or every day at the start, but later on, it would be like, oh, I don't really feel like replying to this email. You don't feel the same excitement. (Hyacinth Interview 2, Line 136)

According to Hyacinth, her initial excitement lasted less than a year. In the interview, she blamed this on 'the fact that she was gone now ... there was just studies, life, there's only so much you can talk about there, and you end up thinking, I've run out of things to talk about! What can I talk about now?' For Hyacinth, who had no online contacts she communicated with regularly at the time of data collection, this was a larger issue. Hyacinth said that her online communication had 'failed' as a whole, 'because you run out of things to talk about'.

As has been previously noted, online, shared interests appear more crucial than in face-to-face communication where relationships may be maintained on the basis of physical proximity alone. Hyacinth too saw this as a specifi-cally online issue, one that she did not experience in face-to-face contact:

> The reason why I enjoy talking to people in person, which is why I prob-ably chat [online] less, is because I really enjoy the face-to-face contact, and you can talk about anything, and it's always instantaneous. It's probably better in terms of developing a friendship, better than email. (Hyacinth Interview 2, Line 140)

Jacob, too, did not have any online contacts he communicated with regularly at the time of data collection. He also described how after going on exchange for the first time he had acquired the email addresses of two Japanese people he met in Japan, but that 'at either end, one of us never wrote back at some point, we just lost contact'. He said that this made him feel both 'relieved and disappointed ... that it's another person that I don't have to keep in constant contact with, but at the same time, it would have been nice to have a Japanese contact'. Furthermore, Jacob's communication with two Japanese researchers that he assisted also ceased immediately after his work on the project stopped, which he too attributed to their being busy. He said 'They're academics in Japan, they're probably busy with their own stuff'.

One striking feature of all of these cases is the role of being (or at least, being perceived to be) 'busy'. This exact wording occurred so many times in the interviews that it was coded as an *in vivo* category. While only tentative conclusions can be drawn on the basis of the present study, as data from both sides is unavailable, it appears that where relationships were built primarily on the basis of proximity at a given time (e.g. a coincidental meeting through exchange programmes), or for instrumental purposes (e.g. Jacob's work-related communication) that had a specific end in sight (as opposed to a language exchange), unless some common interest is found, this relationship will eventually be seen as a burden by at least one party when work, study, or other pressures intervene. This finding highlights the importance of shared goals or interests, outlined in the previous section.

It is important to note, however, that these experiences represent a small portion of the participants' overall relationships, and some participants (for example, Kaylene) managed to maintain lengthy relationships and frequent communication with a large online L2 network. Genna's relationship with Tokio, too, is an excellent example of the importance of shared interests, not physical proximity, for sustained online relationships. From this kind of sus-tained online communication rich opportunities for language acquisition can develop. However, the opportunities for language acquisition which arise from other, non-communicative activities, such as 'lurking' online, should not be ignored either.

Lurking in CMC

'Lurking' without contributing to the discussion was a major part of some participants' online activity. Although this kind of participation is often invisible or silent, it is by no means uncommon. Research by Nonnecke and Preece (2000, 2003) shows that the majority of participants in online communities are lurkers, and cite one study (Mason, 1999) as estimating this figure at close to 90%; and yet Romiszowski and Mason (2004) claim that lurking remains under-theorised and under-researched. They argue that most CMC research has assumed a lack of engagement on the part of lurkers, or 'read only members' (Shibanai, 2007), which this section will challenge.

Reading, listening, and watching were all important parts of participants' online L2 use, including surfing Japanese websites, downloading music and movies, online shopping, and lurking, or reading/listening/watching other users' CMC without contributing. As previously mentioned, Oscar would listen to other players speaking in Japanese when playing Xbox over the Internet while in Japan. He commented 'it [Halo 3] is a first-person-shooter, so you can hear what your team mates are saying, and you'd hear people speaking Japanese'. While this gave Oscar many opportunities to hear spoken Japanese, he never contributed himself. Jacob also lurked on Japanese forums to find urban legends that he could translate for language practice. For Hyacinth, an avid *manga* fan who mostly engaged in activities such as downloading television shows from Japan (which she then passed on to Lucas) and who lacked the confidence to try many interpersonal activities, downloading and shopping online for *manga* were her main uses of the Internet, and were linked to lurking activities. Yet, far from being a passive consumer of popular culture and others' communication, Hyacinth utilised her online activities to actively pursue cultural and language learning goals.

Hyacinth stated in one interview that she started out reading *manga* that had already been translated to English, 'because it's always a great leap trying to comprehend everything at once'. However, English translations of Japanese *manga* often lag far behind the original publication dates and, sooner or later, Hyacinth would run out of English translations to read. At this point, she would then begin reading the series again in its original Japanese language, before reading through the later, as yet untranslated, volumes in Japanese. Hyacinth commented that, when she first started reading a series in Japanese, she would spend most of her time comparing the English and Japanese versions of the *manga*, in addition to using Jim Breen's online dictionary, 'because it's mostly vocabulary that I'm having trouble with, colloquialisms and jargon'. Of course, comparing two *manga* texts side by side on a computer screen is much easier than keeping two books open at once, and may have facilitated Hyacinth's comparisons. However, for all its convenience, reading on a screen can also cause problems. After suffering from eye strain, Hyacinth started purchasing hardcopies online and having them delivered via Amazon Japan (http://amazon.co.jp) and BK1 (http://www.bk1.jp/). Finding a Japanese online store was important, as Hyacinth found that stores that catered primarily for non-Japanese customers were considerably more expensive. Naturally, using a Japanese site required Hyacinth to navigate the store in Japanese and complete the ordering process in her L2.

Even when she switched to hardcopies, Hyacinth's *manga* reading was still tightly bound to her online practices. When she progressed from first reading English translations and then Japanese originals to reading *manga* in Japanese from the outset, Hyacinth lurked on LiveJournal to find recommendations of new *manga*, and received encouragement from a friend in Taiwan via CMC to keep reading. Hyacinth said, 'she does better Japanese than me, and she wants to help urge me on'. She also continued using online dictionaries to aid her reading, in particular where colloquial terms were used. In our second interview, Hyacinth commented that she had recently learned the words '*busaiku*' (plain) and '*bikei*' (gorgeous) by using an online dictionary when reading a *manga*, and that the context helped her to gain a greater understanding of the nuances of these words. She said,

> *busaiku* is someone who is really plain, and then, the other end was the *bikei* which is really gorgeous. I had to look this up because they had put that in *katakana*, and I was thinking when I looked it up it was just plain, you know, dishevelled or something... But what I assumed in the context was that they were pretty hideously plain. (Hyacinth Interview 2, Line 32)

The use of the *katakana* syllabry for words which are normally written in characters is a common means of showing emphasis in *manga*, just like in CMC. However, the colloquial uses of these words appear to have caused Hyacinth some difficulty. In another example, Hyacinth encountered the word, '*serifu*' (line) in *katakana* and said 'that one's usually used for "that's my line!" kind of use. I had never encountered this kind of thing, especially when learning Japanese. You never learn this kind of line ever!' She went on to explain, 'the best thing you learn is like, right now, we're learning about whales, and mixed marriages or something'. While Hyacinth stated that she did enjoy these kinds of topics covered by the textbook, she said of Japanese

'I want to learn it for myself, and I want to learn it so I can actually understand different language in different contexts'. It appears that the greater access to *manga* afforded by the Internet (in terms of social access to recommendations from others, gained by Hyacinth's lurking on blogs and forums, tangible access in the form of downloads and online shopping, and linguistic access to the language used in *manga* via online dictionaries) gave Hyacinth opportunities to be exposed to language of a very different register to that encountered in the classroom, to engage with others' ideas and preferences, and to access resources which assisted her acquisition of new vocabulary and styles of speech.

CMC and Broader Communication

In order to explore the role communication with Japanese contacts via CMC played in the lives of the Australian participants, data was collected on not only their broader online communication, but also their other (offline) L2 use. Comparisons of their L1 and L2 online communication, and their opportunities to use the L2 online and offline, are outlined in the sections below. This section concludes with a discussion of virtual L2 communities.

Modes of online communication

Participants were asked a variety of questions to gauge their use of Japanese in relation to their other online communication. Participants were asked which forms of CMC they used in English (or other languages) and Japanese, as shown in Table 3.2. Overall, participants reported using approximately twice as many types of CMC in their L1 than their L2.

As self-report data, there may be inaccuracies or omissions in Table 3.2 due to limitations on memory. For example, it is likely that all participants used the Internet for web research, yet not all participants reported this. However, the fact that all participants reported use of more types of CMC mediums in English than in Japanese remains consistent across all 12 reports. Wherever a participant reported use of a medium in one language, they were asked whether or not they used it in the other.

Although participants engaged in a greater variety of activities in their L1, variety is also apparent in their L2 uses of the Internet. Even beginner-level students like Cindy, Genna, and Scott all made use of more than one form of CMC in Japanese. Ellise engaged in five different activity types in her L2, more than several of her peers made use of in English.

Table 3.2 Modes of CMC used by Australian participants

Participant (N = 12)	Reported use in English	Years of use (where known)	Reported use in Japanese	Years of use (where known)	% total use
Cindy	Email	8	Email	0	0
	MSN	8	MSN (in the past)	1	13
	Ameba	1	Ameba	1	100
	SMS				
	Online games (Maple Story)				
SUBTOTAL	5		2 (current)		
Genna	Email	7	Email	1	14
	MySpace	2.5	MySpace	1	40
	Ameba	1	Ameba	1	100
	MSN		MSN		
	SMS				
	Forums				
SUBTOTAL	6		4		
Scott	Skype	3	Skype	3	100
	Email		Email		
	Phone email/SMS		Phone email/SMS		
	MSN				
	Facebook				
	Forums				
	MySpace (in the past)				
SUBTOTAL	6 (current)		3		
Lucas	MSN	6	MSN	1	17
	Email	4	Email	1	25
	Facebook	1.5	Facebook	1	67
	SMS				
	Forums (in the past)				
	Online games (WoW in the past)				
SUBTOTAL	4 (current)		3		

(continued)

Table 3.2 Modes of CMC used by Australian participants (Continued)

Participant (N = 12)	Reported use in English	Years of use (where known)	Reported use in Japanese	Years of use (where known)	% total use
Noah	MSN	8	MSN	1	13
	Online games (WoW,	4	Online games	2	50
	etc.)	1	(WoW)	1	100
	Mixi		Mixi		
	Email				
	SMS				
	Web research				
SUBTOTAL	6		3		
Hyacinth	Email: Hotmail	9	Email: Hotmail	6	67
	Gmail	4	Gmail	0	0
	Ameba		Ameba		
	Forums		Forums (read only)		
	Online shopping		Web research		
	Web research		Online shopping		
	Facebook				
	MySpace (in the past)				
	SMS				
	Online games				
	(Ragnarok)				
SUBTOTAL	8 (current)		5		
Ellise	Email	11	Email	4	36
	MSN	10	MSN	4	40
	Facebook	1	Facebook	0.5	50
	Mixi	1	Mixi	1	100
	Phone email/SMS		Phone email/SMS		
	AIM				
SUBTOTAL	6		5		
Zac	Email Facebook	9	Email	3	33
	Mixi	1	Facebook	1	100
	Phone email/SMS	1	Mixi	1	100
	Online games (Phantasy				
	Star in the past)				
SUBTOTAL	4 (current)		3		

Table 3.2 (Continued)

Participant (N = 12)	Reported use in English	Years of use (where known)	Reported use in Japanese	Years of use (where known)	% total use
Jacob	Email MSN (in the past) Phone email/SMS Wiki Gtalk Facebook Online games (first person shooter games)	9	*Email* MSN (in the past) Phone Email (in Japan) Wiki	6	67
SUBTOTAL	6 (current)		2 (current)		
Alisha	Email MSN Facebook Mixi SMS	12 9 1 1	*Email (in vacation)* *MSN (in semester)* Facebook Mixi SMS	9 4 1 1	75 44 100 100
TOTAL	5		4 (current)		
Oscar	Facebook Mixi Phone email/SMS Email Online games (Chess)	1 1	Facebook *Mixi* Phone email (in Japan)	0.5 1	50 100
TOTAL	5		2 (current)		
Kaylene	Email MSN Mixi Phone email/SMS Facebook Yahoo group Own website/wiki	10 9 1	Email MSN *Mixi* Phone email/SMS	6 7 1	60 78 100
SUBTOTAL	7		4		
TOTAL	68		40		
AVERAGE	5.67		3.33		59

Notes: Modes in *italics* represent those reportedly most used by individual participants.

In terms of the most used medium in Japanese, Mixi, email, Ameba, MSN, and Skype were the most frequently used by participants at the time of the interviews. However, as Table 3.2 shows, patterns of use were found to be highly variable. Firstly, as in Cindy's case, participants may switch from one medium to another. Cindy used MSN in the past, and it was her most frequently used medium in Japanese, but she later began using Ameba the most, devoting approximately the same amount of time to its use, despite the vast differences in the technology. Participants' medium choice appears to be largely influenced by their peers, as described previously, and this needs to be taken into consideration. Secondly, as several participants' (e.g. Oscar and Jacob's) use of phone email shows, use can depend on participants' geographical location. Oscar, for example, used mobile phone email when he was on exchange in Japan; however, when he returned to Australia, not owning an Internet-enabled phone, he was unable to continue this practice. Conversely, Jacob, who also did not own an Internet-enabled phone in Australia, began using phone emails in Japanese only when he moved to Japan partway through the data collection period. Finally, as Alisha's case demonstrates, time of year can also affect medium use, particularly in the case of university students. Alisha stated that during the semester she used MSN the most, but during vacation she preferred email, because 'other people aren't on the computer as often ... everyone has to be online at the same time to chat, otherwise [I] just send an email. It's like ringing [on] the phone and they're not there to answer'. Somewhat surprisingly, Alisha stated that most of her contacts were online 'particularly during exam time, or during assignment time'. While for those overseas the Australian academic year is obviously irrelevant, many of Alisha's Japanese contacts were current students at her Australian university. Furthermore, as Alisha commented, 'everyone has to be online at the same time to chat' (even though sending a message to an offline contact is possible in many chat programs, email seems to be preferred), so her own decreased participation in MSN during vacation periods (motivated by the decreased online presence of her non-Japanese contacts) influenced her communication even with those outside of Australia.

As the current study is longitudinal, tracing participants' CMC use for up to four years, it is largely possible to observe participants' patterns of use; however, this does highlight the fact that shorter, cross-sectional studies need to take into account the popularity of particular tools at the time, the geographical location of participants (in cases where availability of technology is an issue), and the time of data collection in relation to the academic or work calendar.

Participants were also asked how long they had spent using their most frequently used (in Japanese) mode of communication in the previous week, as shown in Table 3.3.

Again, answers varied greatly, ranging from less than an hour per week (e.g. Oscar's use of Mixi), to 14 hours a week (Scott's use of Skype). However, although Scott spent 14 hours per week talking to a Japanese NS (his girl-friend), the vast majority of their conversation was actually in English. Genna's 12 hours per week on MySpace were similarly spent using mostly English, as were Cindy's 10 hours on MSN, Zac's eight hours on Facebook, and Alisha's time using email or MSN. Despite these cases, several examples of rather prolific use of Japanese online are apparent.

Firstly, Cindy's use of Ameba stands out. In her interview, Cindy reported that she devoted one hour a day to adding new contacts who had read her blog, and reading theirs. This appears to have been one of Cindy's foremost motivations for maintaining her blog. Users of Ameba can 'stamp' their foot-print (called *peta*) onto another user's blog to indicate that they have visited (and presumably liked the content of the blog). Cindy indicated that she would receive 'like 150 a day or so, ... so I can't read each blog'. Although it is unclear whether each of these 150 visitors to Cindy's blog actually read and evaluated its content, or whether they were simply aiming to collect reciprocal *peta* themselves, Cindy's devotion of an hour each day to this

Table 3.3 Hours of use of most frequently used CMC in Japanese

Participant (N = 12)	Most frequently used CMC in Japanese	Total use
Cindy	MSN (in the past)	10 hours/week
	Ameba	9 hours/week
Genna	MySpace	12 hours/week
Scott	Skype	14 hours/week
Lucas	Email	1 hour/week
Noah	Mixi	Always open
Hyacinth	Email	2 hours/week
Ellise	Mixi	2 hours/week
Zac	Facebook	8 hours/week
	Mixi	<1 hour/week
Jacob	Email	1.5 hours/week
Alisha	Email (in vacation)	6 hours/week
	MSN (in semester)	Always open
Oscar	Mixi	<1 hour/week
Kaylene	Mixi	10.5 hours/week

process not only gave her the opportunity to read a variety of blogs and build a community of (potential) readers, but the *peta* system also provided motivation in the form of a rewards system. Each time the blog owner receives a certain number of *peta*, they obtain a new character.

In addition to responding to *peta*, Cindy said that she spent a further two hours a week on average writing her blog posts, which almost always included Japanese (37/39 blogs). This kind of commitment may appear surprising from a beginning student, however it is obvious from the content of her blogs that Cindy engaged with her audience, directly addressing her readers at times. Cindy commented on her blog on 9 December 2008: 「ペタカラはアイスマンを返変えたよね！(ﾟ∀ﾟ)b　昨晩のペタの方へ、どうもありがとう！！！(笑)」(My *peta* character transformed into an ice man! A big thank you to everyone who sent me *peta* last night!!!).

Next, keeping Mixi constantly open in the background demonstrates how important this line of communication was to Noah. Although he said he does not have the time to be as responsive to Mixi notifications (for example, announcements that one of his friends have posted a new blog, commented on one of his, or sent him a message) during the semester, Noah says that he always has Mixi open during the vacation period, 'just in case I get little notification things'. While Mixi, a form of SNS, would traditionally be categorised as an 'asynchronous' tool, this style of use shows that Noah is treating the medium as a synchronous tool, receiving and responding immediately. This issue will be further discussed in Chapter 4.

Finally, Kaylene's use of Mixi also represents a high level of involvement. Roughly one-third of Kaylene's online time is spent on Mixi, which she uses predominantly in Japanese (16 of Kaylene's 17 blogs were written entirely in Japanese, the remaining one containing some switches to English, and the vast majority of her comments and private messages were likewise in Japanese).

It is evident from these responses that while for some of the participants use of Japanese constituted a rather small part of their online experiences, for others it is an integral part. Of course, time devoted to communicating online depends most importantly on the number of contacts a person has, their contacts' availability, and their relationship.

As a final indication of participants' involvement in communication with NSs of Japanese in respect to their broader online communication practices, participants were also asked about their lists of contacts ('readers' on blogs, 'address books' in email, 'friends' on English-based SNSs, '*mai miku*' on Mixi, and 'buddies' on MSN). These results are displayed in Table 3.4, which includes, where it differs to the total number, participants' estimation of how many 'active contacts' their lists includes – that is, those they have frequent communication with. Overall, the findings in relation to total number of contacts appear not unusual given de Bakker *et al.*'s (2007) finding that around one-third of university students have over 100 friends on their MSN buddy lists.

Interesting changes may be noted, however, in the cases where data is available from both before and after a particular event which caused a change in the demographic makeup of participants' contact base. One such type of event is going to Japan, which presents numerous opportunities to increase one's network, as shown previously. Ellise's use of Facebook and Mixi is one such example, where her Japanese contacts on Facebook increased from just three to 41 over the time she spent in Japan. By comparison, her total number of contacts only increased from 110 to 311. In other words, before her stay in Japan, Ellise's Japanese contacts accounted for only 2.7% of her total list, but at the end of her stay this ratio had increased to 13.2%. Similarly, Ellise's Mixi contact list, which consisted exclusively of Japanese contacts, increased from 19 to 42 during the same period. Jacob's Facebook contact list also grew from 42 to 136 contacts overall. But more surprising was the fact that before leaving Australia Jacob had no Japanese contacts on Facebook whatsoever. Despite this, approximately a year after moving to Japan, this number increased to 28, with Japanese NSs accounting for 20.6% of his total contacts.

It is not only in-country or exchange experiences which can alter the demographics of learners' online contacts. Another example is local immersion. Zac originally collected 12 contacts on his Mixi profile, which he started after living in Japan for a period; however, this profile became inaccessible and was lost, along with all 12 contacts. When Zac managed to re-establish a profile, he was only able to recover two of those original contacts. However, as mentioned above, Zac joined the conversation group MeetUp, which meets face-to-face although it is organised online. After attending this group, and accepting some 'random invites', Zac's contact list grew to almost its former size, or as Zac stated in the interview, 'it's grown from a measly two to now eleven'.

A final factor that can drastically affect the makeup of one's contact list is what some participants referred to as 'culling' – the process of deleting contacts from one's list in order to make communication more manageable. Jacob's Gtalk contact list, for example, was drastically culled from his original MSN contact list of about 20 'buddies'. Such a 'culled' list may give a more accurate picture of who a participant actually communicates with, in comparison with the lists of those who 'collect friends'.

While the numbers of Japanese contacts as a percentage of the Australian participants' total contacts in Table 3.4 may paint their contact with NSs of

Table 3.4 Number of contacts by participant and medium

Participant (N = 12)	Medium	Total contacts (TC)	Active contacts	Total Japanese contacts (JC)	% Japanese NS (JC/TC)
Cindy	Ameba	16	11	14	87.5
	MSN	100	20	2	2
Genna	Ameba	26	7	24	92.3
	MySpace	196	50	3	1.5
	Hotmail/MSN	100	10		
Scott	Gmail	80	40	6	7.5
Lucas	Facebook	141	12	3	2.1
	MSN	70	40	2	2.8
Noah	Mixi	11		8	72
Hyacinth	Ameba	2	1	0	0
	Facebook	108		0	0
	Gmail	100	30	2	2
Ellise	Facebook (before Japan)	110		3	2.7
	Facebook (after Japan)	311		41	13.2
	Mixi (before Japan)	19		19	100
	Mixi (after Japan)	42		42	100
	Hotmail	150		8	5.3
	MSN	100	25	2	2
Zac	Facebook	254	50	12	4.7
	Mixi (old site)	12		12	100
	Mixi (new site – after MeetUp)	2		2	100
	Gmail	11		11	100
		400	20	50	12.5
Jacob	Facebook (before Japan)	42		0	0
	Facebook (in Japan)	136		28	20.6
	Gmail	20		3	15
	Gtalk	5		0	0
Alisha	Facebook	38		3	7.9
	Mixi	7		3	42.9
	Hotmail/MSN	50	15	12	24

Table 3.4 (Continued)

Participant (N = 12)	Medium	Total contacts (TC)	Active contacts	Total Japanese contacts (JC)	% Japanese NS (JC/TC)
Oscar	Facebook	131		3	2.3
	Mixi	13		10	76.9
Kaylene	Facebook	33		8	24.2
	Mixi	11	4	10	90.9
	Hotmail	123	100		
	MSN	28	13	7	25
	Gmail	74	20		

Notes: Cindy also used Yahoo mail, and Lucas Hotmail, but as neither used the address book function their data is not included here.

Japanese as fairly uncommon, it is important to note that most participants have been using the mediums described in this section in English for much longer than they have Japanese and, hence, have had longer to build up a base of English-speakers. Participants in the present study had on average only used CMC in Japanese for 59% of the number of years they had used the same tools in English, as displayed in Table 3.2 previously.

Another more accurate estimation of participants' contact with Japanese NSs overall can be obtained from examining their reports of who they communicated with over the past week, shown in Table 3.5. Only the mediums that they used in the week of the interview are listed.

Table 3.5 demonstrates that while some participants, like Cindy, did not communicate online with any NSs of Japanese in the week of the interview, others interacted with numerous NS contacts. Mixi was used almost exclusively with Japanese contacts, while Facebook appears to have one of the lowest percentages of interactions with Japanese NSs. Possible reasons for this will be explored in the discussion of 'domains' later in this chapter.

Offline L2 communication

In addition to their use of Japanese in the classroom, all participants reported using Japanese in other, offline, contexts. While in some cases their opportunities for interaction were quite limited, several factors appear to facilitate these opportunities, including the use of CMC to aid in organising offline meetings and obtaining Japanese materials. Participants' opportunities

Table 3.5 Australian participants' interactions over the past week

Participant (N = 12)	Medium	Total contacts interacted with in past week	Japanese contacts interacted with in past week	Percentage Japanese NS
Cindy	MSN	6	0	0
Genna	Hotmail	4	1	25
	MySpace	10	3	30
Scott	Skype	1	1	100
	Gmail	5	1	20
Lucas	Hotmail	1	1	100
	Facebook	1	0	0
Noah	Mixi	4	4	100
Hyacinth	Hotmail	2	1	50
Ellise	MSN	5	1	20
	Email	20	5	25
	Mixi	1	1	100
Zac	Mixi	2	1	50
	Facebook	20	2	10
Jacob	Email	10	1	10
Alisha	Email	10	1	10
Oscar	Mixi	3	3	100
Kaylene	Mixi	6	5	83
	Email	10	3	30

for the use of their L2, and contributing factors, are outlined below. The categories of L2 communication were arrived at through the *in vivo* and topical coding of participants' comments in the interviews.

University

For Alisha, university classes acted as a springboard to out-of-classroom communication with NSs of Japanese. Alisha got together with some Japanese friends that she had met in a linguistics class on a regular basis for informal conversations about Japanese language. Importantly, Alisha reports that these meetings were organised through a form of CMC – SMS.

Formalised social activities

Kaylene participated in a formal language exchange, organised by the university, which gave her frequent contact with NSs of Japanese. Like Alisha, she organised this contact via CMC. Zac's involvement in the MeetUp group, which was also organised online, provided similar opportunities. Bible study at Oscar's church enabled him to make a Japanese acquaintance that he met each week and with whom he played Japanese chess (*shōgi*).

Communicating with other NNSs

Prior to meeting Tokio in person, Genna claimed that she had little or no opportunity to use Japanese with NSs in a face-to-face setting. Her only opportunity to speak Japanese was to talk with her younger sister (who had been on a short-term exchange to Japan) while watching Japanese television shows. Likewise, Hyacinth discussed online the *manga* she read with another L2 speaker of Japanese, a friend from Taiwan. In addition to communicating with these NNSs of Japanese in their established networks, Genna and Hyacinth also sought out the advice and expertise of NNSs living in Japan over the Internet. Genna established communication with an American female whom she met online through her Japanese friend Tokio, to whom she could ask questions about dating, safety, and life at an international school. Hyacinth sought the advice of a NNS living in Japan on the blog site LiveJournal regarding CMC medium choice (described later in this chapter).

Work

For Jacob and Zac, who worked at the *manga* library, the opportunity to read *manga* was not the only language learning benefit they gained from this arrangement. Jacob also reported speaking in Japanese with any native Japanese speakers he met as part of his role as a volunteer. Although his part-time job did not relate to Japanese, Lucas said that his main opportunity to speak Japanese outside the classroom was in talking to a workmate to whom he was teaching a few phrases.

Other-mediated communication

Some participants kept in contact with their friends and acquaintances in Japan via non-electronic modes. Cindy wrote letters to Rina, Kaylene posted presents, such as boxed chocolates, at Christmas to several of her close contacts, who would reciprocate, and Scott communicated via mobile phone calls with his girlfriend, Kieko. Lucas also called his friend Hisayo over a landline phone, which he arranged over MSN. As mentioned above, CMC, and email in particular (although some circles appear to be moving towards SNSs such as Facebook or Mixi), can function as a 'passport' to, or a tool for, organising face-to-face communication (as mentioned above), and non-Internet mediated communication (as well as other Internet-mediated communication, as will be shown in Chapter 4). Below is an example of Kaylene's use of email to confirm Chikae's postal address:

Extract 3.2 Kaylene's email to Chikae: 3/12/2007 1:57:28 PM

千歌恵の住所は何？
クリスマスのチョコレートを送りたいから　：）
(What is your address Chikae?
Because I'd like to send you some chocolates for Christmas)

Reading and watching/listening

Ellise and Genna both enjoyed watching Japanese television shows, and Hyacinth, Jacob, and Zac all reported reading *manga* as one of their main uses of Japanese outside the classroom. Naturally, Ellise and Genna's television shows were largely downloaded, and Hyacinth, who unlike Jacob and Zac, did not work at the *manga* library, ordered many *manga* from the Internet, or used CMC to arrange with her Taiwanese friend to have copies sent to her.

The pattern emerging from the above examples clearly shows the integral part Internet use played in participants' L2 use as a whole. CMC facilitated Alisha, Kaylene, and Zac's face-to-face meetings with NSs, and without the Internet, Ellise, Genna, and Hyacinth would have found it difficult to access Japanese media. Yet another emerging pattern is that for some students, particularly those from lower levels, opportunities for face-to-face communication appeared difficult to find in Australia. None of the participants enrolled in levels 1–6 of the Japanese programme at their university reported any regular communication with NSs of Japanese in face-to-face settings. Zac, Jacob, Alisha, Oscar, and Kaylene, all enrolled in level 9 or higher, were the only participants who had face-to-face conversations with local Japanese. Genna, Lucas, and Hyacinth all used Japanese with other NNSs only (until Genna eventually met Tokio face-to-face after meeting online), and Ellise only engaged in reading, watching, or listening to Japanese alone. Noah stated that he mostly spoke to himself in Japanese as he did not really know anyone who understood it in his offline, outside-the-classroom life. Scott also claimed that his language use outside the classroom was mostly limited to 'just saying some stupid words with friends'. Thus, CMC can be seen to play an important role, not only in facilitating face-to-face communication with local Japanese, as seen among the more proficient learners, but also in compensating for a lack of face-to-face communication for lower-level students.

Linguistic Domains and Virtual L2 Community

Academic literature, the popular press, and CMC advertisements alike have claimed that the Internet fosters 'virtual communities'. Thus, it was unsurprising that several participants made reference to this concept in the interviews; however, not all of their comments were positive. Having situated participants' use of CMC in Japanese in terms of their broader online and L2 practices, we now turn to examine how participants themselves viewed their involvement in a virtual L2 community using Mixi, the most frequently used Japanese medium, as a primary case study.

'A place where you can be surrounded by the language'

To some participants, like Genna, who, as mentioned above, reported that she had no opportunities to use Japanese in face-to-face settings outside the classroom, the benefit of communicating in Japanese online was simply that she got to use the language at all. Alisha echoed this sentiment, saying, 'in my everyday life, I don't use the language unless I do it online'. Evidence from Kaylene's experience strengthens this idea of CMC as a surrogate for face-to-face communication. During a fieldwork interview in Japan, Kaylene remarked that she had not been using Mixi recently, 'I think I've made one post since I came to Japan, and since then, I've sort of slacked off'. She explained:

> I used to use it a lot in Australia as Japanese practise, because I felt like I wasn't getting enough practise in Australia, but now I'm working at the museum, and I get to talk to people every day in Japanese, I guess it's not as necessary. (Kaylene-Ruriko Focus-group, Line 238)

Use of CMC among students in Australia for Japanese practise appears common among the participants, even if their main goal is social rather than educational. Alisha's view of the Internet (or, more specifically, her personal 'internet') was 'a place where you can be surrounded by the language without being in a place where you're surrounded by the language! It's a virtual community'.

Mixi, in particular, was highlighted as a virtual L2 community by several participants. Kaylene termed Mixi a 'Japanese forum', and stated that this influenced her language choice: 'I tend to view Mixi as a Japanese forum [and] I've only used English here in the couple of phrases that I wasn't sure about, and when I was talking about the English language'. As previously mentioned, 16 of Kaylene's 17 blogs were written entirely in Japanese. It appears that it was not simply the presence of NSs of Japanese, but also the fact that Mixi was an area of the Internet dominated by Japanese that influenced participants' perceptions about Mixi as a virtual L2 community, and their language choice. Ellise also explained that her reason for choosing to write mostly in Japanese on Mixi was that '99% of people on there can't actually read English'. Accordingly, nine of Ellise's 10 blogs were written entirely in Japanese. Even Sae, one of Ellise's Japanese contacts, said that she used Japanese with Ellise on Mixi precisely 'because it's Mixi'. Ameba also was seen as a virtual L2 community, but of a different kind. Genna said that she chose this medium for her blog because of its use by celebrities and her NNS peers rather than established NS networks. She said, 'musicians and famous people blog on it, and I read some of them, and then made my own account, and I found out Cindy had done it as well, so that helped. I probably wouldn't have gone on with it [otherwise].'

'You're always gonna be a JSL'

While entering a 'Japanese domain' may have had positive immersion-like effects on learners' motivation to read and write in their L2, some participants also retained a strong feeling of being an outsider. As Alisha said, 'You're always gonna be a JSL [Japanese as a Second Language speaker].' In Hyacinth's interviews, and also in a later chat conversation, where she approached the researcher to describe another incident, several instances of negative experiences in online communities were apparent. Based on feedback from other NNSs of Japanese on the blog site LiveJournal, Hyacinth became wary of attempting a number of online activities. Hyacinth described a blogging tool that focused on drawing, one of her main interests. In fact, Hyacinth's own Ameba blog featured many original drawings (five drawings spread over six blog entries). In the interview, Hyacinth said that she had wanted to try this new blog site until she heard 'a lot of negative feedback from people who weren't Japanese, and from the Japanese online circles, communities, they were ostracised'. Hyacinth also heard similar feedback about an online video site that she described as being 'for Japanese people'. She said,

> I remember them saying one person posted a video of them self, and they were mocked to the ends of the earth, and felt really ashamed, because they weren't Japanese. I think there's a kind of pride that comes with them [being Japanese], especially online. (Hyacinth Interview 1, Line 376)

Similarly, Hyacinth was also warned off 2chan, a very popular Japanese Internet forum famous for its distinctive vocabulary and appearance in the film *Densha Otoko*, saying that she thought it was 'dangerous to try as a non-Japanese speaker'. Again, she had heard that 'if you say one word out of line, something wrong, no one will look at you or respect you or anything'.

While Hyacinth said that hearing these rumours may have influenced her decision not to participate more actively online, she claimed that a bigger influence was a lack of confidence:

It's mostly because I'm still not very confident, and it's mostly conversational Japanese, especially the modern speaking ... I find with online Japanese, there are a lot of words that are made just for that online communication, which I always feel sort of hazy about. (Hyacinth Interview 1, Line 388)

Although it is important not to over-emphasise the benefits of the Internet at the expense of ignoring the less positive aspects, Hyacinth's experiences were by no means representative of the group as a whole, and her reluctance to participate online seems to have at least in part been affected by her own self-consciousness and lack of confidence in her Japanese. Even though communicating with one's university teachers in Japanese was common practice among the Australian participants in general, Hyacinth stated that she had never tried to email any of her teachers in Japanese, and was frightened of doing so. Nevertheless, it must be remembered that such negative experiences do occur, and while Hyacinth's reports were not representative of the group, this may be because the others have not ventured into the various online spaces she did.

WebKare

A final example of a negative experience for Hyacinth occurred on the forum of an online game. Almost two months after her final interview, Hyacinth contacted the researcher to describe an experience, this time on a medium she had actually decided to attempt using, called *WebKare* (Web Boyfriend, http://web-kare.jp), an online dating simulator aimed at girls, with a forum attached. Hyacinth joined this website and played the game; however, while she read the forum postings often, she decided not to contribute herself, due to the abusive nature of some posts. Although a large number of Japanese-speaking users were welcoming and helpful to Japanese learners, some members were dissatisfied about the use of other languages, particularly Chinese and Korean, or the 'poor' use of Japanese on the website. Hostility towards language variation on the WebKare forum is evident; for example, in the following post from an anonymous user written in Japanese, which Hyacinth pointed out as typical of the debate:

Extract 3.3 Japanese WebKare posting example

日本語で書きなさい。
ここは日本人のためのサービスです。
日本語が理解できないなら日本のサービスを受ける資格はありません。
中国だの韓国だのそれぞれの国で勝手に暴れなさい。

(Write in Japanese.
This is a service for Japanese people.
If you cannot understand Japanese you have no right to use Japanese services.
Whether you're from China or Korea, go act like savages in your own country.) (Anon. 20/09/2008)

Despite the post's aggressive wording, Hyacinth showed some sympathy to this writer's point of view, stating that she did not understand why people would use a Japanese site 'if you only want to talk in another language'. She said, 'some Japanese users mentioned that some foreign users use "I don't understand Japanese/I'm foreign" as an excuse to avoid confrontation'.

For Hyacinth, an Australian-Chinese-background learner of Japanese, hostility towards Chinese languages affected her motivation to engage in interaction on the forums. Even so, Hyacinth saw the reaction of the 'hostile' Japanese as symptomatic of their online space being invaded: 'I think the frustrations are the invasion of a domain that [is] mostly Japanese'. When asked what made the website a 'Japanese domain', Hyacinth responded 'Generally, the website being completely in Japanese to me suggests that a level of Japanese is required to play it ... especially with instructions in Japanese'.

It is important to note that most of the conversation regarding the use of WebKare in languages other than Japanese was carried out by anonymous users who, like in the post above, chose not to attach their name or avatar to their messages. Levy and Stockwell (2006) state that while anonymity in CMC can have positive effects, such as giving learners more confidence to participate than they may have in face-to-face communication (as noted by Shibanai, 2007 also), negative effects, such as the 'flaming' (hostile or insulting comments) seen above, are also fostered by the affordance of anonymity. As previously mentioned, Ridings *et al.* (2006) attribute lurking behaviour to a lack of trust, which appears fitting here. Given Hyacinth's experiences online, and the hostile environment that she witnessed on WebKare, it is unsurprising that she chose not to contribute to this forum, and instead acted as a read-only member, or lurker.

Mobile phones

Although such negative experiences do not appear widespread, exposure to the kind of environment described above may have severe effects on a learner's desire to attempt communication in their L2. However, some additional factors actually preclude the ability of non-Japanese to communicate at all. In a fieldwork interview in Japan, Jacob reported that his choice of mobile phone was limited to the providers that would actually sell mobile phones to non-Japanese nationals. Furthermore, part-way through the data collection period, Mixi, which previously had required an invitation from a current member in order to join (which may be difficult for learners to obtain), introduced a rule requiring prospective users to have a Japanese mobile phone email address to sign up (a condition excluding many non-residents). One of the top-ranked English articles on this move, available at http://www.tofugu.com/, is titled 'Mixi Now Hates Foreigners: Requires a (Japanese) Mobile Email Address to Join'. As previously seen, also, in order for Ellise to join the Gackt fan club and to be able to access online content she not only had to pay the membership fee, but ask a friend living in Japan, whom she communicated with via mobile email, to act as a proxy, as a Japan-based mailing address was also required.

Likewise, Zac described how he would not have been able to re-create his Mixi account in Australia after it was accidentally lost if it were not for the assistance of his Japanese sister-in-law. She allowed him to use her mobile phone email address, and received the confirmation message that unlocks membership to the site for him. However, obviously, not every learner has a Japanese friend or sister-in-law to help initiate them into Japanese online spaces. Another participant, Cindy, described how she was not so lucky, and, having been unable to sign up to Mixi, eventually gave up and joined a different site, Ameba, instead. Cindy's motivation to blog in Japanese does not appear to have been diminished by this experience, as she went on to blog prolifically on Ameba, posting 35 blogs in the space of a month, only two of which were written exclusively in English, despite the fact that she had only studied Japanese for a short time. However, being a member of the most popular social networking site, Mixi, has specific advantages, as previously mentioned.

L2 identity in a virtual L2 community

Finally, the ways in which participants in the present study chose to signal their status as NNSs on Mixi are of interest in examining their perceived status in the online L2 community, and their motivations for joining. Despite Burkhalter (1999) and Herring's (2003) claims that, so long as language competencies do not indicate otherwise, the signalling of 'race', ethnicity, 'sex', gender, or indeed any other aspect of identity online, appears to be at the participant's discretion, none of the Australian students in the current study attempted to hide or disguise their national identity. Instead, using both the linguistic and visual means highlighted in Chapter 1, they brought them to the fore. This can be seen, for example, in an analysis of SNS profiles. Half of the Australian participants in the current study, Alisha, Ellise, Kaylene, Noah, Oscar, and Zac were members of Mixi, and for five of them

Mixi was their most commonly used CMC medium in Japanese. Mixi profiles may consist of a display photo, list of basic information (e.g. age, sex, and location), self-introduction, and a list of likes and interests, all of which are optional to complete. The remainder of this section will explore the ways in which participants manipulated these four visual and linguistic elements of the profile to develop their online L2 identities.

All six participants who were members of Mixi clearly stated in their profiles that they were not Japanese, or that they were studying Japanese. All listed 「海外オーストラリア」 (Overseas: Australia) as their current address and, additionally, Alisha, Ellise, and Zac explicitly stated their nationality in the body of their profiles. This information often took precedence over other biographic details or interests.

Alisha's profile opened with the statement 「オーストラリア人だ」 (I am Australian). Ellise's profile also started with a statement of nationality: 「私はオーストラリア人とイギリス人ですけれども今オーストラリアに住んでいます！」 (I am Australian and English, however I am living in Australia at the moment!). Zac's profile read 「ザックです。オーストラリア人で２３歳です」 (I'm Zac. I am Australian and 23 years old). Kaylene's approach was a little less direct, simply implying her 'foreignness' by stating 「この日記は、きっと 下手で外国人っぽいな日本語か「ケイリー語」になっちゃうごめんね」 (I'm sorry, this blog will probably end up being very badly written and the Japanese is that of a foreigner, or even 'Kaylese'), referring to herself as a NNS, and her own idiolect as 'Kaylese'.

Some were also careful to emphasise the fact that they were still studying Japanese. Ellise's second line was 「今は大学で日本語を勉強しています」 (I am studying Japanese at university at the moment). Similarly, Oscar stated 「今、日本語と中国語を勉強しています」 (At the moment, I am studying Japanese and Chinese). Noah even gave a whole history of his learning of Japanese, reproduced below:

Extract 3.4 Excerpt from Noah's Mixi profile

私は２００６年から今まで日本語を勉強しています。最初はＲ大学で日本語の勉強を始まったんですが後八ヶ月に卒業しました。短いコースでしたけどすごく楽しくて興味深かった。今はＭ大学で勉強しています。もちろん日本語の勉強を続けています。

(I have been studying Japanese since 2006 up to now. At first, I began studying Japanese at R University, but I graduated after eight months. It was a short course, but a lot of fun and I was very interested. Now, I am studying at M University. Of course, I am continuing with my Japanese study.)

In Tudini's (2003) analysis of Italian learners' chat with NSs as a language learning tool a similar phenomenon was observed, whereby many learners chose to reveal their non-native status early on in their communication. The present study demonstrates that learners are likely to make similar choices outside of the institutional setting also. Finally, several participants also used the Interests section to further focus on language. Ellise, Noah, Oscar, and Zac all listed 「語学」 (language study) as a hobby.

Although a major theme of all six profiles, it would be erroneous to presume that being a 'foreigner'/language learner was the only identity at the forefront of participants' profile construction. Another observable pattern concerns interest in Japanese culture, something all participants took pains to emphasise. Four of the six participants used Japan-related photographs for their display picture; Alisha, a photo of herself in the snow in Japan, Zac, likewise, a photo of himself with a snow sculpture in Japan, Ellise used a *purikura* (Japanese Print Club photo sticker) of herself and a Japanese friend, complete with Japanese graffiti, and Oscar's display photo was a shot of his neighbourhood in Japan (which he described in his profile). All six also listed Japanese-related likes and interests. This may appear unsurprising, given that an interest in Japanese culture is hardly remarkable among students of Japanese, or even among the youth population more generally, as Larson (2003) notes. However, interesting comparisons can be drawn between participants' English-based social networking profiles (in this case, Facebook, the most popular English SNS among participants, will be used as a basis for comparison), and their Japanese (Mixi) profiles.

As can be seen in Table 3.6, none of the participants mentioned any of the Japanese-specific interests that they displayed on Mixi (Japanese television dramas, *karaoke, anime, manga, shogi* chess, alcohol – traditional *sake* or modern Japanese cocktails at the 300 Yen Bar, Japanese foods (e.g. *tantanmen* noodles), video games, or even language learning) in their English Facebook profiles. This demonstrates the context-specificity of participants' identity displays.

Lastly, although all six participants went to great lengths to foreground their NNS status, and emphasise their interest in Japanese culture on Mixi, this does not mean that they cast themselves in a wholly subordinate role. This is clearest in the case of Noah, who positioned himself as a learner of Japanese, but an expert in English:「私は日本で英語の教師にたりたいんです。... feel free to ask me for help with English」(I want to become a teacher of English in Japan). Zac also divulged his aspirations to become an English teacher, offering to speak in English or Japanese with anyone interested:「私の夢は日本で英語教師になりたいです。 そのためにいっぱい日本人の友達を作って、日本語と英語で話したいです。」(My dream is that I want to become

Table 3.6 Australian participants' interests on Mixi and Facebook

Participant	Mixi interests	Facebook interests
Alisha	Swimming, Japanese anime, and music	None listed
Ellise	Sports, *karaoke*, band, cooking, *sake*, shopping, driving, language study, Japanese TV dramas and video games, ice skating, AFL, *tantanmen* noodles, the 300 Yen Bar	Acting, singing, travelling, reading, talking, shopping
Kaylene	Travel, art, language study, reading, internet	Stuff, music
Oscar	Movies, sport, food, travel, language study, reading, TV, video games, internet, Japanese chess	None listed
Noah	Language study, *manga*	*-No profile-*
Zac	Watching movies, sport, watching sport, listening to music, cooking, *sake*, driving, travel, language study, *manga*, TV, video games, internet	*-No profile-*
Lucas	*-No profile-*	Sleeping Eating Video gaming

Source: Pasfield-Neofitou (2011: 104).

an English teacher in Japan. Therefore I want to make a lot of Japanese friends, and talk in Japanese and English.)

Discussion

In examining the social settings of participants' online language use, two major themes emerged. The first is the existence of language or nationality/ethnicity based 'domains', and the second, a sense of belonging (or not belonging) to a 'virtual community'. While the Internet has often been claimed as a monolithic, 'placeless' space, physical location and face-to-face communication with NS peers were found to play an important part in medium choice. Based on an *in vivo* coding of interviews with participants, and the analysis of interaction data collected, language-specific 'forums' or 'domains' were identified. These social settings were found to have both positive and negative effects on the learners in the present study. A sense of being immersed in someone else's space made Alisha feel that she was surrounded by the language, in effect, giving her the opportunity to draw on the contextual resources of a different cultural system in order to facilitate her goal of language acquisition, as will be explored in Chapter 4. However, negative effects were felt also, including Hyacinth's experiences of intolerance towards 'outside' languages or ethnic groups that were not considered part of the social setting of the WebKare forum.

In contrast with many previous studies of CMC, which have emphasised the importance of L2 language production without considering the positive effects of receptive use, the present study has highlighted important opportunities for noticing and potential language acquisition that such activities, including lurking, offer. For many participants, watching Japanese television shows and movies or listening to Japanese music was an important secondary activity carried out while online. For Hyacinth, reading, watching, and listening activities were her major use of Japanese. Although Hyacinth's preference for these types of activities was linked to a lack of confidence in her language ability, and the possible result of some negative experiences online, several opportunities for language learning were identified. Hyacinth made use of resources in her reading to acquire new vocabulary, she engaged with others, sharing television shows and obtaining recommendations of *manga* and, perhaps most substantially, made use of her Japanese to navigate the complex processes of online shopping in her L2.

Building on the exploration of participants' psychobiographies in the previous chapter, this chapter also examined participants' ongoing construction of their identities online. As outlined in Chapter 1, in addition to one's continuous sense of self, which was evident in representations of 'core' identity, people are constantly changing and shaped by external forces, such as those at play in social settings, and are manifested in situated activity. In the situated activity of L2 use in CMC, being an L2 learner was found to be an important identity for many participants, and an aspect of self which they foregrounded in their profiles – notably, their 'Japanese domain' profiles. Participants were found to actively construct online spaces, signalling their interest in Japan to prospective contacts, encouraging the discussion of Japanese language and culture. Participants' language use in these online spaces is examined in the following chapter.

Note

1. A small portion of this chapter was previously published in Pasfield–Neofitou, S.E. (2011) Second language learners' experiences of virtual community and foreignness. *Language Learning & Technology* 15 (2), 92–198.

4   Features of CMC Use

As the previous two chapters demonstrated, participants developed and maintained a wide variety of relationships via CMC. This chapter will examine the features of their CMC use, focusing on the second research question presented in Chapter 1, which examines the ways learners use CMC in their L2, for what purposes, and in what combinations.

Drawing on numerical data from the corpus analysis of participants' CMC interactions, coupled with the coding of both interaction and interview data, this chapter will describe some of the relevant features of participants' situated CMC discourse, including the organisation of conversations, orthographic and code-switching, and types of language use. Where examples are presented from the discourse data, participants' script and spacing choices are retained, including the use of non-standard romanisation. The present chapter concludes with a case study of two learners' longitudinal patterns of language use, drawing together aspects of psychobiography, social setting, and situated activity, before contextual resources are examined in the following chapter.

Organisation of Online Conversations

As mentioned in Chapter 1, the present study makes use of three units of analysis; the e-turn, the turn, and the conversation. The relationship between the turn and e-turn in the present study is modelled according to Sacks *et al.*'s (1974) relationship between the turn and turn construction unit (TCU). Like the e-turn, a TCU is a fundamental segment of speech, describing pieces of conversation which may comprise an entire turn. At the end of each TCU (or e-turn) is a transition relevance place (TRP). Each TRP marks a point where the floor may be shifted to another speaker. In speech, this may be marked through intonation or a small pause, indicating the end of a phrase or clause. At this point, the current speaker will select the next speaker, the next speaker will self-select, or the current speaker will continue. In the case of CMC, each participant decides when to place a TRP by hitting send and completing an e-turn. The end of an e-turn thus opens the possibility for them to select the next person to take the floor by inviting their interlocutor to contribute a turn before relinquishing the floor (current speaker selects next speaker), their interlocutor to take the floor by interjecting with a new e-turn (next speaker self-selects), or for them to continue the turn, by adding another e-turn before their interlocutor has a chance to (current speaker continues). In this way, a single turn may consist of more than one e-turn. Although originally applied to chat (cf. Pasfield-Neofitou, 2006; Thorne, 1999), I extend the notion of the e-turn here to include other forms of text-based CMC – for example, one email can be considered a single e-turn, as may a video upload, or a comment on a BBS, and a series of any of these e-turns from the one sender may be considered a turn. For example, if one email is sent and a reply not received, and the sender follows with another, this may be counted as a single turn. Although a TRP was established at the sending of the first email, the recipient decided not to self-select and, thus, the current turn continues. A total of 2460 e-turns were identified in the data collected for the present study, in 370 separate conversations.

An example of an e-turn and turn in chat is given in Figure 4.1; however, the same concept is applicable to other CMC conversations, for instance, a series of emails. Each of the sections below tagged with the date and time of sending, and the sender's screen name, represent a single e-turn, in addition to the one highlighted.

As in oral conversation, where overlap, false starts, hesitations, interruptions, and minimal responses, which do not constitute turns, occur, a turn in CMC is not as precisely delimited as the e-turn. However, while the e-turn functions well as a clear-cut minimal unit, it is insufficient to stand alone directly underneath the conversation level. While it is true that individual participants choose at what point to hit send, technical and interpersonal constraints are also present. In some chat programs, forums, or mobile phone text messages, the e-turn may be limited to a specific number of characters, forcing the participant to take multiple e-turns to get their turn across.

25/02/2008	21:37:17	Tokio	It's good. Have you got friends?		
25/02/2008	21:27:49	~;*;~daffodil~;*;~	**I met one guy from my sociology class, and we had lunch**	e-turn	turn
25/02/2008	21:37:56	~;*;~daffodil~;*;~	**so, 1 friend!**		
25/02/2008	21:37:58	~;*;~daffodil~;*;~	**lol**		
25/02/2008	21:38:15	Tokio	It's much better than nothing!		

Figure 4.1 Example of a turn and e-turn in Tokio and Genna's chat

On other occasions, particularly in chat or other mediums being used in a fast-paced manner, participants may deliberately break a turn up over several e-turns in order to avoid their contribution being made irrelevant. Importantly, e-turns may become disjointed, and require rejuxtaposition via a number of means.

Constructing e-turns

In face-to-face speech, listeners' predictions of when a speaker may possibly complete a TCU have been proven to be fundamental to the smooth organisation of talk (Liddicoat, 2004). While in programs such as ICQ, users may view each other's messages as they are typed letter by letter, in all forms of CMC collected for the present study, participants were unable to view e-turns in progress. Thus, participants may deliberately split their turn over several e-turns to avoid spending too long typing a reply in a single e-turn, in case the conversation moves on to a new topic before they have a chance to make their contribution. This is not only the case with 'synchronous' modes such as chat, but may also occur in 'asynchronous' modes like email, where a participant may send a short reply to let others know they are working on a longer contribution, to ensure that it is expected and is not superseded by any new topics which might make it redundant. One reason for such messages is that in many forms of CMC interlocutors may be unaware that their partner is even producing a turn until it is sent. A notable exception is MSN, which displays '__ is typing a message', or Gtalk, which shows a symbol of a keyboard. Some users monitor this area of their chat window to ensure that they wait for their interlocutor to finish composing, in order to avoid overlap, which may in turn affect turn-taking organisation (Pasfield-Neofitou, 2006). Even so, in chat conversations in particular, where the time between sending and receiving messages is usually very short, concurrent 'threads' of conversational topics, and disrupted adjacency pairs, as previously mentioned, are common. An example from a chat conversation between Kaylene and Ruriko is given in Figure 4.2.

In this example, three distinct strands or threads of conversation are maintained simultaneously. According to Kaylene, the lines joined by the thin solid grey line were 'talking about the camera', in which Ruriko organised to use Kaylene's webcam. The second thread, joined by a bold solid black line, is about it being 'so cool how they can email phones in Japan', and the third, joined by a grey dotted line, is organising a day and time to use the webcam (related to, but distinct from, the first solid grey thread). Turn adjacency is clearly interrupted, with answers to questions, responses to

	Time	From	Message
1	8:23:03 PM	kay miró	Is that enough time to let people in Japan know you'll be online?
2	8:23:19 PM	kay miró	oh, I forgot... you can email their phone, right?
3	8:23:25 PM	瑠璃子 ((Ruriko))	あ、母の日だけど仕事ある？？ ((Ah, it's Mother's Day but do you have work??))
2	8:23:41 PM	kay miró	かっこいいね ((It's cool))
1	8:24:03 PM	瑠璃子	yes!! maybe it is ok!!
2	8:24:14 PM	瑠璃子	What is cool??
3	8:24:17 PM	kay miró	いいえ、バイトはあしたと土曜日だけ:) ((No, my part time job is only on tomorrow and Saturday :)))
2	8:24:32 PM	kay miró	being able to email people's phones is cool ^^;
3	8:24:57 PM	瑠璃子	Oh, nice!! So what time are you free??
2	8:25:01 PM	瑠璃子	Ah, I got it!!
3	8:25:34 PM	kay miró	anytime you like. I'll probably just be doing homework that day.

Figure 4.2 Turn management in Kaylene and Ruriko's chat
Source: Pasfield-Neofitou (2009a: 45).

comments, and queries about statements delayed, often occurring one to two e-turns later (Pasfield-Neofitou, 2009a). This kind of turn management is markedly different to that observed in face-to-face communication. Greenfield and Subrahmanyam (2003) note that, in order to be considered coherent, adjacent turns in a conversation are normally related in some way to what came before (Grice, 1975; Schegloff & Sacks, 1973), and the ordering of speakers specifies that successive speakers are participating in a single conversational thread (Sacks *et al.*, 1974). Indeed, Liddicoat states that where gaps or overlaps occur (in spoken communication), they can be seen as 'something of interactional significance' (2007: 51). Yet, these rules are not 'fundamental' online. As Kaylene explained:

> I'm just so used to doing that (composing turns that overlap) in [Japanese] chat, because in English [chat], I do that all the time as well, and sometimes we have three conversations going on at a time ... it's because typing takes a long time, and generally, while the other person's reading, you're saying something else anyway, and so, you end up replying to a comment, then typing one out, then replying to one ... they don't usually last long anyway. (cited in Pasfield-Neofitou, 2006: 45)

However, it is not only in relatively fast-paced conversations that such thread overlaps appear. As shown later in the present chapter, overlapping topics or threads may occur in conversations carried out over lengthy periods of time, via a variety of different means, including those such as email that have traditionally been considered 'asynchronous'. It appears that the text-based nature of some CMC modes may help sustain multiple concurrent threads in a way that is not afforded in oral communication, by giving some freedom from the human constraints on memory. Participants may scroll up and check the previous e-turns in a chat conversation, or search their archived emails, for example. Such actions are not possible in face-to-face talk, where one must ask an interlocutor for repetition. Furthermore, the way in which the computer receives and orders text-based messages means that, unlike in oral conversation, where it may not be possible to understand one or all interlocutors if more than one party talks at once, text-based messages are always presented independently, in the order in which they are received. In the example presented in Figure 4.2, it is likely that Kaylene's e-turn at 8:24:17 was being composed at the same time as Ruriko's sent just three seconds earlier at 8:24:14. However, rather than displaying these turns as a jumbled mess of characters, the computer presents them as two distinct e-turns, each tagged with the sender's name. The same occurs, for example, with two emails or two blog comments composed concurrently.

Constructing turns

While every completion of an e-turn represents a technical TRP, that is, it is technically possible for speaker change to occur and even a new conversational thread to intervene, there are several ways that participants may signal that they wish to hold the floor, even though this does not mean that their signals will be read, understood, or accommodated. Participants may decide to split their turns over more than one e-turn for a variety of reasons, including to signal a change in language or topic, as will be explored in the following sections, to ensure that their contribution does not become irrelevant in a fast-paced conversation, or, in some modes of CMC, because a maximum character length has been reached. An e-turn may even be accidentally sent before its intended completion. This is relatively common in Japanese chat, where the Enter key is used to both send a message and select one's desired characters from a list. However, evidence from Toyoda and Harrison's (2002) study appears to suggest that, at least in NSs' use, the places in which turns are split are usually not random, but instead play a role in the organisation of conversation. When NNSs incorrectly segmented a turn, misunderstandings sometimes occurred.

Thus, in order to fully understand the organisation of CMC conversations, it is important to consider management at the levels of the e-turn (where an individual decides where to segment an utterance), the turn (where participants sequence the organisation of e-turns), and the conversation (where participants jointly construct single or multiple threads over any number of turns and e-turns). Examination of language use at only the e-turn level is deceptive in that it does not provide adequate scope for consideration of the ways in which participants jointly and skilfully manage their communication via quoting a previous turn to give the illusion of adjacency, and a number of other linguistic and visual means to effectively re-order e-turns, as will be outlined in the following chapter. The identification of turns, however, fosters a much more sophisticated understanding of CMC conversations.

Conversations in writing

Outlined in Chapter 1, the term 'conversation' is proposed as the top-level unit of analysis, to refer not only to the more conventional chat and Voice Over Internet Protocol (VOIP) conversations, but also conversations via email, SNSs, and so on. As mentioned previously, the conversation-like nature of text-based CMC has been noted in the past, with previous studies considering various modes: 'conversations in writing' or 'speech in writing' (cf. Okamoto, 1998). The use of the term conversations here is not intended to imply that text-based CMC is *identical* to face-to-face conversations, or those carried out via audio-based CMC (e.g. Skype), but rather, should be viewed as shorthand for 'conversations in writing' where appropriate.

Six criteria, based on the analysis of the collected CMC data, interviews with participants, and the literature reviewed in Chapter 1, are utilised for determining the boundaries of a conversation in the present study. The first criterion is *terminology present in the application itself*. When participants use Gmail, the software terms a series of emails a 'conversation' and visually presents it as such, with related emails organised chronologically according to topic. The same is true of chat conversations and so forth. Users choose to contribute to a conversation (as opposed to constructing a stand-alone e-turn) by utilising the organisational capacity of the software. The second, related, criterion applies to more traditional email programs. Participants can choose to *reply to a message* rather than start a new conversation with a different subject line, resulting in email subjects such as 'RE: RE: Your project'. While such replies are not always topically relevant to the original message, participants do often make skilful use of subject lines to organise their communication. A similar phenomenon occurs in, for example, BBSs and blogs, where participants choose where to locate their reply in the hierarchy of messages. Thirdly, *quoting* may be used, either by the attachment of one or more previous messages at the end of a new message, as is often the case automatically in an emailed reply, or through the incorporation of segments of a previous message (chat e-turn, blog, and so on) into the current one. This form of juxtaposing stimulus and response is a technique used to create the 'illusion' of turn adjacency and is evidence of the two messages being part of one conversation. Fourthly, *cohesive features* in the language used, referring to previous utterances more indirectly, are further evidence of belonging. These cohesive features may even include references to utterances produced in a different medium, as will be further explored in the case studies at the end of this chapter. The fifth criterion is *content*. A thread of relevant topics should be evident, although participants may change topics abruptly. *Temporal boundaries* of the conversation may also give an indication of whether several e-turns on unrelated topics are likely to be considered the same 'conversation' by participants. The final and most convincing criteria are *indications from participants themselves* that any given series of messages forms a 'conversation', as revealed through interviews in the present study. Not all criteria need be present to determine the boundaries of a conversation, but the presence of more than one can help to strengthen identification.

Topic, content, and psychological categories factor in to the management and definition of both the turn and the conversation, contrasting with the e-turn, based on a technological category, albeit one influenced by individual and interpersonal factors. However, an important distinction is made between the conversation and turn level, in that conversations are co-constructed through the turn-taking of two or more interlocutors, while management of e-turns into a turn is something performed largely by the individual. An interlocutor may (intentionally or unintentionally) interrupt a series of e-turns intended as a single turn, but the onus is upon the sender to demonstrate the relevance of each e-turn to the next in that turn; for example, via the use of appropriate segmentation, quoting, and so on. Participants' patterns of turn-taking were found to be related to their use of repair (as will be examined in detail in Chapter 5) and their language use, in terms of orthographic and code-switching. These issues will be explored following an introduction to participants' language choices below.

Language Choice

Both Japanese and English were used by all of the Australian participants in their CMC conversations with NSs of Japanese. However, some participants used only one language with specific contacts, or via certain mediums. The influence of the 'domain' in which communication is located, interpersonal factors, and the purpose of communication on language choice will be discussed in the subsections below, providing a context for the examination of orthographic and code-switching in the following section.

In the analysis of participants' interaction data, Nishimura's (1992, 1997) categories of 'Basically English' and 'Basically Japanese' varieties proved useful. Every e-turn in each medium was categorised as either 'English' (containing no code-switching to Japanese), 'Mostly English' (where borrowings or code-switches occurred within an English environment, following English grammatical rules), 'Japanese', 'Mostly Japanese', 'Translation' (where the same statement was repeated in the other language immediately afterward), 'No language' (where, for example, participants posted a blog containing a photo and no linguistic content, or sent a chat message which contained only an emoticon), or 'Other' (where languages other than Japanese and English were used). As can be seen in Table 4.1, arranged in order of the proportion of Japanese use on particular mediums (least to most), overall, the Australian participants' language use with their Japanese interlocutors online was fairly balanced. English or mostly English e-turns accounted for 47% of all e-turns sent by Australian participants, while 48% were composed in Japanese or mostly Japanese. Overall, 74% of the Australian participants' e-turns incorporated some Japanese.

While some caution must be exercised in interpreting these statistics from a small sample, in that they should not be viewed as generalisable to the entire online population of Japanese learners, Table 4.1 provides an important view of participants' language choice. Furthermore, the reliability of participants' perceptions of their own language use as reported in the interviews appears to be confirmed by the corpus analysis performed. To take language choice in email as an example, Alisha described her emails as mostly English, Jacob reported using Japanese or translation, Kaylene stated that she mostly code-switched or used Japanese, and Scott said that his emails were often 95% English, 5% Japanese, or sometimes almost entirely in Chinese. All of these self-assessments turned out to be quite appropriate generalisations when measured against the data, suggesting that participants' self-report data is reasonably reliable.

Facebook appears at the top of the list in Table 4.1, having the least use of Japanese (6% for messages, 27% on the wall) and most use of English (94% for messages, 73% on the wall) with the Japanese participants in the present study, and Mixi Messages (63% Japanese), Mixi Blogs (78% Japanese), and Mobile Phone Messages (88% Japanese) at the bottom. This clear difference in language choice on the SNSs Facebook and Mixi appears to be a result of

Table 4.1 Australian participants' language choice by medium

	Participant (N = 12)	Total e-turns	English	Mostly English	Mostly Japanese	Japanese	Translation	No language	Other
Facebook messages	Alisha	16	63%	31%	6%	0%	0%	0%	0%
				(94%)		(6%)		(0%)	
Facebook wall	Lucas	13	31%	38%	15%	15%	0%	0%	0%
	Ellise	2	0%	100%	0%	0%	0%	0%	0%
	Alisha	2	0%	50%	50%	0%	0%	0%	0%
Average for all 17 e-turns from all 3 participants			**10%**	**63%**	**22%**	**5%**	**0%**	**0%**	**0%**
				(73%)		(27%)		(0%)	
Emails	Cindy	10	100%	0%	0%	0%	0%	0%	0%
	Genna	15	73%	27%	0%	0%	0%	0%	0%
	Scott	10	20%	10%	10%	0%	0%	0%	60%
	Lucas	14	0%	50%	43%	0%	0%	0%	7%
	Jacob	4	50%	0%	0%	25%	25%	0%	0%
	Alisha	40	50%	50%	0%	0%	0%	0%	0%
	Kaylene	45	2%	2%	16%	80%	0%	0%	0%
Average for all 138 e-turns from all 7 participants			**42%**	**20%**	**10%**	**15%**	**3%**	**0%**	**10%**
				(62%)		(25%)		(13%)	
MSN e-turns	Genna	292	90%	3%	0%	3%	0%	3%	0%
	Lucas	238	58%	6%	3%	29%	0%	4%	0%
	Alisha	75	40%	3%	3%	55%	0%	0%	0%
	Kaylene	46	46%	2%	3%	48%	0%	1%	0%

	n							
Average for all 651 e-turns from all 4 participants		59%	4%	2%	34%	0%	2%	0%
		(62%)			(36%)		(2%)	
Ameba blogs	Cindy 39	5%	69%	18%	5%	0%	0%	3%
	Genna 30	0%	13%	50%	30%	3%	3%	0%
	Hyacinth 6	0%	17%	83%	0%	0%	0%	0%
Average for all 75 e-turns from all 3 participants		2%	33%	50%	12%	1%	1%	1%
		(35%)			(62%)		(3%)	
Mixi messages	Oscar 8	0%	25%	0%	63%	13%	0%	0%
		(25%)			(63%)		(13%)	
Mixi blogs	Ellise 10	10%	0%	0%	90%	0%	0%	0%
	Zac 4	25%	50%	0%	0%	25%	0%	0%
	Alisha 5	0%	0%	20%	80%	0%	0%	0%
	Oscar 6	0%	0%	0%	100%	0%	0%	0%
	Kaylene 17	0%	0%	6%	94%	0%	0%	0%
Average for all 42 e-turns from all 5 participants		7%	10%	5%	73%	5%	0%	0%
		(17%)			(78%)		(5%)	
Mobile emails	Kaylene 59	7%	5%	41%	47%	0%	0%	0%
		(12%)			(88%)		(5%)	
Average language use by Australian participants across all mediums		24%	24%	17%	31%	3%	0%	1%
		(47%)			(48%)		(5%)	
Total e-turns that included Japanese					(74%)			

Notes: The above table represents only those e-turns composed by the Australian participants. Genna's MySpace messages, Zac's emails, and Noah's Mixi blogs were excluded from this table, as they each only wrote one. As figures are given as whole percentages, some rows may not equal 100.

participants' viewing them as belonging to different linguistic 'domains', as described in Chapter 3.

Another factor which may have contributed to the frequency of Japanese use on mobile phone emails is the input method utilised on these devices. Kaylene, the only participant whose mobile emails were available for analysis, commented 'I like using Japanese on my mobile phone, 'cause it's a lot easier to type in than English'. She stated that this preference was because her Japanese mobile phone 'doesn't have predictive text for English, so it takes a lot longer to type out'. Kaylene's colleague Watako, who was also present at the focus-group, agreed with Kaylene that it was easier to type in Japanese on the mobile phone.

The participants who used Facebook with NSs of Japanese in the present study, Alisha, Ellise, and Lucas, used predominantly the mostly English variety in their wall postings to their Japanese contacts. All of the participants who were members of Mixi likewise used predominantly Japanese in their blogs, with the exception of Zac, who employed code-switching, translation, and wrote one blog in English. It is important to note, however, that Zac was very interested in translation, enrolled in a translation course, and used his Mixi blog primarily to post and receive feedback on translations he had completed for class assessment. The use of translation will be examined more closely at the end of this section.

With the exception of Lucas, whose use of Japanese in his email communication with Hisayo increased over time as part of a determined effort to practise his L2, as described above, Japanese proficiency did not appear to be linked to language choice. Medium choice, or, more importantly, the linguistic 'domain' in which that medium is seen as being located and interpersonal factors, such as relationship and interlocutor's language choice, have a far greater influence (Pasfield-Neofitou, 2011).

Interpersonal factors

In order to examine participants' language choice according to interpersonal factors, their email correspondence will be used as an example. There are several reasons for this selection. Firstly, email was the most frequently used communication medium in the present study. Ten of the 12 Australians made use of email with Japanese contacts, eight of whom were able to provide interaction data to the researcher. In total, email data was collected from 14 pairs (some of the Australian participants provided data from communication with more than one Japanese contact). Secondly, unlike SNSs, blogs, online games, forums, or websites, email is a relatively 'domainless' mode of communication. Users may select their own email address domain, mail program, and operating language settings, and communication tends to be private rather than displayed for others to see, meaning that users are not influenced by the language of anyone but their own contacts. Therefore, the effect of any interpersonal factors may be more easily determined.

Table 4.2 is arranged in order of Japanese use in emails (least to most). This is calculated based on the pair's total average use, not the individual learner's language production, as language selection is viewed here as negotiated and co-constructed. Furthermore, receptive use of Japanese (e.g. reading an email in Japanese and responding appropriately in English) is also considered an important opportunity for noticing and potential language acquisition.

At first glance, it may appear that learners' level of language is a major influence. The only participant to use English-only 100% of the time was Cindy, a level 1–2 student, and the only participant to use Japanese-only 100% of the time was Kaylene, a post-level 11–12 student. In fact, of the six pairs who use an English variety more than half of the time, three included a level 1–2 student. Of the seven pairs who use a Japanese variety more than half of the time, six involved Kaylene, the only student to have finished level 11–12. Indeed, language proficiency is an important factor; however, as evidenced in the discussion of domains above, it is not the only influence.

As can be seen in Table 4.2, although Cindy and Genna, lower-level students, used English-only or mostly English with their contacts Mei and Tokio, it is noteworthy that Alisha, one of the higher-level students, also used only English and mostly English varieties with Noriko. Zac, another level 9–10 student, also used English varieties most of the time with Fumie. On the other hand, Jacob, also a level 9–10 student, was the only participant aside from Kaylene to participate in an exchange where more than half of the messages were in a Japanese variety. This demonstrates that there is variation in language selection even among students of approximately the same language proficiency.

Kaylene's email use

Kaylene's case is of particular interest, as she exchanged emails with seven contacts who agreed to participate in the present study. In one of these seven exchanges, Kaylene and her contact Ukiko each sent only one email, so their data was excluded from analysis. However, Kaylene's exchanges with her other six contacts demonstrate the influence of interpersonal factors. A certain pattern is observable in terms of Kaylene's language use with her partners of different relationship types or levels of seniority.

The contact with whom Kaylene used the most balanced proportions of English and Japanese was her former LEP, Ruriko. At the time of the first

Table 4.2 Pairs' language choice by relationship

Participant (N = 8)	Contact (N = 14)	Total emails	English	Mostly English	Mostly Japanese	Japanese	Other (inc. trans. & no lang.)
Cindy (level 1–2)	to Mei	10	100% (100%)	0%	0% (0%)	0%	0% (0%)
	from Mei	11	100% (100%)	0%	0% (0%)	0%	0% (0%)
(Mei visited Cindy's school on exchange)							
Genna (level 1–2)	to Tokio	15	73% (100%)	27%	0% (0%)	0%	0% (0%)
	from Tokio	9	67% (100%)	33%	0% (0%)	0%	0% (0%)
(Tokio friended Genna on MySpace)							
Alisha (level 9–10)	to Noriko	40	50% (100%)	50%	0% (0%)	0%	0% (0%)
	From Noriko	58	5% (100%)	95%	0% (0%)	0%	0% (0%)
(Noriko was Alisha's tutor)							
Scott (level 1–2)	to Kieko	10	20% (30%)	10%	10% (10%)	0%	60% (60%)
	from Kieko	7	43% (57%)	14%	0% (0%)	0%	43% (43%)
(Kieko is Scott's girlfriend)							
Zac (level 9–10)	to Fumie	1	100% (100%)	0%	0% (0%)	0%	0% (0%)
	from Fumie	2	50% (50%)	0%	50% (50%)	0%	0% (0%)
(Fumie and Zac met at MeetUp)							
Lucas (level 3–4)	to Hisayo	14	0% (50%)	50%	43% (43%)	0%	7% (7%)
	from Hisayo	24	29% (75%)	46%	8% (8%)	0%	17% (17%)
(Hisayo was Lucas' host sister)							

	N					
Kaylene (level 11–12) to Ruriko	12	0%	0% (25%)	25%	50% (75%)	0% (0%)
from Ruriko	10	0%	30% (30%)	30%	40% (70%)	0% (0%)
(Ruriko was Kaylene's language exchange partner)						
Jacob (level 9–10) to Kō	4	50%	0% (50%)	0%	25% (25%)	25% (25%)
to Kō	0	0%	0% (0%)	0%	100% (100%)	0% (0%)
(Kō requested some manga-related work from Jacob)						
Kaylene to Junko	10	20%	10% (30%)	10%	60% (70%)	0% (0%)
from Junko	140	0%	0% (0%)	10%	80% (90%)	10% (10%)
(Junko is one of Kaylene's work colleagues)						
Kaylene to Chikae	7	14%	0% (14%)	0%	86% (86%)	0% (0%)
from Chikae	5	20%	0% (20%)	0%	80% (80%)	0% (0%)
(Chikae visited Kaylene's university on exchange)						
Kaylene to Ikuko	8	0%	0% (0%)	0%	100% (100%)	0% (0%)
from Ikuko	11	9%	0% (9%)	0%	91% (91%)	0% (0%)
(Ikuko is Kaylene's university advisor)						
Kaylene to Daishi	5	0%	0% (0%)	20%	80% (100%)	0% (0%)
from Daishi	7	0%	0% (0%)	0%	100% (100%)	0% (0%)
(Daishi is one of Kaylene's superiors at the museum)						
Kaylene to Kō	6	0%	0% (0%)	17%	83% (100%)	0% (0%)
from Kō	7	0%	0% (0%)	0%	100% (100%)	0% (0%)
(Kō is one of Kaylene's superiors at the museum)						

Notes: Kaylene's use of email with Ukiko has been excluded from this table, as they each only wrote one.

interview, Kaylene commented that she tried to make her email exchanges with Ruriko roughly equal in terms of language selection. She stated, 'Sometimes it will all be Japanese, and then the next email will be all English'. Likewise, Ruriko claimed that their communication involved both Japanese and English. Although half of the emails Kaylene sent were in only Japanese, half of them contained at least some English. This approximately mirrors Ruriko's language use, as she composed 40% of her messages entirely in Japanese, and the other 60% contained some amount of English.

Kaylene's language use with Junko, a colleague at the *manga* museum where Kaylene worked while in Japan, is quite different. They both used Japanese varieties almost exclusively. Kaylene used even more Japanese with Chikae, whom she had met on exchange. Although on the surface, Kaylene's relationship with Chikae may appear similar to Cindy's relationship with Mei, as both Mei and Chikae visited Australia on educational exchanges, the vast difference in the pairs' language preferences may be explained by the circumstances in which they met, as well as Kaylene and Cindy's respective language learning histories. Kaylene met Chikae in Japan on her first trip as an exchange student to a Japanese university, and then Chikae came to Australia on exchange herself. From the outset, their communication took place in mostly Japanese, and their relationship developed in a Japanese environment. Kaylene, studying Japanese at the time, had a strong motivation to make use of the language. Cindy, however, having never been to Japan herself, met Mei for the first time when Mei visited Australia on exchange. At the time, Cindy had not yet begun studying Japanese; however, Mei was eager to practice English, and said in her follow-up interview that emailing Cindy helps with this aim. Thus, Kaylene and Ruriko's contrasting use of mostly Japanese, given that their relationship was founded in a Japanese environment, and given Kaylene's motivation to practise her L2 from the outset, does not appear surprising.

Importantly, the contacts with whom Kaylene used the most Japanese (more than 95% of the time) were all relationships in which Kaylene was corresponding with someone she considered her superior. In her communication with Ikuko, an advisor to foreign students at the university Kaylene studied at while in Japan, Kaylene used only Japanese all of the time. Likewise, Ikuko used only Japanese to Kaylene, with the exception of one email. The only email Ikuko composed in English was a group email sent out to Kaylene and five other foreign students. Thus, it appears that Ikuko's communication with foreign students, in her capacity as an advisor, was not limited to Japanese, even though she and Kaylene used only Japanese in their private correspondence.

The two Japanese participants with whom Kaylene used the most Japanese were both work colleagues at the *manga* museum where she worked while in Japan, and, importantly, who were also her superiors. All of Kaylene's communication with Daishi and Kō, also a university professor, was conducted in a Japanese variety; a large portion in only Japanese. Jacob also corresponded with Kō, in his capacity working at a *manga* library in Australia before he left for Japan, and described Kō as a 'bigwig in a Japanese university'. For this reason, Jacob said that he made a concerted effort to ensure his Japanese was properly proofread and corrected before sending emails to Kō. Although Jacob's use of Japanese with Kō was not as frequent as Kaylene's, it is still reasonably high (72.5%, much higher than the other level 9–10 students' use of Japanese in emails in the present study). It is important to note that while those in subordinate roles may try to accommodate their superior's perceived language preferences or needs, sometimes the imbalance of power may cause the learner to feel concerned about their L2 use, and avoid it. In his communication with Kō, Jacob was concerned that his use of Japanese may inconvenience Kō if it was difficult to understand. Therefore, on the occasions when he could not get anyone to proofread his draft email, Jacob would write in English, despite Kō's lack of English proficiency. When Kō visited Australia on a work-related trip, Jacob noticed that he was accompanied by graduate-student interpreters, and their presence seems to have influenced his language choice at times. Jacob explained that when he was emailing Kō and his colleagues, 'if it was something I could say in Japanese, I'd write it in Japanese, but [when] it was a lot of organising things, I thought it was better off if their end translated it'.

A number of psychobiographical and interpersonal factors have been suggested to influence language choice. The variation in terms of Kaylene's language use with her seven contacts participating in the present study may be at least partly explained by a number of factors. The language backgrounds of Kaylene's contacts are summarised in Table 4.3, with details of their language use in emails with Kaylene.

One of the most striking features of Table 4.3 is that the female participants, with whom Kaylene used the least Japanese, are grouped at the top. However, with such a small sample, it would be premature to assume that Kaylene's language choice was based on her interlocutor's gender alone. Furthermore, there is no difference between Kaylene's use of Japanese in emails to Ikuko or to either Daishi or Kō. Additionally, Daishi and Kō share many other biographical factors (similar ages, similar levels of English, and the same work position in relation to Kaylene) in addition to gender, which must be considered. Proximity of age also does not appear to account for language use as well as relationship type was found to. Instead, it may simply be that

Table 4.3 Kaylene's contacts

	Gender	Age	English proficiency	% Japanese varieties to Kaylene	% Japanese varieties from Kaylene	Relationship type
Ruriko	F	23	TOEIC 875	70	75	Language exchange partner
Junko	F	40	Very Good	90	70	Museum colleague
Chikae	F	23	Eiken 2	80	86	Friend at Australian uni
Ikuko	F	40	TOEIC 895	91	100	University administration
Daishi	M	39	Little/None	100	100	Museum boss
Kō	M	34	Little/None	100	100	Museum boss

certain types of relationships are more likely to develop among people of a similar age or gender.

Perhaps the most seemingly important of the factors above is Kaylene's interlocutors' proficiency in English. However, as was the case with the Australian participants, this does not seem to entirely explain language selection either. Although Daishi and Kō both have little or no reported English ability, necessitating their exclusive use of Japanese with Kaylene, the other participants are scattered in terms of language ability, and high levels of English proficiency do not necessarily match with high levels of use. Ikuko, for example, has the highest score of any participant in the present study on a standardised test, and makes use of English frequently in her role as an advisor to international students; however, Kaylene uses exclusively Japanese with her. Thus it appears that unless an interlocutor's proficiency in one's L1 is minimal or non-existent, the pair's relationship and the individuals' desire to use their respective L2s are more important.

The co-construction of language choice

As mentioned at the beginning of this section, there is evidence to suggest that language choice is very much co-constructed. The reciprocal use of language is evident in the data from not only Kaylene and her partners, but also other participants in the present study. Not considering Kaylene's email communication with Ukiko (which consisted of only two messages), or Zac's communication with Fumie (only three messages), participants accommodated one another's language choices. Cindy and Mei both used English exclusively. Genna and Tokio's language use was also very similar, with both using only English around two-thirds of the time, and mostly English in the other third. Although Noriko introduced Japanese words in many of her emails, both Alisha and Noriko each used English or mostly English varieties in all of their emails. The majority of Scott and Kieko's messages were bi- or trilingual involving Cantonese, with Scott composing such emails 60% of the time, and Kieko, 43% of the time. They each wrote monolingual English emails more frequently than mostly English emails with some Japanese. Lucas and Hisayo both used the mostly English variety more than any other, and Kaylene and her contacts, as seen in Table 4.2, exhibited similar patterns.

The only pair in which participants' language choices did not appear similar was Jacob and Kō. The above mentioned factors, including Jacob's anxiety about using his L2 with Kō, and Kō's lack of English proficiency may help to explain this non-reciprocal use of language varieties. Jacob explained 'I want to make sure I'm presenting myself clearly'. While he opted to avoid using Japanese when he felt the language required was too difficult and he had no one to check his language, Kō's limited English proficiency meant that he continued to use exclusively Japanese. Thus, the pair relied on third parties (Kō's translators, and Jacob's proofreaders) to maintain their communication.

Overall, however, participants' convergence in terms of language choice appears to support Giles *et al.*'s theory of communication accommodation, which posits that when language users seek approval in a social situation, they are likely to converge with their interlocutor in terms of language choice, dialect, and paralinguistic features (Giles *et al.*, 1991). Given that the participants in the present study were involved in social and collegial relationships, it is unsurprising that such convergence would take place. Participants' use of paralinguistic features in their emails and other communication, described below, also suggests that participants actively accommodated each other's communication styles.

Paralinguistic features

Two main varieties of paralinguistic features were found in participants' emails, Japanese or 'Asian' style (*'emoji'*), e.g. ^_^, and 'Western' style ('smileys'), e.g. :) text art and emoticons (cf. Katsuno & Yano, 2007; K.M. Lee, 2007), and may be considered a third 'code'. More detailed categorisations of paralinguistic features in Japanese–English online communication are included in Pasfield-Neofitou (2006, 2007d). Importantly, emoticon use was viewed as making communication more intimate in Tokaji (1997), while non-inclusion of emoticons was perceived as giving communication a more serious tone. Murase and Inoue (2003) and Baron (2004) also found that females used emoticons much more frequently than males. Taking the example again of email, the most commonly used 'domainless' medium, participants' average use per email of paralinguistic features (of either kind) is displayed in the graph presented in Figure 4.3.

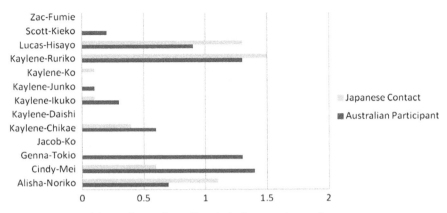

Figure 4.3 Participants' use of paralinguistic features in email

As can be seen in Figure 4.3, in the three pairs involving Zac and Fumie, Kaylene and Daishi, and Jacob and Kō, both interlocutors refrained from using paralinguistic features entirely. In the three pairs involving Scott and Kieko, Kaylene and Kō, and Kaylene and Junko, one participant did not use any paralinguistic features at all, while their partner used them very sparingly – an average of less than 0.2 per email in each case (often a single email containing an isolated emoticon). Meanwhile, in the five pairs involving Lucas and Hisayo, Kaylene and Ruriko, Kaylene and Ikuko, Cindy and Mei, and Alisha and Noriko, both interlocutors made use of paralinguistic features, at a very similar frequency. Overall, there was an average difference of just 0.3 paralinguistic features per email within each pair.

The only pair in which the use of paralinguistic features was not reciprocal was Genna and Tokio. While Tokio did not use any paralinguistic features in his emails to Genna, she had the third highest use of paralinguistic features among Australian participants in her emails to him. This divergent use may be explained by considering Genna and Tokio's psychobiographical backgrounds. Tokio's non-use of emoticons does not appear unusual given his gender and age. Genna's particularly high use of paralinguistic features, despite Tokio's non-use, may be explained by the fact that she showed great interest in *emoji*, including those featured in the movie *Densha Otoko*, which she discussed with Tokio via MSN and email at great length. She also blogged about the meanings of various *emoji* on her Ameba blog, indicating a personal interest in these particular paralinguistic features. This interest is supported by the fact that of the 19 paralinguistic features Genna used in her emails to Tokio, 12 were Japanese-style.

On the whole, both participants' language choice and use of paralinguistic features appears reasonably reciprocal, suggesting that interpersonal factors are indeed highly important in determining code selection.

Translation and bridgework

Although accounting for only around 3% of the total e-turns collected, as indicated in Table 4.1, translation was a technique used by several participants for a variety of reasons, including both enjoyment and instrumental purposes related to university or work. Another major reason was as a safeguard against miscommunication as shown in the example in Extract 4.1 from Kaylene on 27 February 2008:

Extract 4.1 Kaylene's use of translation in chat

1 kay says:

最初の一ヶ月は大学の寮だけど、研究生は寮で住むのが、まあ、ダメと言えないが、普通に 研究生のためじゃない寮だから、その後、自分でどこか探さなきゃ。 ◄─────── Original

(The first month will be the university dorm, but research students living there is, well, I can't say it's forbidden, but it's not normally a dorm for research students, so after that, I have to find somewhere by myself.)
2 kay says:

それ意味をなす？

(Does that make sense?)
3 kay says:
Research students are not forbidden, but not really allowed to live there, so I have to find somewhere else to stay after the first month or so. ◄─────── Translation

Notes: Times of messages received are not available for the conversation above due to a technical problem with Kaylene's computer. However, e-turns are numbered in the order they were received.

Similarly, Jacob reported that when he initially emails someone in Japanese, he does so with an English translation appended, in case problems in character encoding cause the Japanese not to display correctly. In one example an email Jacob sent to Kō turned out as pages of nonsensical symbols such as '√◆縺。縺ッ2'. Again, it is important to note that, like Zac, Kaylene and Jacob were both very interested in translation, and had undertaken the same translation course. Furthermore, Kaylene had completed an honours project in translation, and, when she travelled to Japan part-way through the data collection period, received regular requests via email to assist with translation for the *manga* museum where she worked.

Finally, some 'bridging' blogs of the type Herring *et al.* (2007) describe, through which multilingual users, like those in the present study, provide bridges between cultures, as outlined in Chapter 1, were found in the data. Both Zac and Genna maintained bilingual blogs that included translation as a means of making their content comprehensible and accessible to a wider audience. For Zac, who, as mentioned above, aspired to become an English teacher, a desire to give the Japanese readers of his blog a 'challenge' appears to have been part of his motivation, along with catering for his target readership. In his Mixi blog on 28 August 2008, Zac described that day's basketball game in English, and then in Japanese. However, the English version contained more detail than the Japanese, including game statistics. He explained: 'I know that a lot of my friends are girls, and a lot of them don't really play sports, so I was trying to make it short and sweet in the Japanese version'. However, Zac claimed that he made the English version a little more difficult because he wanted them to have a challenge, 'if they need to ask me questions, it kind of challenges their reading, and I wanted them to have a challenge'. This goal is consistent with Zac's positioning of himself as an aspiring English teacher in his Mixi profile, and demonstrates also the effect of (at least, perceived) interlocutor language preference. Genna, on the other hand, had an audience of not only the Japanese readers of her blog she met online, but also her fellow university students Cindy and Hyacinth, which appears to have influenced her choice to maintain a bilingual blog.

Code and Orthographic Switching

As the above sections on language choice suggest, code-switching was remarkably prevalent in the discourse data, with the majority of communication being carried out in more than one language. This demonstrates that code-switching should be considered a normal product of bilingual language use in not only face-to-face, but also online settings.

In order to type in Japanese using a Western keyboard, the use of software called an 'Input Method Editor' (IME) is necessary. On a Mac, this software may be referred to as simply 'Input Method', but as the majority of participants in the present study used Windows-based PCs, the term IME will be utilised. As previously explained, the IME converts what the user types in the Roman alphabet into *hiragana* syllables on the screen. After hitting the Space Bar, the user may convert the *hiragana* to either *katakana* (collectively termed 'kana') or Japanese characters (commonly referred to as 'kanji') by selecting from a list of candidates that are a phonetic match.

There are several ways to switch between orthographies via the IME, including via mouse (the input method can be changed by clicking on an icon on the language bar), or keyboard (shortcuts to switch between Japanese and English include holding down the 'ALT' and tilde (~) keys simultaneously, or hitting F10). My previous research (Pasfield-Neofitou, 2006: 52) also showed that some users prefer to avoid switching the IME by either typing in capitals (typing in all uppercase will allow the user to type in English while in the Japanese IME; however, if the user begins typing in lowercase again, the computer will default to Japanese), or by simply avoiding code-switching altogether, continuing in whichever language a conversation was initiated in for as long as possible.

In most instances, participants in the present study made use of the Japanese input method when they wrote in Japanese, meaning that there was an orthographic switch as well as a code-switch to perform. However code-switching does not always necessitate an orthographic switch. It is possible for participants to code-switch from English to Japanese without changing their orthography, by using romanisation. An example of code-switching in two comments on Ellise and Eri's Facebook wall are excerpted in Extract 4.2. In the first comment, Eri performs a code-switch (from English to Japanese) without an orthographic switch. That is, she uses romanisation for the Japanese translation in the second line. In the second comment, however, Ellise makes both a code-switch (from English to Japanese) and an orthographic switch, changing the IME from English to Japanese to write 「先生」 (sensei, teacher).

Extract 4.2 Code and orthographic switching in two Facebook comments

Eri Yamamoto wrote
at 8:54am on October 10th, 2007
Happy Birthday Elli!!
Otanjoubi Omedetou!!!

Ellise Richardson (Australia) wrote
at 12:03am on October 12th, 2007
hahahaha! I seeee! Thanks 先生!

Table 4.4 depicts the frequent code-switching practices of 10 Australian participants and 16 of their contacts who consented to participate in the present study. Noah and Hyacinth did not have any private communication during the data collection period with any Japanese contacts who agreed to participate in the present study, and therefore do not appear in the table.

Table 4.4 Use of code-switching (CS) in participants' CMC conversations

Participant (n = 10)	Contact(s) (n = 16)	Medium	Number of conversations	Total monolingual	Total CS	% CS
Alisha	Eri	FB messages	1	0	1	100
		FB wall	1	0	1	100
		Mixi messages	1	1	0	0
		MSN chat	1	0	1	100
	Noriko	Email	41	0	41	100
		FB messages	9	0	9	100
		FB wall	1	0	1	100
Cindy	Mei	Email	9	9	0	0
Elli	Eri	FB wall	1	0	1	100
Genna	Tokio	Email	9	5	4	44
		MSN chat	3	0	2	67
		MS comments	1	0	1	100
Jacob	Kō	Email	2	0	2	100
Kaylene	Chikae	Email	4	3	1	25
		Mobile email	1	0	1	100
	Daishi	Email	4	3	1	25
	Ikuko	Email	9	9	0	0
	Junko	Email	11	8	3	27
	Kō	Email	2	1	1	50
	Ruriko	Email	9	2	7	78
		Mobile email	9	2	7	78
		MSN chat	4	0	4	100
	Ukiko	Email	1	0	1	100
		Mobile email	22	9	13	59
	Watako	Mobile email	9	6	3	33
Lucas	Hisayo	Email	24	5	19	79
		FB wall	11	3	8	73
		MSN chat	9	0	9	100
Oscar	Yoshio	Mixi messages	6	3	3	50
Scott	Kieko	Email	13	3	10	77
Zac	Fumie	Email	1	0	1	100
					Average	**70**

Language choice on blogs and their respective comments are also excluded, as these conversations often include comments from users who are not participants in the present study, and whose communication therefore cannot be analysed, but nevertheless may have influenced the language choice of participants (for this reason, Atsuko and Sae do not appear in the table either, as their only communication with the Australian participants in the present study was via blog comments).

Having identified the factors which affected participants' language selection overall (in various domains and with various interlocutors at the conversation level), the following subsections will examine participants' code-switching behaviour at the micro-level (within the turn or e-turn). In order to do this, Auer's (1984, 1995, 1998) CA approach, successfully employed by Kötter (2003) in the analysis of tandem language learning in an instructed MOO setting, is adopted. Auer defines two functions of code-switching, namely, participant-related and discourse-related. Participant-related functions are characterised as those which signal attributes of the speaker, such as preference and competence, and are highly linked to a person's psychobiography. Discourse-related functions provide cues for the organisation of conversation, such as topic change, and are dependent on the situated activity taking place. This distinction appears useful in examining learners' use of CMC, where partners with differing language proficiency levels employ two languages, and where the organisation of conversation, as related in Chapter 1, may be extremely complex. A single code-switch may also have both participant- and discourse-related functions.

Motivations for code-switching online

Participants appeared to be highly aware of their code-switching behaviour, in both face-to-face and online situations. Alisha even remarked upon her use of code-switching with another friend, Aika, in an email to Noriko. She stated:

Extract 4.3 Excerpt from Alisha's email to Noriko on code-switching

Aika and I usually speak in English. Sometimes when she speaks in English I will try and respond in Japanese and sometimes this leads to a code-switch to the conversation being in Japanese but when I speak English she usually responds in English. Unless there is a particular expression or feeling that she feels she needs to express in Japanese.

In the Extract 4.3, Alisha demonstrates not only her awareness of her own and Aika's use of code-switching, but also her understanding of the reasons for this use. Alisha sometimes switches to Japanese in order to practise her L2, a participant-related function, while she observes Aika's switching to Japanese as fulfilling a discourse-related function.

Alisha was equally conscious of her use of code-switching in CMC in general. In her first interview, Alisha said, 'I use MSN, code-switching there. I don't always speak in Japanese, and I don't always speak in English. It's a mix. Even [with people who] study Japanese . . . and I sometimes code-switch in SMS'.

As can be seen from Table 4.1, code-switching was employed by participants across a number of different CMC mediums. Kaylene mentioned her use of code-switching with Ruriko via email in her first interview also, saying 'It's a mixture. Even in the same email, we'll code-switch.' Elli also stated that she mixed both Japanese and English in her emails to Madoka, one of her Japanese contacts who did not participate in the present study. Elli commented, 'I always take advantage of the fact that she can speak English, but I like to use Japanese sometimes, just to make it a little easier on her, not that my Japanese is great at all times . . . but just to show that I'm trying'.

Both participant-related and discourse-related switches were identified in the present study, although it would be misleading to quantify them, as interview data to ascertain participants' motivations was not available for all instances. One example from Genna is excerpted in Extract 4.4.

Extract 4.4 Genna's code-mixing of Japanese and English

I liked 学校へ行こう. Variety shows are my 一番好き X3 The set's on some of the TV shows are so colourful, it makes my eyes hurt XD
(I liked *Let's Go to School*. Variety shows are my favourite X3 The set's on some of the TV shows are so colourful, it makes my eyes hurt XD)

I like 山田 from 電車男, but he needs to relax more! poor guy is so up-tight!
(I like Yamada from *Train Man*, but he needs to relax more! Poor guy is so up-tight!)

In her emails to Tokio, Genna mostly used Japanese only for brief borrowings, in particular proper nouns such as the names of television shows and people, with only occasional borrowings of other items. However, in Extract 4.4 Genna not only used Japanese where it made sense in the discourse to do so (in citing names and titles), but also where she was able to, stating that 'Variety shows are my 一番好き'. Genna explained in the interview that she had done so as a concerted effort to use Japanese, because of Tokio's encouragement: 'Tokio keeps saying to me, write to me in Japanese!'

It appears that, for Genna, code-switching to Japanese was not simply the most logical selection, but also a way to practise her L2, and appease Tokio. Thus, her switches fulfilled both participant- and discourse-related functions. Genna's switches to English in this segment, however, appear to be fulfilling a primarily participant-related function, in that Genna stated she was 'too lazy' to try and write the whole email in Japanese, after having composed a blog on Ameba entirely in Japanese earlier that day. Examination of this extract shows that choice of code is motivated by not only participant-related factors which are tied to one's psychobiographical experiences (e.g. being encouraged to use more Japanese, being exhausted by writing a blog in Japanese earlier in the day), but also discourse-related factors which are particular to the situated activity at hand (e.g. the topic of Japanese television shows).

Liebscher and Dailey-O'Cain (2005) state that, until their own research on learners' code-switching in a content-based learning environment, learners' code-switching was thought of as mainly or solely participant-related. However, the current study also found examples of learners switching language for discourse-related functions. In addition to the above example of Genna's use of Japanese in order to discuss Japanese dramas, a number of possibly discourse-related code-switches were identified. Ruriko used English in her discussion of daylight savings, an Australian time change not present in Japan. Kaylene was also found to switch into English in her predominantly Japanese chat conversation with Ruriko in order to quote an utterance which was originally made in English:

Extract 4.5 Kaylene's code-switch to English

48 kay says:

でも、多分いつか、観光のために行く 😊

(But, maybe someday, I will go for sightseeing)

49 kay says:

「Come when i'm there and i'll show you round」と言ったから、Tashは、今年の終わりぐらい行きたいと言ってくれた。出来たらいいな。

(Because I said 'Come when I'm there and I'll show you round', Tash told me she wanted to go around the end of this year.)

Kaylene said in a follow-up interview 'I always just speak to Tash in English, so I put it in English'. Other discourse-related functions of code-switching include changing languages to distinguish between different threads, a practice which will be analysed in the subsection below.

Types of code-switching online

As Auer's (1984, 1995, 1998) approach is based on CA, close attention is paid to where in an interaction code-switching takes place, and its relevance to the turn-taking system (Sacks *et al.*, 1974). In face-to-face speech, one type of code-switching is 'tag switching', where a tag, exclamation, formulaic expression, or discourse particle from one language is placed into an utterance in another language. Others are 'inter-sentential switching', occurring outside the sentence or clause level, and 'intra-sentential switching', occurring within the level of the sentence or clause. Interestingly, in the case of CMC, code-switching can also be observed at the level of the e-turn, with switching occurring either within or outside the boundaries of the e-turn. This is of particular importance in the analysis of chat, where e-turns are often limited in length (e.g. a maximum of 400 characters) and conversations usually fast-paced. A segment of a chat conversation including both inter- and intra- (in this case, tag) e-turn switching is posited in Extract 4.6.

Extract 4.6 Inter- and intra- e-turn switching in Kaylene and Ruriko's chat

24/04/2006	10:58:43 PM	瑠璃子 (Ruriko)	ありがとう☆but... I wanna be ... (Thank you☆but... I wanna be...)	Examples of intra e-turn switching
24/04/2006	10:59:02 PM	瑠璃子	sexy woman!!笑 (sexy woman!! lol)	
24/04/2006	10:59:42 PM	kay miró	i'm sure you're boyfriend thinks you are ^_^	
24/04/2006	10:59:57 PM	kay miró	hey at least you're not like me, my mind is like a child lol...	Inter e-turn switching
24/04/2006	11:00:17 PM	kay miró	私本当に子供っぽい。。。 ^_^; (I am really childish... ^^;)	
24/04/2006	11:00:29 PM	瑠璃子	no!!!!!!	

Extract 4.6 consists of three separate turns (segments consisting of one or more e-turns, before a shift in speaker occurs), made up of six individual e-turns (individual blocks of text tagged with the sender's name). Ruriko's turns are shaded in white and Kaylene's in grey. In each of her e-turns at 10:58:43 PM and 10:59:02 PM, Ruriko employs intra e-turn switching; in the first, from Japanese to English, and in the second, English to Japanese. Kaylene, on the other hand, composes one e-turn in English at 10:59:57 PM, and then follows it with a turn in Japanese at 11:00:17 PM, an example of inter e-turn switching.

Numerical analyses of participants' MSN conversations suggest that inter e-turn switching was used the most frequently by most participants in the present study. There may be several reasons for this, and Auer's (1984, 1995, 1998) personal and discourse-related functions appear relevant in choosing whether or not to perform an orthographic switch, when to start and end an e-turn, and whether or not to combine a switch in orthography with a new e-turn. The present study identifies a technology-related factor related to the personal-related function, which may influence orthographic and, in turn, code-switching choices. Just as language competency is considered, so must be a user's technical competency. However, this cannot simply be considered a personal-related factor, as issues of access must also be examined.

Participant and technology-related factors

In the present study, four pairs, or eight participants, engaged in MSN chat conversations. Of those eight, six showed a preference for inter e-turn switching. The degree of preference depended on a number of factors, but overall it was found that those with the most uses of inter e-turn switches in each pair were the NNSs of Japanese. Alisha employed inter e-turn code-switching 76.5% of the time compared to Eri's 20%. Genna used inter e-turn switching 71.5% of the time, while Tokio did so only 12.5%. In the other two pairs, differences were not as pronounced, but still significant. Kaylene made use of inter e-turn switching 86.1% of the time compared to Ruriko's 78%, and Lucas used inter e-turn switching 77% of the time compared to Hisayo's 60%. Thus, it appears that inter e-turn switching was preferred by those who were less familiar with switching between the Japanese and English orthographies, while those with greater familiarity (mostly the NSs of Japanese) switched freely within e-turns.

The similarities between Kaylene and Ruriko, and Lucas and Hisayo's choice of code-switching method can be explained by examining their computer proficiency. While Kaylene was a very proficient computer user, Ruriko was not as confident, especially when using an Australian computer. In fact, in one of their early chats in 2006, Ruriko was using a computer at her Australian university dormitory and needed to ask Kaylene how to swap between orthographies on an Australian computer. While on a Japanese keyboard there is a dedicated button to switch between character sets, a special key combination is required when using a Western keyboard, as described above.

In the case of Lucas and Hisayo, taking a closer look at Lucas' computer proficiency may explain their similarities. Lucas did not learn how to type in Japanese until April of 2007. Thus, some of their chat conversations do not make use of the Japanese orthography; rather, all switches to Japanese are made in romanisation. When using romanisation, their preferences were remarkably similar: Lucas used inter e-turn switching 66% of the time and intra e-turn switching 34%, while Hisayo used inter e-turn switching 60.3% of the time and intra e-turn switching 39.7% of the time. When using the Japanese orthography, however, Lucas' use of intra e-turn switching dropped to just 17.5%, approximately half of its previous proportion, while Hisayo's remained stable, at 60.5%. This phenomenon is explored below.

The cases of Ruriko and Lucas' code-switching choices suggest that typing proficiency is a very relevant factor. All of the non-Japanese NSs strongly preferred inter e-turn switching (>71.5% of code-switches were performed inter e-turn), while all of the Japanese NS either preferred intra e-turn switching, or only slightly preferred inter e-turn switching. While proficiency in Japanese typing does not necessarily go hand in hand with being a NS of Japanese (as Ruriko's example demonstrates, as access to familiar technology was more important in her case) it does stand to reason that the Japanese participants in the present study would be more familiar with typing in Japanese. Importantly, the Japanese participants who were situated in Japan had the added advantage of having a keyboard specifically designed for the use of Japanese. Although the user still normally types in the Roman alphabet, Japanese keyboards feature a 'henkan' (conversion) key not found on Western keyboards, specifically to facilitate the swapping between character sets.

Because of the complex processes involved in performing both a code and orthographic switch, participants may have opted to code-switch in-between rather than mid e-turn during their chat conversations, in order to make use of the extra time afforded. In my previous research (Pasfield-Neofitou, 2006), it was found that Jacob, who is a participant in the present study also, routinely deleted his contributions in chat without sending them, because he could not type quickly enough to avoid having his interlocutor change the topic before he sent his reply. Setting the IME at the beginning of an e-turn, and continuing in that language for the remainder of the e-turn, is less time consuming than swapping between the different orthographic methods several times during the composition of an e-turn, and may explain the Australian participants' preference for this type of code-switching. This interpretation of the chat data is substantiated by consideration of participants' uses of other mediums. As only Lucas and Hisayo's most recent communication via MSN was available in its full data log format with time stamping, their average response times across a number of mediums will be used for illustrative purposes.

While in the present study participants' MSN chat conversations had the fastest average turnaround between messages sent and replies received

Table 4.5 Lucas' use of intra e-turn code-switching

Mode of communication	Average response time	% of intra e-turn switches
MSN	1.22 minutes	17.5 (in Japanese orthography)
		39.5 (in romanisation)
Facebook wall	3.38 days	53.8
Email	4.88 days	100

(Lucas and Hisayo's most recent chat, for example, consisted of 32 turns, composed across 44 e-turns, over the span of 39 minutes, equivalent to a reply every 1.22 minutes), time was not always as pressing a factor in participants' communication mediated via other modes. Lucas and Hisayo's average time between sent and received Facebook wall messages was 3.38 days. Some of their replies were quite prompt and were sent within the same day; however, on the whole, the time pressure was much less. Their average time between sent and received emails was 4.88 days.

Increased response time was found to correlate with increased use of intra-, as opposed to inter-, e-turn switching, as Lucas' case, presented in Table 4.5, demonstrates.

Evidence from the interviews also suggests that time is a very relevant factor. Genna and Tokio's use of email and MySpace was often quite fast-paced, to the extent that Genna described their use of MySpace comments as 'chatting', despite the fact that communication via this medium would traditionally be described as 'asynchronous' and 'written'. When explaining her use of Japanese on MySpace, she said that she would occasionally switch to Japanese for personal and discourse-related functions, 'perhaps the odd word, if I know the word for it in Japanese that sort of fits the situation better than the English', and that in these situations she would use romanisation, 'only because it's quicker, but sometimes I'll try *hiragana*'.

Discourse-related factors

Discourse-related functions of inter e-turn code- (and orthographic) switching were also found. In MSN, as in other forms of CMC, the construction of a new e-turn may signal a reply to a different thread, or a shift in topic. Use of a different language may perform a discourse-related function here, where different scripts are utilised to visually and linguistically define threads of conversation. Where topics overlap, participants may use different languages to differentiate between threads, as the example in Extract 4.7 from an MSN chat conversation between Kaylene and Ruriko demonstrates.

Extract 4.7 Kaylene and Ruriko's use of code-switching and e-turns in threads

24/04/2006	11:25:40 PM	瑠璃子	I finished one essay today!!
24/04/2006	11:26:13 PM	瑠璃子	B u t I have still two more essay in this week.
24/04/2006	11:26:34 PM	瑠璃子	but I'm hapy:)
24/04/2006	11:26:46 PM	kay miró	あそうなの。　　　…私は病気の時だけ、how do you say 'to check your weight' in Japanese¿ (Oh is that right.　　…Only when I am sick, how do you say 'to check your weight' in Japanese¿)
24/04/2006	11:26:58 PM	kay miró	yay! well done!
24/04/2006	11:27:43 PM	kay miró	essays are evil. ...but it feels good to have them finished :)
24/04/2006	11:28:23 PM	瑠璃子	’ 体重を計る’ だよ:) (It's 'check your weight')
24/04/2006	11:28:53 PM	瑠璃子	yes, you're right;)
24/04/2006	11:29:09 PM	kay miró	ありがとう♥。　　…じゃ～あ、私は病気の時だけ、体重を計る。 (Thank you .... We~ll, Only when I am sick, I check my weight.)

In this segment of chat, Ruriko and Kaylene use different languages to distinguish between different threads. The topic of their thread in English (shaded in grey) is Ruriko's having finished her essay, and the topic of their thread in Japanese (shaded in white) is weighing oneself. At 11:25:40 PM, Ruriko begins a turn consisting of three e-turns, about having finished her essay, ending at 11:26:34 PM. While Ruriko was constructing this turn, Kaylene was composing her own e-turn related to an earlier topic, in which Ruriko was describing her custom of weighing herself each day while she was in Japan. Kaylene responds 「あそうなの」 ('Oh is that right') to Ruriko's previous description of her weighing practices, and goes on to explain her own. However, mid-way through composing her e-turn, Kaylene realises that she does not know how to say 'check your weight' in Japanese, and is forced to perform a participant-related code-switch to English in order to ask for Ruriko's assistance. While waiting for Ruriko to aid her in finishing this utterance, Kaylene reads and responds to the thread that Ruriko has started about her essay. In order to do this, she starts a new e-turn and replies to Ruriko's English thread in English. Ruriko then responds to Kaylene's request for language assistance, composing not only the target form 「体重を計る」 ('Check your weight'), but the entire e-turn in Japanese. Then, she composes a new e-turn in English to reply to the essay thread. This example demonstrates the ways in which code and orthographic switching, combined with the skilful management of e-turns, can be used to manage multiple conversational threads concurrently.

It should be noted that overlapping threads of conversation occurred in other modes of communication utilised in the present study also, including PC and phone emails; however, perhaps because of the ability to indicate to which message one is replying in the subject line (e.g. 'RE: Today is Yukimi's birthday!!') and the often slower time frame, code-switching was seldom employed to distinguish between threads on modes other than chat in the present study.

Orthographic switching

As mentioned above, in order to switch between Japanese and English, participants in the present study often had to perform an intermediate change – an orthographic switch. While it is possible to represent Japanese in English characters by using romanisation, most participants preferred to use the Japanese *kana* and characters. Alisha stated that large sections of romanisation were difficult to read, and she would only use it as a last resort: 'Sometimes it's hard to understand the *romaji* (romanisation), but at that point in time I was staying at my sister's place, and her computer can't read Japanese at all'. In some cases, having to use romanisation meant that Alisha refrained from using Japanese almost entirely. Describing her university email account, which at the time was unable to send or receive Japanese emails, Alisha said 'that email account doesn't allow you to view Japanese, so they're always in English, often with, *ganbatte ne* (good luck) and *jya ne* (see ya) and stuff like that, but we often write in English'. One other participant who reported that he frequently engaged in code-switching, but did not switch orthography, was Scott. Like Alisha, Scott's code-switches were mostly tag switches, such as 'have a nice day kie-chan. love you so dayo much'.

In the above example, Scott switches to Japanese for the diminutive suffix '*-chan*', which he affixes to his nickname for Kieko, forming '*kie-chan*', at the end of the first sentence. In the second sentence, Scott uses '*dayo*', a sentence-final particle (consisting of the copula *da* and particle *yo*) that indicates the speaker's strong conviction, often translated as 'you know'. Although in Japanese '*dayo*' would normally occur at the end of a sentence, Scott has used it in the same position that an English intensifier, such as 'very', would occur. Scott recounted his learning of '*dayo*' in one of the interviews, explaining that he saw a beer advertisement on television, in which a Japanese comedian says, '*kimochi ii dayo*' ('that feels good'). From this point onwards, Scott said, 'almost every email that I've sent to Kieko, including to her phone, would have *dayo* in it'. In the second interview, Scott confirmed that he and Kieko would use '*dayo*' frequently, both in their spoken (via Skype) and text-based communication (e.g. email). He said, 'we always use *dayo* for everything'. As one of the first segments of Japanese that Scott learnt, it appears that *'dayo'* is particularly entrenched in his and Kieko's communication, like Alisha and Noriko's use of *'ganbatte ne'* and *'jya ne'*. It appears that for these short borrowings and tag switches, the participants did not deem orthographic switching as necessary as it would be for lengthier segments of text.

Where the Japanese orthography was not available, as in the case of Alisha's use of email above, or difficult to use, that is, where technology-related factors were involved, code-switching to Japanese was often avoided by the Australian participants entirely. Hyacinth said that she did not email her Japanese friends often 'because I don't really like the input system on the PC. I always find trouble when you first change to the Japanese input system … you've gotta fiddle with it or something, and I've never really [been taught] how to make it work formally'.

Finally, the use of multiple languages concurrently may result in orthographic deviations of the type noted in Chapter 3. When Kaylene was chatting with two different contacts (one in English, and one in Japanese) in two separate windows simultaneously, she forgot to switch the IME back to Japanese before continuing her message to Ruriko, 「奨学金も大学のプレースメントmo絶対もらった」 (I definitely received my scholarship and my university placement). This example constitutes an (albeit, unintentional) orthographic switch (*mo*), without a code-switch. Thus, when considering the situated activity of online communication between two users, even when engaged in a private, closed chat conversation, it is important to also consider any other activities they may be engaging in simultaneously, including concurrent conversations in other languages, in order to understand orthography and code selection.

Thus, in addition to participant- and discourse-related functions, such as language and typing proficiency or topic of conversation, technology-related functions, such as access to a Japanese keyboard, availability of the IME, problems with Japanese encoding, and availability of predictive text in each language, may also influence orthographic switching. In turn, language and code-switching choices may also be affected by the availability or usability of a particular input method, as the inability to use the most appropriate orthography may result in avoidance of that language.

'Synchronicity' and Genre of Language Use

Having explored the features of participants' CMC use in terms of the interrelated areas of language choice, code, and orthographic switching, the present section will describe the types of language use participants engaged in more generally, in terms of synchronicity and genre. This section will serve as a background to the two case studies presented at the end of the chapter.

The majority of activities reported by participants were text-based, with the exception of Scott's use of Skype (of which no examples could be collected), and Kaylene's uploading of videos she made to Mixi (which, while directed at a Japanese audience, either contained no language or were filmed in English). However, the distinction between 'talking' and 'writing' here, categories based on an *in vivo* coding of participants' own descriptions during the interviews, is more subtle than a simple differentiation between audio and text-based communication. Nor is it a clear-cut distinction between synchronous and asynchronous tools, as is suggested in Crystal's statement that 'We "write" emails, not "speak" them' (2006: 32). Rather, participants distinguished between 'talking' and 'writing' in terms of degree of synchronicity, based on use rather than solely on medium choice.

As described in Chapter 1, mediums such as blogs, email, and SMS have traditionally been classified as asynchronous, and chat and online games as synchronous. Yet, interview data in the current study from several participants shows that whether a medium is text or audio based, or classified as synchronous or asynchronous by researchers, does not entail that users will think about and use the medium in a predictable manner. For example, the use of MySpace and email, both text-based, 'asynchronous' forms of CMC, was described as 'chatting' by Genna. She said, 'we'll just be chatting, and if there's a slight problem in their sentence or something, I'll just say, oh this sentence should have been written like this'. Note her use of not only the term 'chatting', but also 'say', in direct opposition to Crystal's seemingly innocuous and common-sense suggestion that emails are not spoken. When asked what she meant by 'chatting', Genna responded, 'MySpace commenting, or emails'. Similarly, when asked by the researcher, attempting to probe her use of MSN, commonly known as 'chat', 'Did you chat with any Japanese people?' Ellise responded, 'On Mixi, I did.' Noah also reported using Mixi in a synchronous fashion, keeping it open in the background so that he could immediately respond to any notifications, as described above. Once again, Mixi, an SNS like MySpace, would normally fall under the heading 'asynchronous', demonstrating how traditional models of categorisation fail to account for Ellise and Noah's use. Likewise, 'synchronous' tools such as chat may be used in an 'asynchronous' or 'written' way, through the use of sending offline messages, where a chat message will be displayed the next time the user logs in. For these kinds of reasons, Sealey and Carter's (2004) view of CMC as emergent from speaking, writing, technology, and human behaviour, is of great value.

As emphasised throughout the current volume, it appears that rather than static categorisations of CMC mediums assigned by researchers, a more flexible approach to conceptualising modes of communication is needed. Among the mediums utilised by participants in the present study, Gmail is one example of a medium changing in response to users' preferences, as it now incorporates chat functionality into email, and Facebook also has introduced chat to its other social-networking tools. These factors combined mean that it is increasingly difficult to locate any given tool under just one heading, and, instead, instances of use should be examined, rather than classified on the basis of tool type alone.

Another way of conceptualising CMC use is according to genre, as highlighted by de Nooy and Hanna (2009). This model accounts for differences in individuals' communication. For example, Oscar's Mixi messages were largely modelled on the traditional letter or formal email. For Oscar, communication on Mixi was definitely a written activity. Oscar said, 'I find that I write too long. My messages are usually too long, not just in Japanese, but in English as well'. Furthermore, Oscar expressed his concern that people may be bored by his writing, stating that it takes up time, and, interestingly, noted his dissatisfaction with the short replies he receives:

> Most people send really short things, and even if I wrote heaps, they might send to me one sentence, or a two- or maybe three-sentence reply ... maybe they're going through their emails [quickly], maybe they just can't be bothered. To me, they really didn't put much thought into it. Maybe I shouldn't. Maybe that's the way it should be done. (Oscar Interview 2, Lines 230–232)

Although Oscar here uses the term 'email', he was pointing on the screen to his Mixi messages which are similar to email and often called 'emails', but are a distinct service incorporated in the SNS. Oscar stated that Yoshio, whom he had met on exchange, while 'not as bad as some', would sometimes reply with just two or so words, and never responded to his messages on Mixi with messages of a similar length. Analysis of both participants' messages shows that Oscar's perception was borne out by the data – his Japanese emails were on average 177 characters long, while Yoshio's were approximately a quarter of this length, at just 45 characters. Likewise, Oscar's mostly English variety emails at 168 characters were also considerably longer than Yoshio's at only 116 characters. However, Oscar and Yoshio's messages did not differ just quantitatively, but also qualitatively.

An in-depth analysis of both Oscar and Yoshio's messages shows that each had adopted a different genre. Oscar appears to have been influenced by the traditional email format, which may explain his usage of the term 'email' to refer to Mixi messages above. Most of his messages had a formal opening and/or closing (5/6 messages), and he rarely used emoticons or *emoji*, only one in all six messages, and then it was a pre-set emoticon included standard in Mixi. Conversely, Yoshio only signed his name to a message once, never used formulaic openings/closings, and employed laughter e.g. haha (笑) and complex *emoji*, e.g. ()° □°)」 at least once per message. In terms of style and length, Yoshio's messages were far more similar to the kinds of e-turns seen in other participants' MSN chats than emails. Yet, it is important to recognise that these genres are not static, and, like general trends in terms of CMC mode preference, preferred ways of making use of these mediums can also change over time. Oscar commented in the interview that his contacts in general (not only Japanese) had not always written such short messages, but that, now, most of his peers would 'rather have short ones'.

Case Studies of Two Learners' Longitudinal Patterns of CMC

In order to provide a more complete picture of participants' longitudinal patterns of CMC use and examine the ways in which users' communication may span a number of different mediums and language varieties, and change over time, this section takes two participants, Lucas and Kaylene, as case studies, drawing on their archived communication. Lucas and Kaylene were each able to provide data from three separate years (2006–2008), and both had at least one contact who took part in the emailed interviews. Two of Kaylene's contacts (Ruriko and Watako) even took part in focus-group sessions in Japan with Kaylene and the researcher, making her case particularly rich for analysis.

Although there are more instances of communication from these participants to analyse (294 involving Kaylene, and 93 involving Lucas), this does not mean their CMC use was unusual. In large part, the greater amount of data is because these participants had more years of communication archived than others. Their use in fact appears 'average' among participants in the study. Both use PCs, as did 11/12 of the Australian participants. Their total daily computer use was approximately average, with Lucas using the PC for around three hours a day, and Kaylene for four or so, the same as half of the Australians. The number of computers used by participants regularly was two to three, and Lucas and Kaylene used two and three respectively. The average number of CMC modes used in Japanese was 3.33, and Lucas and Kaylene used three and four respectively. Lucas used MSN, Facebook, and most frequently, email, while Kaylene used email, MSN, phone email or SMS, and most frequently (when in Australia) Mixi. None of these modes were unusual among the sample.

Despite these similarities with the other participants, Kaylene and Lucas as individuals have some differences which make them interesting for cross-case analysis. Firstly, they differ demographically in terms of their gender and age (Kaylene is one of the eldest participants at 28 years, while Lucas is one of the youngest at 19). Like half of the participants, Lucas states that English and Chinese are his native languages, while Kaylene, like the other half, claims English-only. At the time of interview, Kaylene had finished her undergraduate course and completed level 12 Japanese. Lucas, on the other hand, had only just finished a first-year sequence in level 1–2 Japanese. Of those who had been to Japan (all except two participants), Lucas had the least amount of time there, just two weeks on a high school trip. Kaylene, on the other hand, had been for the longest, having spent over a year studying at a Japanese university. They also differed in terms of how many hours a week they spent using their most frequently used in Japanese CMC mode. Lucas was at the low end of the scale, making use of email for approximately one hour a week. On the other hand, Kaylene was at the high end of the scale, using Mixi, which was the CMC mode she used most often in Japanese, for 10.5 hours a week. Importantly, Kaylene has a large and robust network of relationships, of a type described by Boissevain (1974) as 'multiplex', in that it contains diversity of linkages. Lucas, on the other hand, has only one current Japanese contact, Hisayo. This relationship is from an exchange, a very typical relationship representative of those examined in the current volume.

The robustness of Kaylene's network is probably at least in part due to her variety of life experiences – time spent in a Japanese university, participation in the LEP, work at the *manga* library, and so on. Importantly, Kaylene was one of four participants who went to Japan part-way through the data collection process, so it is possible to observe how her patterns of use and relationships changed during this period. While the data collected from Lucas covers his transition from high school to university, Kaylene's data covers her transition from university to the workplace. Thus, each provides an important perspective on learners' uses of CMC over time.

Case 1: Lucas

Lucas and Hisayo's email communication, as described above, began with Hisayo's introduction of herself and her family to Lucas in an email on 2 March 2006, prior to his going on exchange. After Lucas returned to

Australia, they continued to email one another, exchanging photos from Lucas' time in Japan. Over the course of their communication, Lucas and Hisayo made use of three forms of CMC, namely, email, MSN, and Facebook, as well as non-CMC modes, such as telephone calls and postal mail. A timeline detailing their patterns of communication between March 2006 and August 2008 (when data collection ceased) is given in Figure 4.4.

Several defining experiences in Lucas and Hisayo's psychobiographies, and the social setting in which their communication was situated, appear to have influenced their choice of language and medium. These events are analysed below.

Language choice

Lucas and Hisayo's patterns of language selection varied over the three years. The most observable pattern is a progression toward the use of more Japanese. This occurred after a number of changes to Lucas' psychobiographical trajectory. When they first met, Lucas had never studied Japanese. Even so, Hisayo did introduce some Japanese into her emails to Lucas. Most frequent was her use of greetings, such as 'konbanwa' (good evening). By August 2006, although he was still not enrolled in any Japanese course, Lucas began to reciprocate Hisayo's use of Japanese greetings. From 12 August onwards, all of Hisayo and Lucas' emails for the remainder of 2006, except for two, contained at least some Japanese.

One major event which altered the overall pattern of both Lucas and Hisayo's language choice was of course Lucas' enrollment in a Japanese course at university. In 2007, Lucas began studying Japanese, and around this time started experimenting with typing in Japanese. Previously, all of Lucas' use of Japanese had been typed in romanisation. As he did not know how to use the IME, Lucas made use of a word processor called NJStar to compose messages to Hisayo. From there, he would paste the text into emails or chat conversations. His excitement at typing in Japanese is evident. Lucas even changed his screen name on MSN to include the word 「すごい」 (sugoi, great) in hiragana. On 28 and 29 March, Lucas made repeated attempts to demonstrate his new ability to Hisayo. When Hisayo appeared to be online via MSN on 28 March 2007, Lucas greeted her in Japanese. When she had not replied a minute and a half later, he switched to English, asking 'could you see the above message?'. The next evening, Lucas made a similar attempt, and, after again receiving no reply, repeated his greeting in romanisation. Eventually, on 1 April 2007, Hisayo contacted Lucas via MSN, and once more he greeted her in the same way, to which she replied with surprise 'why can u type in Japanese?'. Although at this point in time Lucas had only been formally studying Japanese for a month, one-third of his messages (14/21 e-turns) in their conversation on 1 April were composed

			Email	MSN	Facebook	Non-CMC
2006	Mar	2	H (E)			(Lucas' exchange to Japan)
		?	L (E)			
		20	H (ME)			
		?	L (E)			
		28	H (E)			
		?	L (E)			
	Apr	11	H (ME)			
		?				Lucas called
		29	H (E)			
	May–Jun					
	Jul	17	H (E)			
		?	L (E)			
	Aug	2	H (ME)			
		12	L (ME)			
		18	H (ME)			
	Sep	3	L (ME)			
		16	H (ME)			
	Oct	21	L (ME)			
	Nov	8	H (E)			
		?	L (ME)			
		23	H (E)			
		?				Lucas sent photos
	Dec					
2007	Jan	23	H (ME)			
		?				Lucas called
	Feb	5	H (E)			
		?				Lucas called
		?				(Hisayo stays with Lucas)
		19	L + H (ME)	L (ME)		
		20		L (ME)		
	Mar	5		L (J)*		(Lucas begins studying Japanese)
		6		H (ME) + L (MJ)*		
		28		L (MJ)*		
		29		L (MJ)*		
	Apr	1		L (ME)		
		4		H (ME)		
		8	L (ME)			
		10	H (ME)			
	May	2		H (ME)		
		4	L (MJ)			(Lucas learns to type Japanese)
		5	H (MJ)			

Figure 4.4 Timeline of Lucas and Hisayo's communication

Notes: Initials (H = Hisayo, L = Lucas) indicate sender, or, in the case of MSN, who initiated the conversation. Asterisks indicate that a conversation was attempted, but the recipient did not respond. Abbreviations in parentheses indicate language, E = English, ME = Mostly English, MJ = Mostly Japanese and J = Japanese. Monolingual English communications are presented in bold text, while monolingual Japanese communications are given in italics.

in Japanese. This pattern continued for the remainder of 2007. Every conversation, across all three modes of communication (email, MSN, and Facebook), that Hisayo and Lucas engaged in for the rest of the year contained at least some Japanese. This represents a large increase in the pair's Japanese use in comparison with their previous year. Comparing emails for example, between March (when Lucas and Hisayo began communicating) and December of 2006, Lucas and Hisayo exchanged 19 emails, most of which were in English. Yet between

Jun	21	L (MJ)			Lucas sends birthday present and card
	24	H (ME)			
	?	H (ME)			Hisayo sends ecard
	28		L (ME)		
Jul	5	L (ME)	L (ME)		
	12	H (ME)			
	31	H (ME)			
Aug–Sep	?	L (ME)			
Oct	12			H (ME)	
	14			L (ME)	
	26			H (ME)	
Nov	1			*L (J)*	
	4			H (ME)	
	5			L (ME)	
	6		H (ME)		
	29			*H (J)*	
Dec	?				Hisayo and Lucas exchange Christmas gifts
Jan	4			**H (E)**	
	5			L, L (ME)	
Feb	15			H (ME) + L (ME)	
	21			**H (E)**	
	23			L (MJ)	
Mar	5			H (MJ)	
	19	L (MJ)			
	25			*L (J)*	
	27	H (MJ)			
Apr	4	L (MJ)			
	10	H (ME)			
	11	L (ME)			
	14	**H (E)**			
	22	L (MJ)			(Lucas and Hisayo participate in an emailing project for Lucas' university Japanese course.)
	29	H (ME)			
May	?	L (MJ)			
	17	H (ME)			
	18	L (MJ), L (ME)			
Jun	10			H (MJ)	
	11			**L (E)**	
Jul	18			H (ME)	
	19			L (ME)	
	23			H (ME)	
	24			L + H (MJ)	
Aug	4			L (ME)	
	5			H (ME)	
	17			H(MJ) + L(ME) + H(MJ)	

(left margin: 2008)

Figure 4.4 (Continued)

March (when Lucas began studying Japanese) and December of 2007, Lucas and Hisayo exchanged 11 emails, all of which contained Japanese.

On 4 May 2007, Lucas attended a computer lab session as part of his level 1 course. Lucas immediately made use of his newfound ability to compose emails and communicate via other CMC using the IME, rather than having to copy-and-paste from NJStar. During class time, Lucas composed an email to Hisayo, reproduced in Chapter 2. The greater ease afforded by using the IME to compose messages in Japanese is readily apparent. The average time it took Lucas to respond to one of Hisayo's messages on MSN when he wrote in Japanese using NJStar was almost two minutes. However, after taking the typing class and learning to use the IME, which allowed him to compose his messages directly in MSN, the time taken decreased to an average of 60 seconds. Although Lucas was a highly motivated and diligent student, it is likely that his increased speed was a result of not only his improving language ability, but also the fact that he no longer had to copy-and-paste his messages between two windows.

During 2008, Lucas and Hisayo's language choice appears to have largely balanced out. All four language varieties identified (English/mostly English, Japanese/mostly Japanese) were observed in the period from January to August 2008, when data collection ceased. The pair exchanged six messages in English via email and Facebook, one in Japanese, and 13 in each of the mostly Japanese and mostly English varieties, suggesting that for this pair code-switching became the norm. In previous years, Lucas and Hisayo's uses of email and Facebook consisted of monolingual messages a third of the time (33% in 2006–2007), but in 2008 this decreased to just over a fifth (21%).

Medium choice

The first major occurrence to influence medium choice was of course Lucas' trip to Japan. Host families were provided with the email addresses of the exchange students, among other details, and Hisayo decided to email the student who had been assigned to stay with her family, Lucas, and introduce herself as his host sister, in March 2006. After Lucas' trip, their communication via email continued based on Hisayo's planned trip to Australia. In addition to reporting on their day-to-day lives and matters of cultural interest in both Japan and Australia (festivals, tourist attractions, celebrations, and so on), Lucas and Hisayo also found overlapping areas of interest, such as reading and playing video games, to discuss. These shared interests helped to sustain their communication long after Lucas' departure. At times, their email communication was supplemented by telephone calls. Each of their phone conversations (in April 2006, January and February 2007) were organised via email, demonstrating its use as a 'passport' to other mediums, including offline modes of communication, identified in Chapter 3.

The next major psychobiographical occurrence to fundamentally change the pattern of their medium choice occurred in 2007, when this time Hisayo stayed with Lucas and his family in Australia. After this second face-to-face encounter, they began using MSN in February. At first, their use of MSN appears to have replaced email, as Lucas and Hisayo used chat exclusively, although by April they returned to using primarily email. The trigger for this change appears to have been a technical consideration. Lucas used email to send Hisayo some digital photos from her time in Australia. Although it is possible to send photos via MSN, it is more complex and time-consuming than through email. Thus, Lucas' choice of medium appears to be related to this factor. Also, as previously mentioned, Lucas made several attempts to initiate conversation with Hisayo which failed. Although Hisayo appeared to be online, she was in fact away from the computer and did not respond to his initial greeting or prompts. Thus, Lucas' switch to email may also have been a result of Hisayo's unavailability for chat. Although the pair continued to use MSN sporadically whenever they both happened to be online at the same time, their main mode of communication remained email until they began using a third form of CMC, the SNS Facebook.

Lucas and Hisayo's move to Facebook was influenced by an important shift in the social setting of their communication. Lucas noticed that his friends, including Hisayo, were making a switch from MySpace to Facebook. In an interview, Lucas said 'you move on from MySpace to Facebook, everyone started moving to Facebook'. Although they never communicated via MySpace, both Hisayo and Lucas did maintain MySpace profiles until they moved to Facebook. This switch was part of a larger move at the social level, and examining the broader social setting at the time may help to explain this shift in Lucas and Hisayo's situated activity.

Facebook was originally created for university students in the US, but opened up to the general public in September 2006. In May 2007, four months before Lucas and Hisayo moved over, the *New York Times* ran an article entitled 'Facebook Expands into MySpace's Territory' (Stone, 2007), describing how in the eight months since going public, Facebook had doubled its membership to 24 million users. By July 2007, *PCWorld* was asking, 'Is Facebook the New MySpace?' (Sullivan, 2007). In the article, Sullivan likens SNSs to clubs, stating that every few years a different club would become incredibly popular, leaving the previous hot spot nearly empty.

Like many others, Hisayo and Lucas began using Facebook in late 2007, when Lucas found Hisayo's profile and sent her a friend request. In an interview, Lucas reported that he used Facebook very frequently at the time, logging in at least once a day. He stated that:

> At first, it was actually an addiction. It's sort of like an obligation to go on, see who has replied, see who you can reply to. Nowadays, I tend to use it less. I probably do go on it a couple of times a week, when I'm bored. But I wouldn't go on it every day. (Lucas Interview 3, Line 242)

For the five months spanning October 2007 and March 2008, Facebook appears to have replaced Hisayo and Lucas' use of email, as was the case when they first began using MSN. However, on 19 March Lucas switched back to

2008	Date	Email	Mixi blogs	Mixi comments	Mixi messages	MSN	Mobile
Jan	31		C5 (J)				
Feb	1	K to R ph, K to C (J)		K, C on C5 (J)			
	2	R ph to K (MJ)					
	3	K to R ph (MJ)					
	5	C to K (J)					
	9	R ph to K (J)					
	11	K to R ph (J)					
	17	R ph to K (MJ)					
	19			1 on K15			
	20	K to R ph (MJ)		K on K15 (J)			
	25	R ph to K (J)					
	26	K to R ph (MJ)					
	27					K&R (MJ)	
Mar	2	K to C (J)	K16 (J)	1, U on K16 (J)			
	3	U to K (E)		2 on K16		K to U (J)	
	4			1 on K16			
	5	K to U (MJ)		R on K16 (MJ)			
Apr	6					U to K, K to U (J)	
	23	C to K (J)				U to K, K to U (MJ)	
	24	K to C (J)				C to K (J)	
	25					K to C (J)	
	26					C to K, K to C, C to K (J)	
	27					K to C, C to K (J)	
	29	J to K (J) + K to J (E)					
May	1					U to K (MJ)	
	5	J to K (J) + K to J (ME)					
	6	K to J, J to K, J to K (J), K to J (E), J to K (J)				U to K, K to U (J), U to K (MJ)	
	7					K to U (MJ)	
	12	K to J, J to K, K to J (J)					
	15					U to K (MJ)	
	17					K to U (MJ)	
	19					U to K (ME)	
	21	K to J (J)	K17 (J)	1, C on K17 (J)			
	22			K (J), 1 on K17			
	23	J to K, J to K (J)					
	26	K to J (J)			K to R (MJ)	K to U (J)	
	27	I to K, K to I (J)					
	28	I to K, K to I, I to K, K to I (J)					
	30	I to K, K to I (J)				K to R, K to U (MJ), K to U (J), K to U (E), U to K (ME)	
	31					U to K, K to U, K to U (J), K to U (ME)	
Jun	1					R to K, U to K (MJ)	
	2	I to K, K to I (J)					
	3	I to K, K to I, I to K (J)					
	5	K to I (J)					
	10					K to U (MJ)	
	13					U to K (MJ)	
	14					U to K (ME), K to U (MJ)	
	26					K to U (J)	
	27					U to K (MJ)	

Figure 4.5 Time line of Kaylene's CMC use

email in order to announce that he was going to Japan. Although he did go on to reply to one of Hisayo's previous posts on his Facebook wall, Lucas and Hisayo continued to use email for some time after this switch, for a number of reasons. Firstly, after Hisayo replied to Lucas' announcement on 27 March, Lucas used email on 4 April in order to invite Hisayo to participate in the present study. Most participants made use of email to invite their contacts to join the study, as forwarding an explanatory email from the researcher was required.

After negotiating their joint participation in the present study via email, Lucas had another request for Hisayo. As will be examined in the next chapter, for his level 3–4 course Lucas was required to take part in an emailing project for assessment. Students could either email a Japanese friend, or be paired up with a student at a university in Japan. Lucas decided to invite Hisayo to participate. Hence, they continued to make use of email for the duration of the project. Hisayo and Lucas had agreed to correct one another's emails, and on 18th May, Lucas sent through the last of his corrections for Hisayo. The project complete, the pair switched back to Facebook for the remainder of the data collection period.

The above longitudinal analysis of Lucas and Hisayo's communication demonstrates how psychobiographical factors, such as overseas travel or enrolment in a language course, and social settings, such as the shift from MySpace to Facebook, may influence medium and language choice over time. A case study of an advanced learner, Kaylene, is given below.

Case 2: Kaylene

Kaylene's patterns of L2 use online are somewhat more complex than Lucas', probably owing to her communication with a larger number of contacts, and the fact that she is a higher-level language student. Although data from three years (2006–2008) was available for Kaylene also, the six months starting January 2008 (three months before Kaylene's arrival in Japan) through to June 2008 (three months after) have been selected for in-depth analysis. During this six-month period, Kaylene communicated with five Japanese NSs who agreed to participate in the current study, via six different CMC modes, as depicted in the timeline in Figure 4.5. Due to the complexity

Figure 4.5 Timeline of Kaylene's CMC use (Continued)
Notes: Initials represent as follows, K = Kaylene, R = Ruriko, C = Chikae, U = Ukiko, J = Junko, I = Ikuko. Blogs are numbered to demonstrate the link to comments. Where contacts who did not participate in the present study commented on a blog, the number of non-participant commenters is indicated with a numeral. Abbreviations in parentheses indicate language, E = English, ME = Mostly English, MJ = Mostly Japanese and J = Japanese. Monolingual English communications are presented in bold text, while monolingual Japanese communications are given in italics.

of Kaylene's communication with her Japanese contacts, non-CMC modes of communication have been excluded from this timeline. However, it is important to note that, like Lucas, Kaylene did make use of a number of forms of non-CMC modes with her Japanese contacts. Her use of such modes with one contact, Ruriko, will be considered separately.

Over this period of time, the major change in Kaylene's psychobiography, and the social setting in which her communication was situated, was of course her move to Japan (indicated by the horizontal line in Figure 4.5), which influenced her frequency of CMC use and patterns of language and medium choice.

Frequency of CMC use

There are two obvious differences between Kaylene's use of CMC in Australia and Japan. Firstly, her amount of communication increased dramatically upon her arrival. In January, Kaylene did not communicate with any of her Japanese contacts (although she later read Chikae's blog posted on 31 January), and, again, had no communication in March either. In her last three months in Australia, Kaylene sent seven emails (and received six), read and commented on one of her friends' blogs, received one comment (which she replied to) on one of her past blogs, and participated in one conversation via MSN. In her first three months in Japan however, Kaylene sent 18 emails (and received 17), wrote two blogs, on which she received a total of 9 comments (which she replied to), sent two Mixi messages (and received one), and sent 19 phone emails (and received 17).

The number of contacts with whom Kaylene communicated also increased, which explains in part her overall increased frequency of CMC use. This appears to be attributable to two distinct phenomena. First of all, based on an opportunity to meet face-to-face once again, Kaylene's communication with some Japanese contacts that she already knew was rekindled. Her interaction with Ukiko is one such example, where the pair recommenced their communication after Kaylene's announcement on her Mixi blog on 2 April that she was in Japan. Prior to this, the pair had not had any contact in almost four months. Secondly, as was observed in Chapter 2, time in Japan provides opportunities to form new acquaintances, and in Kaylene's case she developed new relationships at both work and university, increasing her total number of L2 contacts.

Medium choice

The second most striking feature of Kaylene's communication in Japan is her use of mobile phone email. While in Australia Kaylene did not own a mobile capable of using email, this quickly became her main use of CMC with Japanese contacts while in Japan. Over the three-month period depicted above, Kaylene sent/received 36 emails via phone, compared with 35 emails via PC. The difference is much more marked, however, when calculating the total number of emails sent and received via phone and PC up to November 2008 (when data collection ceased). PC emails accounted for around 40% of Kaylene's total emails (68/162), while approximately 60% were sent via phone. Her use of PC email was never entirely replaced by mobile email, however; as is evidenced in her parallel use of these mediums. Some days she made use of both forms of email in one day.

Kaylene's parallel use of PC and phone email can be understood by considering with whom, and for what purposes, she used each of PC and phone email. While in Australia Kaylene made use of email in Japanese primarily with her friends Chikae (an ex-exchange student) and Ruriko (a former LEP), in Japan, she was much more likely to contact both via phone email. Although Kaylene contacted Chikae, and another friend/LEP, Ukiko, via PC email during her first month in Japan, this quickly changed, and for the remainder of the data collection period Kaylene no longer exchanged PC emails with any of her Japanese friends. Instead, PC email became Kaylene's professional mode of communication. While in Japan, Kaylene undertook a Masters preparation course at a Japanese university, and worked at a *manga* museum. From May 2008 onwards, all of Kaylene's communication via PC email was in either in regards to university administration (with Ikuko) or communication with *manga* museum staff, mostly translation requests. Although later in the year Kaylene did begin using phone email with Watako, a colleague at the *manga* museum, it is important to note that this was a social rather than professional use, and thus in keeping with Kaylene's established pattern of use.

Language choice

A shift in Kaylene's language use via email occurred approximately a month after she arrived in Japan. While previously her emails had been a mixture of Japanese and mostly Japanese varieties, with the occasional English-only message, from May onwards all of her emails, with the exception of three to Junko (which contained English translations Junko had requested), were composed entirely in Japanese. This continued on for the remainder of the data collection period.

While it may appear, based on an analysis of Kaylene's PC email use alone, that as she spent more time in Japan her use of Japanese simply increased as a result of being immersed in a Japanese-speaking social setting on a daily basis, it is important to consider the shift in medium demographics. Although Kaylene did use only Japanese in her communication with the staff at the *manga* museum and Ikuko from her university, her patterns of language use with her friends with whom she previously used PC email (but had shifted to phone email) remained relatively unchanged, despite the shift in medium. Roughly half of Kaylene's sent and received emails were composed entirely in Japanese both before and after her move. Thus it appears that Kaylene's move to Japan alone did not significantly influence her use of Japanese, but that her entry into new institutions (the *manga* museum and her Japanese university), in which Japanese was the norm, did.

Conversations via multiple modes of communication

One other interesting aspect of Kaylene's patterns of CMC use is the use of multiple modes of communication within a single conversation or communicative thread. Of all Kaylene's Japanese contacts, she was able to provide interaction data with Ruriko for the longest period of time, so their case has been selected for analysis. (Email data from April 2006–October 2007 was unavailable, and is indicated by black shading.)

As the timeline in Figure 4.6 shows, Kaylene and Ruriko tended to carry out conversational threads via a single medium. They also tended to reply to each other's Mixi blogs using the built-in commenting function directly on the blog page. However, in one case, Ruriko replied to Kaylene's fifth blog (K5) using a private Mixi message. Several of Kaylene and Ruriko's conversational threads spanned multiple modes of communication in this fashion, even involving non-CMC mediums. In December 2007, Kaylene and Ruriko organised to send each other Christmas gifts via email, posted their gifts with cards simultaneously, and then replied to the gifts and cards using email. On 26 May 2008, Kaylene sent Ruriko a message via Mixi and, when she did not receive a reply, sent a follow-up email via mobile phone on 30 May. In her next mobile email, Ruriko responded to both Kaylene's Mixi message and mobile email. This thread of communication (number 14 in Figure 4.6), mostly relating to Kaylene and Ruriko's planning of a holiday together, culminated in a face-to-face meeting on the day that they began their trip. On 2 August 2008, the day they had decided to meet, Ruriko sent Kaylene three mobile emails in a row. Kaylene later explained that, as she was crossing a road on her way to meet Ruriko at the time, she did not hear the noise her phone made when receiving Rurkio's first email at 9:59 AM, informing her that she was waiting in a specific location. It was not until Kaylene received Ruriko's second email at 10:04 AM asking where Kaylene was that she discovered the original email. Seeing Ruriko's seemingly concerned message, Kaylene decided to call Ruriko immediately, rather than send her another message. When they eventually met face-to-face, Ruriko greeted Kaylene via another mobile phone email, 「はろ一♥」 (Hallo), signalling that she had made visual contact. From here, they shifted to spoken, face-to-face communication. This thread of communication spanned four modes of communication – a Mixi message, mobile phone emails, a phone call, and a face-to-face meeting.

As previously mentioned, Kaylene and Ruriko also used some modes of CMC to arrange other CMC use. In February 2008, Kaylene and Ruriko organised an MSN chat conversation via email. In September 2008, Kaylene made a yoga video for Ruriko and asked her via mobile phone email whether she would prefer it to be uploaded to Mixi or sent to her PC (Hotmail) account. At this time, Ruriko was experiencing some difficulties with her Internet access, and did not receive Kaylene's email until Kaylene re-sent it to her other mobile email account later. (Ruriko used both a Softbank and Docomo phone at the time of data collection.) While waiting for Ruriko's reply, Kaylene uploaded the video to Mixi, which Ruriko later watched and commented on. Before watching the video, however, Ruriko confirmed via mobile email that she preferred to watch the video on Mixi, and Kaylene re-confirmed that she had already uploaded it. This thread of communication, represented by number 16 in Figure 4.6, spanned three forms of communication – mobile phone messages, Mixi video, and Mixi comments (four if Ruriko's two phone email accounts are counted separately).

The ways in which Kaylene and Ruriko's conversational threads were found to span different mediums suggests that it is impossible to account for the development of topics and outcome of conversations based on the analysis of a single mode of communication, such as chat, alone. Although some individuals may communicate exclusively via one mode of communication, all participants in the present study made use of multiple forms of communication, including CMC and non-CMC modes. While studies focusing on a single mode of CMC are valuable, the evidence presented here suggests that it is important to view this communication as part of a complex system of interaction, rather than an insulated medium. A study of Kaylene and Ruriko's use of chat, for example, could benefit from an analysis of their emails from 1–26 February 2008, in order to examine the lengthy process of organising a date and time for the chat engaged in via email, prior to the chat conversation itself. Without this context, Kaylene and Ruriko's chat conversation may appear serendipitous and brief. Indeed, nothing in the text of their chat itself hints at the nine emails composed over 26 days that it took to organise this 1.5 hour chat session.

Discussion

Having examined participants' psychobiographies and the social settings of their CMC use in Chapters 2 and 3, this chapter turned to analyse the

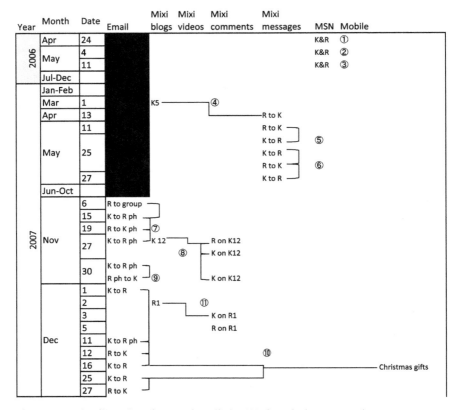

Figure 4.6 Timeline of Kaylene and Ruriko's CMC threads (2006–2008)

features of participants' situated CMC activity, in terms of conversational organisation, language choice, orthographic and code-switching, and types of language use. Lucas and Kaylene's patterns of situated language use via CMC, taking into consideration aspects of their psychobiographies and social settings, were then explored in depth.

Although it has been stated that it is unclear 'how participants cope with the vagaries of turn-taking' online (Crystal, 2011: 25), utilising the three units of analysis proposed in Chapter 1, this chapter demonstrated the ways in which e-turns are consciously ordered into turns by individuals, and turns are co-constructed into conversations by pairs or groups. Participants' patterns of turn-taking were found to be related to their language choice in terms of orthographic and code-switching, as described above, and also related to their use of repair, as will be examined in the following chapter.

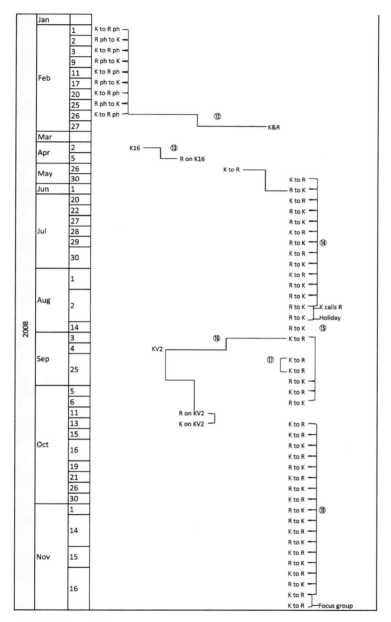

Figure 4.6 (Continued)

Expanding upon the concept of 'domains' identified in the previous chapter, language choice was found to be influenced by the 'domain' in which interaction takes place. Participants' use of English and Japanese on Facebook and Mixi were found to correspond with their identification of these modes as English and Japanese domains respectively. Language choice was also found to be affected by interpersonal relationships, both in terms of participants' relative status, and their respective motivations. Overall, participants' language choice and use of paralinguistic features tended to converge, with participants adopting similar styles of CMC use, suggesting that in most of the pairs under study here, participants wished to reduce the social distance between them. This is unsurprising given that the majority of the relationships under examination in the present study are social in nature (except for Kaylene and Jacob's professional contacts, with whom they used predominantly Japanese).

The use of both code and orthographic switching in CMC was highlighted, and both participant and discourse-related functions of code-switching identified, suggesting that learners' use of code-switching in CMC is similar to learners' and other bilinguals' use of code-switching in other non-institutionalised settings. The extra technical step involved in code-switching between languages which employ different orthographies was found to affect participants' structure of code-switching, in terms of where in a conversation switches took place. Two types of code-switching were identified, namely inter and intra e-turn switching. In fast-paced conversations, inter e-turn switching was preferred, especially by NNSs and others unfamiliar with typing in Japanese. Based on this analysis, it was suggested that, when orthographic switching is employed with a code-switch, it may be easier for users to switch language between e-turns, rather than attempting to change the input method in the middle of composing an e-turn. Switching languages and orthographies during an e-turn takes time, and may render one's contribution irrelevant to the conversation if it takes too long to type. Another possible reason for the prevalence of code-switching at the e-turn boundary, rather than within it, may be that participants used new e-turns to signal new topics, or replies to different threads, and, in some cases, these new turns may trigger a discourse-related switch in language, as was the case in Kaylene and Ruriko's conversation, where overlapping threads of conversation were maintained in two different languages simultaneously. In fact, making use of two different languages appears to have aided participants in distinguishing between concurrent threads. In general, although participants appear to prefer to read Japanese in *kana* and characters rather than in romanisation, technical constraints in some cases made this impossible. Furthermore, particularly in the case of brief borrowings or tag-switching, avoidance of orthographic switching appears common, because, as Genna explained, it is faster to continue typing in English letters.

Language use overall was also categorised, with participants distinguishing between 'talking' and 'writing' in terms of degree of synchronicity, based on their use rather than solely on medium 'type'. Participants' descriptions of their own CMC use and actual evidence from their interactions, appears to challenge the fundamental traditional categorisations of CMC.

Finally, the case studies of Lucas and Kaylene examined their language and medium choice in context, and demonstrate the complex ways in which participants' use of multiple technologies interact. Their situated CMC activity was analysed through the lens of their psychobiographies, as related in Chapter 2, and the social settings of their communication, analysed in Chapter 3, drawing upon the concepts of the e-turn, turn, and conversation outlined in the present chapter. Consideration of key events in Lucas and Kaylene's psychobiographies, and shifts in the social settings of their CMC activity, were found to provide powerful explanations of their language and medium choice. Kaylene and Ruriko's conversational threads were taken as a further in-depth case study, and were found to span a number of different mediums, highlighting the importance of considering both CMC and non-CMC modes of communication when seeking to understand CMC use. Their case also demonstrated how the use of any CMC tool should be considered as part of a complex system of interaction, rather than thought of as an isolated medium. Participants' use of contextual resources, and opportunities for language use and acquisition within their systems of interaction via CMC, will be examined in the following chapter.

5   Use of Contextual Resources and SLA Opportunities

Following the analysis of participants' psychobiographies in Chapter 2, and examination of their interactions with a focus on social setting and situated CMC use in Chapters 3 and 4, this chapter will describe the rich opportunities for language use and acquisition that may develop in the situations described above. This chapter will address the third and final research question posed at the beginning of this book, which aims to examine how participation in online communication provides opportunities for language acquisition. In order to describe opportunities for language acquisition, and demonstrate the extremely valuable forms of language learning, practise, guidance, and assistance afforded in CMC, this chapter will draw on an analytical coding of the interaction and interview data, utilising nodes drawn from both the data itself and the previous studies described in Chapter 1. By focusing further on the situated activity of CMC, and on the use of contextual resources, this chapter concludes the examination of the four domains identified by Layder (1993).

Widening Opportunities for Language Use

A number of opportunities and benefits for widening language use via CMC were identified in the present research, including participants gaining an audience, challenging themselves, accessing authentic materials, and applying classroom learning. These themes emerged from the NVivo coding of the interviews, cited by participants as benefits of CMC use, and are considered 'contextual resources'. Sealey and Carter (2004) use 'contextual resources' to refer to the distribution of material and cultural capital, and the subsequent widening in opportunities for language use. In the case of the situated CMC activity described here, relevant capital includes, in addition to language and education, computers, dictionaries, glossaries, translators, textbooks, reference books, game software, browser plugins, word processors, websites, and mobile phones. Another important resource for language learners is of course the NSs or 'expert' peers with whom they interact, and the language that results from these interactions and is stored as an artefact by the computer.

Because this chapter focuses on learners' L2 use and opportunities for language acquisition, where correction was present an attempt has been made to translate the errors in participants' communication data. Where it was impossible to reflect the error in English, ungrammaticality is indicated with an asterisk (*).

Gaining an Audience and Challenges

Challenging oneself and gaining an authentic audience are two of the most important benefits of CMC use (Chun, 1998; Johnson & Brine, 1999; Pasfield-Neofitou, 2008; Underwood, 1987). As emphasised in Chapter 1, interaction and authentic contexts for communication have long been considered crucial to SLA, across a number of theoretical perspectives, including both social and interactionist accounts. In a social account of artefacts and cultures-of-use in NS–NNS CMC, Thorne (2003) draws on van Lier's (1996) observation that language activity is authentic when it is an expression of one's genuine feelings and beliefs and is intrinsically motivated. Thorne states that authenticity in the communicative process is deeply implicated in language development. In the area of interactionist CMC research, Chapelle (1998) makes use of a model based on Krashen (1982) and Long (1996), and observes that an authentic audience for learners' linguistic output is important so that they attempt to use language for meaning construction, rather than simply practising.

Describing his thrill at having written a lengthy blog, Noah said, 'I just looked at this massive block of Japanese like, "I wrote that". I don't know if it's correct, but ... wow, I wrote this massive block.' Both Noah and Hyacinth started their blogs (on Mixi and Ameba respectively) as a test of their linguistic ability, or, in Noah's words 'to see if I could do it'. However, despite the sense of achievement gained from confirming their ability to write a lengthy piece in Japanese, both Noah and Hyacinth did not continue blogging. Noah wrote only one blog, and Hyacinth, although she wrote six over the span of less than a month, described it as a 'once off', and stopped posting after just 26 days.

What really seemed to motivate the Australian participants to continue with their efforts to use Japanese was confirmation that they were being 'heard' and understood. Cindy said that she tried to blog as much as possible on Ameba, and judged her success in communicating based on the responses from her readers, commenting that her blog seemed 'okay, since other people can read it'. As mentioned in Chapter 3, Cindy spent a great deal of time collecting *peta* stamps from her visitors. Similarly, Zac said that he felt good when he received a compliment on one of his blogs stating that his Japanese was 'great'. Having an active audience appears to be important.

Tutor/tutee roles

In addition to the Australians gaining motivation via their virtual 'immersion' in a Japanese 'domain' online, or feeling a sense of achievement in their own communicative successes, the Japanese participants played a very active role. Noriko, Alisha's former teacher, and Tokio, who was considerably older than Genna, each took on a rather teacherly stance in their communication, and offered study advice and support. Noriko encouraged Alisha to use Japanese not only in CMC with her, but also in offline settings. In an email on 16 August 2007, she asked 'How's Japanese class going? Who's your teacher this semester? Ganbatte ne! (Good luck!) Are you doing language exchange this semester, too? Oh, did you join the Japanese club?' This type of questioning and encouragement appeared frequently in Noriko's emails to Alisha, and may be related to their shared history. As described in Chapter 2, Noriko observed Alisha's Japanese class at university as an intern teacher and, later, Alisha employed Noriko as a private tutor. After Noriko left Australia, it appears that they maintained this tutor/tutee relationship via CMC.

Genna also actively constructed a tutor/tutee relationship with Tokio. She would report her efforts at university Japanese study to him, telling him about her assignments and the results of her tests. On 7 April 2008, Tokio enquired whether Genna had finished her homework that weekend, and the next day she responded, 'I did all my homework like a good girl, lol'. Tokio also encouraged Genna, and offered to answer any questions she may have about Japanese. However, while Alisha and Noriko's relationship appears to have been a one-way teacher–student relationship, deeply rooted in the shared experiences in their psychobiographies, Genna and Tokio engaged in more reciprocal teaching. Tokio, who had moved to Australia to undertake a university course, also reported his assignment results to Genna, who encouraged him in his use of English. It appears that while engagement in teacherly behaviour via CMC may be a natural extension of participants' offline relationships, as was the case with Alisha and Noriko, participants may also co-construct their own language learning setting online, as Genna and Tokio appear to have done. Although Genna and Tokio met via MySpace, not in a classroom setting like Alisha and Noriko, they both had experiences of tutoring others. It is possible that these experiences may have influenced their online communication together. In this way, participants' psychobiographies can be seen to influence the types of communication they engage in.

Peer learning

It was not only Japanese contacts that acted as an audience for participants' L2 use, however. Hyacinth, Genna, and Cindy all wrote Ameba blogs, and seem to have viewed each other as their primary audience, at least at the outset, even though they set up their accounts principally to practise Japanese, and invited their Japanese contacts to view their posts. The three, Genna and Cindy in particular, would borrow photos from each other's blogs and reappropriate topics. For example, Genna posted a blog called 'BLOOD meet and greet' (written in English and Japanese) on 10 June 2008 about a band event that all three girls attended. The next day, Cindy used the same photo in a blog called 「前日」 (previous day). Although physical proximity is not necessary for sustained contact and successful communication, as is demonstrated by Kaylene's lengthy relationships with overseas contacts, borrowing and appropriation of this kind would not be possible without the shared experience Genna and Cindy engaged in. While previous studies have demonstrated that pairing learners with other learners for the purpose of language practise alone may not be effective (Hanna & de Nooy, 2003), in cases where users are engaging in L2 use of their own volition with other NNSs, the benefits of such communication should not be dismissed. Genna and Cindy had the multi-layered benefits of mutual support from a peer at the same level (for example, they would comment on each other's blogs when no entries had been posted in a while, explicitly encouraging each other's further participation), access to blogs by an expert NNS (Hyacinth, enrolled several levels above the other two), and access to blogs by and comments from NSs of Japanese, as outlined above. The importance of such models of communication is described below.

Use of authentic models

As highlighted in the theories discussed previously, in addition to participation, simply gaining exposure to authentic communication is very important for foreign language learners who are not geographically located in an area where their L2 is widely spoken. Gilmore (2004) highlights the need for learners to be presented with realistic models of communication, unlike those in their textbooks, which are limited by what is readily teachable, and CMC may provide one such avenue. In particular, SNSs allow learners to access examples of candid NS–NS communication in their L2 in a previously unprecedented way, where private social interactions are brought into a public setting.

One of the most interesting features of online discourse, especially on SNSs, websites, BBSs, and forums is that much of it is simultaneously conceived of as both 'public' and 'private' (boyd & Heer, 2006). By browsing comments left on a profile, wall, or even lurking on a BBS, like Hyacinth did, as described in Chapter 3, users can see what boyd terms 'public' private conversation, where a comment normally directed to the owner of the page is visible to other visitors. The present subsection will demonstrate how access to such intimate communication can be highly beneficial for language learners in the acquisition of sociolinguistic competence in performing certain speech acts, as emphasised in Canale and Swain's (1980) model of communicative competence.

In one example in the present study, Lucas wanted to congratulate Hisayo on her birthday. Although he had already sent her a card through the regular postal system, he was concerned that it would not reach her in time and so decided to send her an email greeting on the day, reproduced below.

Extract 5.1 Lucas' email birthday greeting to Hisayo

```
こんにちは久代さん！
  ^    |
 /_\   |    誕生日オメデトー！！楽しいの誕生日になりますよ！       |
(^O^) < |                                                        |
        |_____|
```

(Hello Hisayo-san
Happy birthday-!! *Have a fun birthday!)

Lucas explained that he had been trying to think of ways to say 'Happy Birthday' other than the standard *'otanjyōbi omedetō'*, and had logged in to Facebook to find examples of what Hisayo's Japanese friends had been saying. Although the second phrase contains grammatical errors, introduced when Lucas typed the phrase himself from memory (the addition of the unnecessary particle の, and the omission of the long vowel-sound う in よう), he was successful in sending a message that was both longer and more expressive (hoping that she would have an enjoyable day) than a simple *'otanjyōbi omedetō'* would have conveyed.

In another example, exchanging emails with Noriko gave Alisha the opportunity to model her own emails on Noriko's messages. At the beginning of their correspondence in 2006, Alisha always used English openings and closings, such as 'Hey Noriko'/'See you soon then.' Yet, Noriko consistently used *'Noriko yori'* (From Noriko) as the closing of her emails, which Alisha started using later in the year, *'Alisha yori'*. On 26 November 2006, Noriko introduced the opening line *'Alisha e'* (To Alisha), which Alisha then adopted in her own emails as well, *'Noriko e'*. Although it is unclear whether Alisha was learning these formulaic expressions for the first time, or simply gained the confidence to make active use of them through Noriko's repetition, her increased use of Japanese is apparent.

Looking to his Japanese peers' Mixi blogs as models also helped Oscar overcome his anxiety about communicating in an L2 publicly. After reading his peers' blogs, Oscar said:

> When I first started using Mixi, I'd use my electronic dictionary quite a bit when I wanted to say stuff, but now I'm thinking, well, if you look at the way Japanese people write their ones, it's not even grammatically correct. It's just ... the very bare bones. They drop particles; they do funny things to the end of words and whatnot. So it doesn't really matter if it's grammatically correct, just make sure there's no miscommunication. (Oscar Interview 2, Line 42)

It is remarkable that Oscar formed this impression through CMC rather than while he was on exchange at a Japanese university for a year, despite features such as particle dropping being present in face-to-face speech too. Perhaps it was the visual nature of his interaction on Mixi that promoted his noticing, where non-standard forms are clearly marked. As discussed in Chapter 1, orthographic and other variations upon 'standard' language in Japanese CMC are constructed through the use of different symbols, such as → or ～ to indicate a long sound, or differently sized characters, such as さあぁ, which may make these features easier to recognise via CMC due to their distinct nature when written graphically. Crystal (2011) claims that positive links have been made between the use of textisms and L1 English literacy in pre-teens, given that understanding and utilising innovative language play requires and promotes a high level of linguistic awareness. The present study demonstrates that a similar phenomenon may be at play in L2 settings also.

In their interviews, some participants reported having learnt specific lexical items, or new meanings of words, from their online communication. Lucas reported having learnt a new word, 返事 (*henji*, reply), from his email communication with Hisayo. When he later composed an email himself, he searched through Hisayo's emails to find a model phrasing. Jacob also said that in addition to learning words specifically related to sending and receiving email, such as 届く(*todoku*, arrive), he learned an alternative meaning for the word 大変 (*taihen*, terribly) through emailing his Japanese colleague, and received a lot of input to dispel his initial assumptions about its use. While Jacob stated that he had only ever learnt to use *taihen* in a negative sense, such as 'terribly wrong' or 'terrible news', he learnt a new, positive sense through examples he received in Kō's emails, such as 「今回送っていただいた報告には大変刺激を受けました。」 (I took <u>great</u> inspiration from the report that you sent last time). In our interview, Jacob was able to formulate a grammatically acceptable phrase using this newly acquired sense, '*taihen ureshī desu*' (I am <u>very</u> happy). Furthermore, this example was one that he had not received from Kō, but had made up himself, based on his revised assumptions from Kō's usage.

Scott also reported learning Japanese from his interactions with Kieko; in his case, the grammatical construct *mashō*, a verb ending which indicates volition or invitation. He said in an interview that although in class they only ever used the formal non-past (*masu*) form of verbs, Kieko had taught him the *mashō* auxiliary verb ending in a Skype conversation, with the example *nomimashō* (let's drink). He was later able to conjugate the verb *ikimasu* which he had learnt in class, to form 「行きましょう」 (*ikimashō*, let's go) in an email.

Although CMC provided an opportunity for participants to supplement their classroom learning, as shown in this example, it also gave them the chance to make use of what they had formally studied, in an authentic communicative situation. The next subsection will explore the affordances of situated CMC activity for applying classroom learning.

Applying classroom learning

Practising linguistic and cultural knowledge learnt in the classroom in meaningful ways, as emphasised in theories of situated learning (Lave & Wenger, 1991), is a common aim of instructed CMC use (cf. Chung et al., 2006). In the informal setting of the present study, several of the Australian participants talked excitedly about the opportunities they had gained or created to practise classroom learning in their online communication. Scott said that the majority of his use of Japanese with Kieko was 'all the stuff that I've learnt in class'. Cindy reported that her motivation for starting a blog was to practise Japanese, and Noah joined Mixi for the same reason. Zac also added that he did not feel that his eight hours (four of level 10 classes, and four of an advanced reading unit) of Japanese instruction per week was enough, and, for this reason, supplemented his university education with his MeetUp membership and internet use. Lucas, too, commented that incorporating what he had studied into his emails to Hisayo helped him to consolidate the lecture content, and, as previously mentioned in his case study, was able to participate in the email project with her.

One specific example of an opportunity to apply classroom learning in authentic communication online is evident in Ellise's use of the phrase *koto ni narimashita* (it was decided). Ellise said that she had studied the phrase that year, and was thrilled to be able to use it in a blog post announcing her acceptance to a Japanese university. She said, 'I was like, oh wow! I can actually use stuff I learnt'.

In addition to Zac's use of Mixi blogs to obtain feedback from NS peer 'experts' previously mentioned, other learners also looked for feedback on, or support for, assignments or university-endorsed activities online. Alisha, in particular, appears to have utilised CMC frequently for this purpose. After attending a consultation session with her Japanese teacher related to her essay and oral presentation topic choice, she then consulted Noriko, her former tutor, via email. For her essay, Alisha chose to write about Mixi and its effect on the Japanese population, 'in regards to people becoming silent (reticent) and their increasing use of indirect communication', a choice obviously influenced by Alisha's own participation in this medium. Having seen a *kabuki* play in Japan with Noriko (also arranged via email), Alisha decided to do her oral presentation on this form of traditional Japanese theatre. Throughout the two-month process of preparation for the presentation, Noriko showed interest in Alisha's topic, provided her with encouragement and support, and even forwarded her a link to a website on *kabuki*. By the time Alisha was about to present, their roles as 'expert' and 'novice' had switched, and it was Alisha who ended up teaching Noriko about *kabuki*. This was not the only example of Australian participants teaching their Japanese contacts about aspects of Japanese culture – Kaylene also taught several of her blog readers complicated aspects of the Japanese paper-folding craft *origami*.

Alisha also sought advice on her entry in a Japanese speech contest, posting a list of six possible topics in Japanese related to religion in Japan, and asking 「面白いですか。みんな、どういう意見ですか？　どんな提案でも歓迎だ。本当だ。😊」(Are they interesting? Everyone, what is your opinion? Any kind of suggestion is welcome. Really.) She obtained two responses to this blog entry providing advice on which topics might be of most interest, as well as some recommendations of books to read on the various topics.

Finally, involvement in CMC also assisted with accessing authentic materials and resources for use in university courses. As Larson (2003) points out, language teachers are no longer the arbiters of access to the culture and language they teach. The Internet has drastically facilitated access to Japanese materials, and students in the present study showed more advanced ways of searching for relevant information than simply logging on to a Japanese culture website or performing a Google search. Participants' uses of these materials will be described in detail below; however, one example related to education is Alisha's use of Mixi to find advertisements targeted at Japanese people her age for a university assignment.

Engagement in CMC was found to afford participants the opportunity to consolidate their knowledge of the L2, and make use of it in situated activity. Furthermore, participating in CMC afforded learners new opportunities to perform their own research on the target language and culture, and obtain feedback from sources other than their teacher, which will be further explored below. In this way, participants' CMC use was informed by their classroom learning and, in turn, their classroom learning was enriched and solidified by their CMC use. Another way in which classroom learning influenced participants' CMC use is in the area of tools. Textbooks were reported by Lucas and Ellise as useful resources to draw upon when engaging in CMC, and participants' use of other resources, such as online dictionaries, was found to be influenced by the formal instruction teachers provided on their use. These issues will be described in the following section in order to further answer Sealey and Carter's (2004: 197) question of how people are 'differently resourced'.

Dictionaries and Other Resources

One of the most important affordances of situated CMC activity as opposed to face-to-face communication is the ability to use dictionaries and other resources relatively privately. Oscar, pointing at his electronic dictionary during an interview, said 'if you carry this around everywhere, looking up words when you're in a conversation, it looks nerdy'. He reported that he was told by his guitar circle members while on exchange, 'don't do it, it looks bad'. CMC, however, affords learners the opportunity to look up words online or in a separate dictionary without their interlocutor's knowledge. Similar findings were reported in studies of Japanese (Freiermuth & Jarrel, 2006) and Korean students communicating in English, who stated that having the freedom to use a dictionary made them feel less pressure and nerves while chatting (Chung et al., 2006). Although some of my previous research has considered the use of dictionaries by learners of Japanese in CMC contexts (Pasfield-Neofitou, 2007a, 2007b, 2007c, 2009a, 2009b), on the whole, there appears to be little research on the use of dictionaries by learners of non-alphabetic languages, despite the groundbreaking innovations new forms of resources offer students, such as being able to easily look up a character without knowing its pronunciation.

Through examination of their interaction, and interviews with each of the 12 Australians, it was discovered that participants used a surprisingly wide variety of reference materials to support their communication and learning. These resources included a range of dictionaries (paper, electronic, and online) as well as textbooks and other reference books, game software, and browser plugins.

Following Pasfield-Neofitou (2009b), paper (also 'print' or 'hard copy') dictionaries are defined here as dictionaries in a printed book form. Electronic (also 'pocket automatic' or 'computerised bilingual') dictionaries are hand-held computers, similar in size to a calculator, which contain integrated reference materials such as a Japanese monolingual, Japanese–English, English–Japanese, and an in-depth character dictionary. Finally, online dictionaries are usually free to use, searchable dictionaries accessible via the Internet.

The use of dictionaries, and other resources such as Microsoft's IME Pad (which allows the user to draw characters on their computer screen) and Nintendo's dictionary software (which allows the user to utilise their hand-held game system as an electronic dictionary), takes on a particular importance in the study and use of Japanese, including the use of Japanese in the situated activity of CMC. As previously mentioned, Japanese consists of not only the two sets of *kana* symbols, *hiragana* and *katakana*, but, as Gottlieb (1993) notes, in order to be 'literate' in Japanese, one would also need to be familiar with at least 1945 characters and the roman alphabet, which may be used to write either Japanese or English words. An authentic example of all four is given in Figure 5.1, excerpted from a chat conversation between Alisha and Eri on 25 August 2008.

In most paper dictionaries, the 46 *hiragana* syllables are used to index all words. Thus, learners must know the phonetic reading of characters in order to look them up in *hiragana*-based dictionaries. Character or *'kanji'* dictionaries are a notable exception, where characters are looked up using the number of strokes or radical. However, these dictionaries are intended primarily to facilitate the use of other *hiragana*-indexed dictionaries, and do not usually contain detailed definitions or examples. Thus, electronic and online dictionaries, which provide alternate and integrated ways of searching for words, as will be outlined below, constitute an extremely important resource for learners of non-alphabet languages such as Japanese. A list of the dictionaries and other tools participants reported using is given in Table 5.1.

フランスの王妃Marie Antoinette   (France's Queen, Marie Antoinette)

Katakana   Characters

Hiragana   Roman alphabet

Figure 5.1 Example of writing systems from Alisha and Eri's chat

Table 5.1 Resources used during CMC interactions

Participant (N=12)	Name of resource	Printed resources			Digital resources							
		Paper-based			Non-computer		Software	Computer-based				
								Internet				
		Paper Dictionaries	Textbooks	Reference Books	Electronic Dictionaries	Game Software	Word Processors	Online Dictionaries	Online Translators	Online Glossaries	Browser Plugins	Total
Cindy	WWWJDIC							*				2
	Denshi Jisho							*				
Genna	Babelfish								*			2
	Denshi Jisho							*				
Scott	-											0
Lucas	Yookoso		*									3
	NJStar						*					
	Denshi Jisho							*				
Noah	Rikai chan										*	1
Hyacinth	WWWJDIC							*				1
Ellise	Lighthouse dictionary	*										5
	Word						*					
	J Bridge		*									
	Complete Japanese Verb Guide			*								
	Babelfish								*			

Participant	Resource	Used	Total
Zac	Kanji Sonomama Rakubiki Jiten	*	4
	Rikai	*	
	Reading Tutor	*	
	Denshi Jisho	*	
Jacob	WWWJDIC	*	2
	Eijiro	*	
Alisha	Eijiro	*	3
	Reading Tutor	*	
	Unspecified elec. dictionary	*	
Oscar	Cannon Wordtank G90	*	1
Kaylene	Eijiro	*	4
	WWWJDIC	*	
	Rikai chan	*	
	Unspecified elec. dictionary	*	
Total	(Average = 2.33 per participant)	1 2 1 3 1 2 10 2 4 2	**28**

As the data in Table 5.1 relies on participants' memories, it must be noted that participants may have used more tools than those mentioned above. However, it is clear that most participants made use of multiple resources. Scott was the only participant to not report use of any resources; however, as previously mentioned, his case is unusual in that his communication was mostly with his girlfriend. Scott's communication with Kieko was conducted mostly in English or Chinese, as described above, and he made use of Japanese only when he wanted to practise what he had already acquired. He explained in the interview, 'I've never used a dictionary [in communicating with Kieko online], because it's usually all the stuff that I've learnt in class'. For others, however, who were more motivated to 'challenge' themselves, and those whose interlocutors did not have such a high level of English, or who did not share a lingua franca (such as Scott and Kieko's use of Chinese), the use of dictionaries and other resources appears more crucial.

In Table 5.1, several categories of tools may be distinguished. Firstly, the resources may be defined as either printed or digital. Such a distinction is important in that printed and digital texts require quite different styles of consultation, as will be further explained. Secondly, the digital resources may be categorised as either computer-based or non-computer-based. When considering the use of resources to support CMC, this distinction is especially significant. Computer-based resources usually allow the user to copy-and-paste, while non-computer-based digital resources require the user to re-enter what is written, introducing the possibility of reproduction errors, and, unless a stylus is available, necessitating the recognition of the reading of characters. Finally, computer-based texts may be categorised as either Internet- or software-based. Internet-based tools are distinctive in that they require the user to be online and are normally accessed through a browser, and, more importantly, are typically updated more frequently than software-based resources. Software-based resources, on the other hand, need to be installed on the user's computer. Participants' patterns of use (or non-use) of the abovementioned resources will be outlined below.

Paper-based printed resources

Of the references participants reported using, three kinds of paper-based printed resources were identified: paper dictionaries, reference books, and textbooks. Only two Australian participants, Lucas and Ellise, reported using paper-based resources, both of whom were students of intermediate-level Japanese. As can be seen in Table 5.1, while Lucas made use of only his textbook, *Yookoso* (Tohsaku, 2006), in terms of printed materials, Ellise used a hard-copy dictionary (Kenkyusha's *Lighthouse*), and a reference book

(Tuttle's *The Complete Japanese Verb Guide*) in addition to her textbook, *J Bridge* (Koyama, 2007).

Paper or hard-copy dictionaries are usually familiar to students who use monolingual dictionaries in their first language, and their advantages include their ability to be browsed more easily than their electronic or online counterparts. As Ellise remarked, 'paper's a bit easier to use, as you can kinda flip through it', and such browsing may allow students to notice other vocabulary along the way (Pasfield-Neofitou, 2009b). Overall, Ellise reported that she used her paper dictionary 'mainly to check the *kanji*' characters she was using in her blogs were correct, and her verb book to look up complex conjugations. On the other hand, Ellise used her textbook to confirm the structure of grammar patterns she had studied in class. Lucas, too, said that he used his textbook to look up 'how to use the grammar points'. He remarked that this was a relatively efficient way of finding what he was looking for, as 'all I had to do was look at the glossary or index, flip to the page, and have a quick look'. In one example, Lucas described how he used his textbook to find the sentence ending と思います (*to omoimasu*, I think), for use in the phrase 「とてもいいテレビゲームと思います」 (I think it's a very good video game), which he composed in an email to Hisayo. He explained that although he had studied the construction in conjunction with adjectives, he was unsure how to make use of *to omoimasu* in this particular utterance 'because [very good video game] was a noun'.

One clear similarity between both Lucas and Ellise's uses of paper-based printed resources is that, in all cases, the two were drawing on them for support in production, not to aid their understanding of others' utterances. Ellise confirmed in her interview that she would use the paper dictionary if she was writing something herself; however, would make use of a computer-based source if she needed to copy-and-paste something that someone else had written.

Non-computer-based digital resources

Even though they are digital, non-computer-based digital resources also do not afford the use of copy-and-paste because they remain external to the computer or device though which interaction is taking place. A quarter of the Australian participants reported using non-computer-based digital resources while engaging in CMC. Two types of such resources were identified in the present study, electronic dictionaries, described above, and game software, in this case for the Nintendo DS hand-held game system.

One highly practical advantage of electronic dictionaries over paper is the ease of cross-referencing. Rather than needing to look up a character in a separate *kanji* dictionary, and then look it up again in the *hiragana*-indexed Japanese-to-English dictionary, users can move between dictionaries quickly and easily through the use of the 'Jump' function. The portability of electronic dictionaries is another of their major advantages over paper dictionaries. Despite their increased ease of use over paper dictionaries in terms of finding characters, electronic dictionaries, like paper dictionaries, were still used mostly for looking up words for production, not to look up unknown vocabulary in a text the user was reading. Alisha confirmed that she used her dictionary 'more often for what I want to say'. Furthermore, the cost of electronic dictionaries can also be prohibitive. Yonally and Gilfert (1995) suggest that electronic dictionaries cost on average between ¥10,000 and ¥50,000 (approximately US$100–$500), a figure which, fieldwork for the present study confirms, does not appear to have changed dramatically. In an interview, Ellise spoke of her plans to research electronic dictionaries before her upcoming trip to Japan, as she wanted to ensure that she got 'the right one'. Being able to input characters with a stylus (rather than having to look them up using stroke count or radical) was an important feature for her. Another drawback is the necessity of batteries, and the fragility of the technology. Kaylene reported that she used her electronic dictionary only 'very occasionally', because 'my electronic dictionary is dying at the moment, so it's just easier to use the online one'.

A second type of non-computer-based digital resource identified was game software, used on a portable games system, in this case Nintendo's DS, although other examples exist. At the time of data collection, two applications were available for the DS: 『楽引き辞典』 (*Rakubiki jiten*, Easy-to-use Dictionary) and 『漢字そのまま楽引き辞典』 (*Kanji sono mama Rakubiki jiten*, Characters just like that Easy-to-use Dictionary). Zac carried his DS with him everywhere, and because of the function in *Kanji sono mama* that allowed him to look up characters simply by drawing them on the screen, was able to look up difficult characters comparatively easily by using the DS stylus.

Software-based digital resources

Some participants reported utilising software-based resources, that is, tools like a word processor or browser plugin that must be installed on the user's computer. As previously outlined, Lucas stated that while communicating online, he made use of a 'special word processor for writing Japanese', called NJStar, which he explained 'comes with a dictionary for writing Japanese, so you just highlight a word, and the meaning pops up'. Lucas reported that he would compose emails in the word processor; 'that's pretty much how I write my emails, and then I copy-and-paste that'. Ellise, too, used a word processor, Microsoft Word, to aid in her online communication in Japanese, using it to look up the readings of Japanese characters using the 'Reconvert' function. She said 'I put it in Word, and changed it to Japanese, then you right click, and it comes up with all the Japanese readings on the side'. Such resources were used mostly for reading, as Ellise stated, 'usually with my own stuff, I don't have to look up much, but with what he writes, um. . .!'

The second form of software-based digital resources identified in the present study are plugins, programs that interact with a host application, usually a web browser, to provide a specific function, such as, in this case, making available glosses of Japanese words in the browser pane. In the current research, participants reported using two specific plugins, Rikai-chan, a Rikai-based glossary plugin for the browser Firefox, and a plugin for WoW, which enabled the viewing of Japanese characters in in-game conversation. This plugin was used only by Noah, but as he had stopped playing WoW in Japanese by the time of the data collection, no evidence of his use was available for analysis. However, Rikai-chan was used by both Noah and Kaylene at the time of the study.

Noah said of Rikai-chan 'it helps. A lot. With the insane *kanji*'. This was the only resource Noah, an advanced student, reported making use of at the time of data collection, as he claimed that he already knew most of the words that he wanted to write in Japanese, and only needed Rikai-chan to read what others wrote. The only way in which Noah checked the accuracy of his own utterances was by ensuring that the correct characters appeared when he used the character conversion function in the IME. Although no participants reported the IME as a specific resource that they made use of, as it is rather different in nature to the other resources described here (users must make use of the IME in order to input Japanese characters), its usefulness to confirm that the word one has typed is spelled correctly, if the correct characters appear upon hitting conversion, should not be underestimated. However, users may find it difficult to select the correct character from the multitude suggested by the IME (indeed, this led to some errors in the present study, as will be demonstrated later). Despite Noah's reliance on Rikai-chan as his sole resource, Kaylene found that utilising a number of resources maximised the benefits, and helped to overcome some of the technical constraints that she faced, especially as she found that Rikai-chan had some compatibility problems with Gmail at the time.

One of the greatest advantages of all computer-based resources (both software-based and the Internet-based tools described in the next subsection) is the ability to cut-and-paste to and from a text one is reading or writing. Alisha stated in her interview that when she encountered anything she did not understand while communicating with Noriko, 'particularly if it's in Japanese script, I just cut and paste it into an online dictionary'. This eliminates the need for users to spend lengthy amounts of time looking up individual characters by stroke count or radical element before finding the reading that would enable them to look up the word in a traditional paper dictionary.

Internet-based digital resources

Unsurprisingly, online resources were the most commonly used in the present study, with 10 out of the 12 Australian participants making use of at least one kind of online resource via their computer. These Internet-based digital resources can be divided into several categories, and in the present study I make use of the categorisation I have developed elsewhere (Pasfield-Neofitou, 2009b), consisting of three types. First are 'dictionaries', where a word is searched for and a list of possible translations produced. Second are 'glossaries', where text is input into a box, and glosses are provided for individual words or characters with readings and meanings, often using mouse-over tool tips. Third are 'translators', where text is input into a box and the website provides a translation. Denshi Jisho (http://www.jisho.org/) is one example of an online dictionary, and was used by three participants in the present study. Rikai (http://www.rikai.com/perl/Home.pl), which was used in its various forms by a further three participants, is an example of a glossary. Finally, Babelfish (http://babelfish.yahoo.com/), used by two participants, is an example of a translator. Although, like the various types of paper-based resources, each of these has different uses, they are most often discussed under the umbrella term 'online dictionaries'.

As Li (2006) notes, many students are understandably reluctant to pay large sums of money for study resources. A survey I conducted of 55 paper dictionaries available at the participants' university at the time of research showed that students would need to spend upwards of $200 on paper resources to obtain a similar quality and quantity of information that is available freely online (Pasfield-Neofitou, 2009b). Electronic dictionaries, as shown in the previous subsection, are costly also. As online dictionaries are free to use, there are virtually no constraints on the number of tools one might consult. Kaylene reported that she kept two or three online dictionaries, Eijiro (http://www.alc.co.jp/), Jim Breen's WWWJDIC (http://www.csse.monash.edu.au/~jwb/cgi-bin/wwwjdic.cgi?1C), and occasionally Rikai, open every time she used Japanese online, saying that she 'opened them straight away, in case I needed them'. Kaylene was a regular multi-tasker, and commented:

I have a billion things open on the computer at once, I usually at least have, when I'm emailing, the browser open, and because I use Firefox, I usually have a few tabs open, so if I'm typing in Japanese, then I'll often want to look things up, so I'll have Jim Breen's website open, as well as Eijiro, or sometimes Rikai. (Kaylene-Watako Focus-group, Line 157)

This appears to be a common strategy, with Zac, too, stating that he would keep Denshi Jisho, Rikai, and Reading Tutor (http://language.tiu. ac.jp/index_e.html) open while reading a Japanese text, 'just to make sure that I'm getting the full picture'.

Alisha, likewise, outlined her strategy for attempting searches in multiple resources, stating, 'usually I just use Reading Tutor. If that's no good, Eijiro, the one that translators use.' Jacob, too, mentioned that he used more than one source regularly, in his case, WWWJDIC and Eijiro (otherwise known as ALC). He said:

alc.co.jp is pretty essential for when I'm emailing somebody in Japanese, because it searches sentences rather than just vocab, so I can see an example sentence, and I can just copy-and-paste that and change the vocab around to what I'm writing about. [I use WWWJDIC] if it's not available in ALC, or if I'm just looking up one word, it's usually good for that. (Jacob Interview 2, Line 56)

As these examples demonstrate, most participants had a sophisticated understanding of the different uses of different tools. Glossaries or translators like Reading Tutor may be useful to obtain a 'big picture' in Zac's words, of what someone else has written, while dictionaries such as ALC and WWWJDIC prove useful for looking up single words and obtaining sample sentences, as Jacob points out. Further, because there are virtually no space or memory restrictions, online dictionaries often contain far more example sentences than offline tools (Pasfield-Neofitou, 2009b). The importance of examples to guide word choice is highlighted by Genna, who said, 'I look at the sentences, and see what sentences are close to what I'm trying to say'. Hyacinth too said that she found WWWJDIC easy to use because 'it has examples of how a word is used'. Many Internet-based dictionaries, like WWWJDIC, are regularly updated, or, like Eijiro, source their words from the media and Internet, and, hence, are more likely to include newly coined words than a paper or electronic dictionary, which may eventually need to be replaced.

As noted above, in terms of use, Internet-based digital resources were often used to aid participants' reading of others' utterances, something that paper resources were not used for in the present study. Kaylene reported that she used an online dictionary to look up 迷路 (*meiro*, labyrinth), which appeared in Ruriko's utterance 「何の動画なのかな？？迷路？？」 (What's your video of?? The labyrinth??) in their chat on 27 February 2008, referring to a video of a maze Kaylene had posted on Mixi. One month later, Kaylene was still able to recall the meaning of this word in context. In fact, Kaylene appears to have retained passive knowledge of a substantial portion of the vocabulary and characters she researched using various online tools. Some of this retained knowledge is demonstrated in Kaylene's explanation of how she went about writing her blog entitled 「レゴの遊ぶと離婚の思い出」 (Play with Lego and memories of divorce) on 28 January 2008, two months before the interview:

> I used Eijiro a fair bit for this one, because I wanted to look up things like the Japanese term for Lego blocks … I already knew *rikon* (divorce) but I wanted to look up things like 'material possessions', when people break up possessions when they get divorced, *kyōyōbutsu* (common property) … [Now] if I saw it, I would know what it meant, but if I needed to use it, I might need to look it up again. But then, in the dictionary, when you see the different examples, I would know which one I'd used before. (Kaylene Interview 2, Lines 292–298)

The role of mobile phones

Internet-enabled mobile phones were also found to be useful as stand-alone resources, or in facilitating the use of computer-based resources. Oscar used his mobile phone as a dictionary while engaging in face-to-face communication in Japan, to disguise the fact that he was using a dictionary, after he was told that using his electronic dictionary made him look 'nerdy'. More relevant to the current study, Kaylene reported her use of a mobile phone in conjunction with other forms of CMC. While the characters used in Japanese pose a particular problem for learners when used in person or place names because they cannot reliably be found in standard dictionaries, Kaylene came up with some innovative ways of solving this problem using CMC tools. When meeting someone for the first time in Japan, Kaylene would ask her interlocutor to send their details to her mobile via Bluetooth in order to obtain the correct characters for their name immediately after she heard the pronunciation. Secondly, when friends would email meeting plans to her mobile that contained the name of a place written in characters, Kaylene reported that she would forward the email to her PC email account, and then look the name up in Wikipedia.

Website research to support language acquisition and communication

Kaylene's use of Wikipedia to look up vocabulary in CMC use was by no means exceptional. Ellise and Lucas also utilised websites, but to find specific lexical items for their own active use. For example, Ellise made use of a Japanese university website to check the characters for the university name. Such websites proved much more useful than the various types of dictionaries and other generalised resources mentioned above when trying to find proper nouns, such as game titles or university names, in particular.

Describing his recent emails to Hisayo, Lucas reported that he used websites, including Nintendo's http://nintendo.co.jp and http://wii.com/jp/, which he found via a Google search, to find the names of his favourite Nintendo games, including『おどるメイドインワリオ』(Dance Made in Wario), called 'Wario Ware: Smooth Moves' in English. In the process, he learnt the verb *odoru* (dance), which he was able to remember correctly a month later.

Non-use of resource materials

Scott may have been the only learner who reported that he never used resource materials; however, several other participants noted constraints on their use. Alisha commented, 'I don't usually have time to sit there with a dictionary' when writing an email. Likewise, Zac stated that he code-switched to English in his Mixi blog when he was not sure of the word in Japanese. This non-use of resources appears to be related to not wanting to interrupt one's 'flow' of writing. Zac elaborated on his choice to use the word 'finals' in English also, saying 'I just didn't know how to write it in Japanese at the time, and I was just going with the flow and didn't want to use jisho. org to look it up'.

Ellise also noted that she 'couldn't be bothered to look up all the words' at times, and, in those cases, opted to write in English. She described how one Mixi blog, about her involvement in a university theatre group play, required so much vocabulary that she did not know in Japanese (such as the word for 'audition', and vocabulary to explain the plot of *The Crucible*), that she opted to write the blog entirely in English, although all of her other blogs were written entirely in Japanese. Part of Ellise's reluctance to look up a large number of words may be related to her preference for paper, as opposed to online, dictionaries. As outlined above, paper and electronic dictionaries and other non-computer resources may be more difficult to use than computer-based resources in an online setting. This is because, firstly, the user cannot simply copy-and-paste the target word to the text they are composing.

A second reason is that rather than just switching to another window on the screen, the user must switch their attention to an entirely different object, from the computer or mobile phone screen to a book or secondary small electronic device. However, it is likely that Ellise's seemingly unusual preference for paper dictionaries over online dictionaries is based on the unsatisfactory experiences she had using online dictionaries. Ellise reported in an interview that she had tried a few dictionaries and translators after performing a Google search, but did not find any suitable.

One of the translators that Ellise tried using and was dissatisfied with was Babelfish. Ellise used Babelfish as both a translator and dictionary, saying that she used it 'when I've got a big chunk of stuff, or one *kanji* or word and I don't know what it is'. While Babelfish can be useful in gaining an understanding of the general gist of a text at hand, it is not ideally used as a dictionary. Furthermore, it is a general, rather than specialised, translator, which provides translation services between approximately 40 different language pairs. While students like Zac, Jacob, Alisha, and Kaylene, who had undertaken the specialised translation unit (level 10 at the focus university), had extensive knowledge of online dictionaries and translators, and showed evidence of utilising a variety of online tools, Ellise had not yet received any explicit instruction in her formal education regarding the use of such tools. Oscar, who also did not use any online resources, had not undertaken the translation unit either, despite his enrolment in levels 11–12 at the time of data collection, owing to the fact that he undertook an equivalent level language course on exchange in Japan. Thus, it appears that specific guidance from teachers may benefit students' use of resources outside the classroom.

Opportunities for Planning and Revision

There is much evidence to suggest that pre-task and within-task planning aids learners to produce more complex language in task-based settings (Foster & Skehan, 1996; Mehnert, 1998; Skehan & Foster, 2005; Tavakoli & Skehan, 2005; Wendel, 1997; Yuan & Ellis, 2003). As noted in the discussion of situated activity, CMC may also afford great opportunities for planning in informal (i.e. social rather than task-based) communication, in part due to the relatively slower pace in comparison with face-to-face speech (as documented by Greenfield & Subrahmanyam, 2003; Pasfield-Neofitou, 2007b; Toyoda & Harrison, 2002). Not only do participants have the opportunity to complete planning prior to their interaction, but, because of the normally more relaxed pace, during the interaction itself. As shown above, while engaging in situated CMC, participants had the time to consciously apply classroom learning in their communication online, and make use of diction-aries and other resources to carefully construct their utterances, freed of the pressure of being seen as 'nerdy' by referring to a dictionary frequently.

Two distinct types of planning can be identified in participants' CMC use. The first is pre-interaction planning, where, prior to sending an email, for example, or posting a blog, the participant has the opportunity to con-sider how to express the content they will need to encode. The second is planning that takes place during a conversation, such as the use of dictionar-ies and other resources between or in the construction of e-turns, in relative privacy, as opposed to directly facing an interlocutor. Examples of both types have been given throughout the present analysis. Pre-interaction planning, where participants made use of planning strategies before engaging in a con-versation, include Kaylene's use of a dictionary to find divorce-related vocab-ulary before writing a blog on the topic, Ellise's research on her Japanese university's website before announcing her acceptance there, Lucas' viewing of model birthday greetings on Hisayo's page before composing his own greeting, and Jacob's planning to seek proofreading. During interaction strat-egies, used where participants were already engaged in a conversation, include the use of dictionaries and other tools to look up words that became relevant throughout the course of the interaction, and self-initiated self-repair before the message is sent (re-typing a misspelt word, for example). Forms of self-repair will be further explored in the next section.

Furthermore, participants' use of CMC was also found to exhibit excel-lent opportunities for revision after a given interaction. According to Levy and Stockwell (2006), some of the most important affordances of new tech-nology are the ability to communicate at a distance and to aid memory. As Sealey and Carter (2004) state, writing (and electronic discourse by exten-sion) allows for the production of texts, which can lead to their contempla-tion, the development of thought, make memory more durable, and enable critical engagement with language. Here, it is argued that audio recordings, made possible by, for example, Scott's use of Skype (although no examples were available for analysis), and video recordings, for example, those Kaylene shared on Mixi, provide similar affordances. As noted in the methodology described in Chapter 1, all participants in the present study were already making use of the various archiving functions available to them. Indeed, chats, emails, and even blog postings and SNS comments are usually saved automatically, unless the user makes the choice to delete (or 'cull', as described in Chapter 3) them, representing a record of participants' communication, and a portfolio of their own L2 development. Perhaps most importantly, archived communication also constitutes yet another resource upon which users can draw in future conversation. Such a use can be seen in the case of

Lucas, described earlier, who reported that he reviewed his previous email communication with Hisayo to find the word *henji* (reply) so that he could close his own email correctly. He said 'she had sent that in an email to me earlier ... so I looked it up, and voila!' In this way, archived communication may not only aid memory by providing a durable record of past conversations, but also constitute an excellent resource in which learners can find uses of the words and phrases they wish to use, within an authentic context immediately relevant to their situation. Other ways in which participants received assistance from their partners are outlined below.

Repair and Corrective Feedback in CMC

Communication in the target language is a prerequisite for language learning, and the importance of authentic social interaction is emphasised in all major theories of SLA (including, notably, Krashen's (1982) Input Hypothesis, Long's (1983, 1996) Interaction Hypothesis, and Sociocultural Theory). In fact, sociocultural SLA prefers to talk about 'participation' in interaction rather than 'acquisition' (Sfard, 1998), with the view that taking part in social activity constitutes development (Ellis, 2009). In CMC, like any situated activity, various forms of assistance, negotiation, and accommodation make increased participation possible for learners.

As Sealey and Carter (2004) describe, electronic discourse may be conceptualised as a cultural emergent property of speech, writing, and human interaction with technology. As emergent properties cannot be reduced to any one of their constituent elements, it follows that situated CMC activity is likely to exhibit some different kinds of affordances and constraints relating to the provision of assistance, than those associated with situated activity in face-to-face settings. Accordingly, this section will explore the affordances and constraints of situated CMC activity identified in the present study, with specific reference to discourse repair, peer editing, and feedback, three key issues identified in the literature reviewed in Chapter 1, and which also emerged in the coding of data.

Discourse repair

As detailed in Chapter 1, discourse repair has been the topic of much research in the area of CMC (Beauvois, 1998; Coniam & Wong, 2004; Darhower, 2002; Schwienhorst, 2002; Shekary & Tahririan, 2006; Smith, 2003), and is an important component of any communication. The usefulness of examining repair in applied linguistics research has been highlighted by Schegloff *et al.* (2002), and Foster and Ohta (2005) have identified repair and other forms of assistance as one of the ways learners gain access to the language being learned. Additionally, repair may provide opportunities for negotiation of meaning and form, leading to the possibility of language acquisition (Ellis, 2009), as will be demonstrated in the present subsection. In the context of CMC, Chung *et al.* (2006) have argued that engaging in discourse repair provides learners with the conditions necessary to support complex language learning, and Schwienhorst's (2002) study of repair in CMC showed that it can increase learners' awareness of the learning process, and force them to understand language learning as a social process of inter-dependence. However, little attention has been paid to the unique features of repair in online communication, especially in naturalistic settings.

Schegloff (2000) defines repair as a practice for dealing with problems in speaking, hearing, or understanding the conversation. In the case of text-based CMC, this may also be thought of as reading, writing, and understanding. Schegloff finds it useful to distinguish *who* initiates repair (*self*, the speaker of the trouble-source turn, or *other*), and *where* the repair is initiated (with Schegloff observing that virtually all repair occurs in a very narrow window of opportunity, generally within three turns of the source of trouble). Repair usually occurs in the same turn as the trouble-source, the turn after the trouble-source, or the turn after that. In speech, Schegloff (1992) argued that third position repair may be thought of as the last systematically provided opportunity to catch divergent understandings and other troubles.

Self-initiated repair in the first position may occur when the speaker realises a problem in the turn they are producing (T1), and initiates repair before relinquishing the floor. Alternatively, second position repair occurs when the receiver of T1 finds a problem in the turn, and addresses it in the next turn, (T2). This is considered the basic position for other-initiated repair. Finally, third position repair is self-initiated, and occurs when the receiver of T1 finds no problem warranting repair in the next turn position, and thus produces a T2; however, this T2 demonstrates the understanding that has been accorded, which the speaker of T1 may perceive as problematic, and then repair occurs in the third position (T3). Repair may comprise four components, although not all need be present. The components identified by Schegloff include, (1) initiation of the repair (e.g. 'no'), (2) an agreement or acceptance component, if the speaker of T2 has perceived T1 as a complaint, (3) rejection, where the speaker rejects the prior turn, and (4) repair proper.

Schegloff (2000) later described another position in which 'other'-initiated repair may occur – fourth position, due to the recurrence of repairs initiated by the NNS in NS–NNS conversation at a position later than that previously claimed to be the basic repair position for other-initiated repair (namely, next turn or T2). If repair is not attempted within three or sometimes four turns, then it becomes 'next relevant'. When repair becomes next relevant, it may never again be relevant. Darhower (2002) argues that evidence from MOOs corroborates Schegloff's findings regarding relevance in the chatroom as well, as a breakdown which occurred in one chat in line 23 was still not recovered by line 37, rendering the shared communicative context beyond repair. However, the present subsection will show how participants in the current study manipulated the organisation of their conversations in order to recreate relevance and perform repair. The ability to effectively restructure the conversation to perform repair in CMC, as will be seen in some of the examples below, by creating the illusion of adjacency, is crucial in chat communication in particular, where different threads commonly overlap, and e-turns pertaining to a different topic regularly intervene, delaying responses and interrupting adjacency pairs, as argued in Chapter 1.

In text-based CMC, where a written record is visible, repair may occur well after the third or fourth position, aided by the ability to cut-and-paste the relevant portion of text (T1, or the 'trouble-source turn') and to highlight via a variety of linguistic and symbolic means (which appear largely uninvestigated) precisely where misunderstanding or breakdown occurred. An overview of the instances of repair identified in the corpus is given in Table 5.2.

In total, only 22 instances of repair were identified in the corpus of 370 conversations, an average of 0.06 per conversation. Furthermore, only seven pairs appeared to engage in repair at all. Two of the pairs involved the same Australian interlocutor, meaning that, in total, only five of the 12 Australian participants engaged in repair identifiable from the collected data. Assuming that all instances of repair were identified, this is far below the level observed by Shekary and Tahririan (2006), who found an average of

Table 5.2 Instances of repair identified in the corpus

Participant (N = 12)	Self-initiated self-repair	Other-initiated self-repair	Self-initiated other-repair	Other-initiated other-repair	Total
Alisha–Eri	4		2		6
Alisha–Noriko		1	2		3
Ellise–Sae			1		1
Genna–Tokio			2		2
Kaylene–Ukiko				1	1
Kaylene–Chikae			1	1	2
Lucas–Hisayo		2	3	2	7
Total	4	3	11	4	22

89.49 language-related episodes per 10,000 words in their study of eight dyads. While accurate estimates of the number of 'words' in the Japanese–English (and, on occasion, other-language) conversations presented here are difficult to arrive at for comparative purposes, it is clear that the levels of repair identified in the present study were much lower. This suggests that repair or engagement in language-related conversation, especially when other-initiated, should not be assumed as a given of CMC use. Rather, Shekary and Tahririan's participants' high levels of engagement in repair and language-related conversation appear to be a likely result of both the institutional setting, and the successful pre-treatment session applied, as previously mentioned. As Norrick (1991) notes, in everyday conversation between individuals of approximately equal status other-correction constitutes a possible face-threatening act, because it entails a judgement by one participant about a gap in the other's linguistic or cultural knowledge. Research on social bilingual conversations has found that correction between adults is not the norm, in contrast with the frequent use of repair in instructional settings such as the language classroom, or even semi-instructional settings such as a language exchange. Rather, Schegloff *et al.* (1977) state that there is a preference for self-correction and, in most forms of CMC, participants are able to revise their utterances before sending, as outlined in the previous section, and, thus, there may be no trace of this correction in the resulting output, as O'Rourke (2008) and Smith (2008) point out in the case of chat logs. In studies focusing on learners in educational environments, a number of supplementary methods of data collection, such as keystroke logs, screen-capture, eye-tracking, and video recording (in addition to the retrospective interviews conducted with participants in the present study) may be employed in order to capture participants' pre-send corrections (O'Rourke, 2008). As previously described, such methods were not deemed appropriate in the out-of-class context of the present study, where participants made use of various computers in locations as diverse as work and home, and even mobile devices. It appears safe to say, however, as Smith claims (2008: 90), 'if there are instances of self-repair that appear on the chat logs' (and I would argue this potentially extends to other types of conversations, for example, on SNS walls) 'there must be many more that are attempted, but edited out before the message is sent to the interlocutor'. Indeed, the relatively low frequency of repair uncovered in the data collected may be due to the fact that other-initiated or other-repair is often relatively uncommon in social interactions between adults, with self-initiated self-repair preferred, but not all instances of self-initiated self-repair may be reflected in the log files collected.

One interesting finding, however, is that the instances of repair that were identified were spread across a number of mediums, as demonstrated in

Table 5.3 Instances of repair according to medium

Participant (N = 12)	Self-initiated self-repair	Other-initiated self-repair	Self-initiated other-repair	Other-initiated other-repair	Total
Email		1	2	1	4
Chat	4	2	5	1	12
Mixi			2	2	4
Facebook			2		2
Total	4	3	11	4	22

Table 5.3. What is noteworthy here is the fact that repair was undertaken in both private (email, chat) and public (Mixi, Facebook) forums.

The following subsections will describe participants' attitudes and expectations in terms of repair and highlight the features of repair in situated CMC activity, particularly regarding the strategies used to initiate repair, and make the achievement of an outcome explicit where cues such as tone of voice are not available in a text-based setting. Then, specific instances of repair and resulting language learning opportunities will be discussed.

Attitudes and expectations towards repair

It has been noted that many users of monolingual informal CMC, 'are happy to send messages with no revision at all, not caring if typing errors, spelling mistakes, and other anomalies are included in their messages' (Crystal, 2006: 49). In fact, misspellings and other inconsistencies with 'standard' language are conceived of by many as a natural feature of monolingual informal CMC (Crystal, 2001a), and the same appears to be true of bilingual informal CMC, even when the participants are also engaged in formal language learning.

Oscar stated in his interview that he 'couldn't be bothered' correcting his friend and former classmate, Yoshio. Sae also said, regarding Ellise's Mixi communication, that 'there are a lot of what you would call mistakes, however, I felt that it was okay as I could understand what she meant'. Thus, it appears that negotiation of meaning, where a problem in understanding or a breakdown has occurred, was carried out when problems arose; negotiation of form, or repair without the occurrence of communicative difficulty, was usually avoided, as is also true of face-to-face speech (Ellis, 2009).

Features of repair strategies

Although repair was, on the whole, infrequent, a range of strategies were employed by participants to initiate repair, signalling an error or lack of understanding, and a repair outcome. The types of strategies coded in the present corpus are summarised in Table 5.4, each with an example.

It is apparent from Table 5.4 that participants employed a variety of strategies (linguistic, visual, and repetition, and some more sophisticated combinations) in order to achieve successful negotiation. The ability to use copy-and-paste and to explicitly quote previous text may facilitate noticing, and affords the restructuring of conversations so that after a problem-source e-turn followed by divergent e-turns turns may be restored to relevance, and repair may occur. In the subsections below, examples have been selected to demonstrate the types of repair strategies identified above, grouped according to who initiated the repair, and whose utterance was the subject of the repair.

Table 5.4 Categorisation of repair strategies

Type	Description	Examples
Linguistic	Explicit statement of error	ちがう (Alisha, chat) (wrong)
	Apology for error	ごめんなさい(Ellise, blog) (I'm sorry)
	Hesitation	あの[う](Lucas, chat) (umm)
Visual (often used with at least partial repetition)	Graphical indication of error, repair, or uncertain portion of text	← (Hisayo, wall) → (Chikae, comment) ≫ (Alisha, chat) * (Eri, chat)
Repetition	Direct repetition using copy-and-paste	わり (Alisha, chat)
	Repetition in different script	hiragana (Lucas, chat)
	Use of quotation marks	"..." 「 」 (Alisha, chat)
	Use of greater-than symbol to indicate quotation	> (Noriko, email)
	Use of symbols to replace whole repetition	~ (Alisha, chat)
Combined	Emoticon (combined with linguistic means)	>＿< (Ellise, blog) ... (Lucas, chat; Ellise, blog)
	Graphical hesitation (combined with linguistic means)	? (Alisha, chat)
	Indication of question (combined with repetition)	

Types of repair

Self-initiated self-repair

Self-initiated self-repair tended to be marked explicitly in some way. One strategy involved signalling the error with an utterance like 「ちがう」 *chigau*, 'no' or 'wrong'), or even apologising, elements both identified in spoken conversation by Schegloff (1992). In Alisha's chat with Eri, she employed self-initiated self-repair primarily for the purposes of correcting character selection. In a chat on 25 August 2008, Alisha apparently misread the characters 「漫画」 (*manga*, a comic) as the graphically and semantically similar 「映画」 (*eiga*, a movie), a reading that was plausible in the context of their discussion (about *The Rose of Versailles*, which is both the title of a *manga* series and a movie). Alisha then typed 'eiga kara?' which was converted to 「映画から」 (from a movie?), but it was not until she hit Enter that she realised her mistake, noticing the difference between the characters in her and Eri's utterances. She self-corrected, quickly sending 「ちがう」 (no) and 「漫画 から」 from a *manga*) shortly thereafter.

Extract 5.2 Example of self-initiated self-repair (character recognition)

10. erri says:

ああ、ベルサイユのばらっていう漫画の主人公だよ。

(Ah, it's the main character of a *manga* called The Rose of Versailles)
11. Alisha says:

うんん、そうだ。忙しい。

(Mmm, yeah. Busy.)
12. erri says:

そうだよね。

(That would be right.)
13. Alisha says:

映画から?   ◄────── Problem-source ⎤

(From a movie?)
14. Alisha says:

ちがう   ◄────── Initiation   ⎥ 3 e-turns, 1 turn

(No)
15. Alisha says:

漫画から   ◄──────   ⎤ Outcome
(From a manga)   ⎦

Notes: Times of messages received are not available for the conversation above due to a technical problem with Alisha's computer. However, e-turns are numbered in the order they were received.

This example clearly shows the three parts defined by Schegloff, problem-source, initiation, and outcome. Although Alisha divided these between three separate e-turns, they form a single turn, constituting an example of self-initiated self-repair in a single turn. The fact that this turn consists of three e-turns is not simply a technological artefact, however. It is only after hitting send at the end of the e-turn in line 13, creating a TRP by ending the e-turn, that Alisha realises her mistake, by looking back at Eri's original utterance in line 10 which she had misread. She then claims the floor back with a place-holding e-turn at line 14, in order to signal that she is continuing her turn. It is obvious that Alisha' s use of the three e-turns to undertake this repair is not an arbitrary splitting of a single turn into three lines, but, rather, a deliberate strategy to hold the floor at line 14 after she notices her mistake in line 13, in order to repair the error in line 15.

Later in the same conversation, Alisha apologised for some other typing mistakes. When she accidentally typed 'kanisai' instead of 'kudasai' (please), the symbols were converted to the characters 「官委細」 (bureaucrat details).

Extract 5.3 Example of self-initiated self-repair (Japanese typing error)

21. Alisha says:

その漫画について少し話して管委細。

(Talk about that *manga* bureaucratic details.)
22. erri says:

もちろん。

(Of course.)
23. Alisha says:

ごめん。〜てください。

(Sorry. 〜 please.)

At the next-turn position (line 22), Eri did not find the mistaken conversion warranting of repair, apparently understanding Alisha's request (as is evidenced through her agreement to explain the *manga*). However, Alisha initiated repair herself in the third position (line 23). Alisha apologised for the mistype and corrected herself, making use of the tilde (~) as a stand-in for the first portion of her sentence, rather than repeating the whole phrase, thus eliminating the need for her to either re-type or copy-and-paste her original utterance, while effectively highlighting the changed portion. Despite Alisha's use of the tilde to save time, it appears that she spent so long typing both the apology acknowledging her error and the correction, that Eri had the time to self-select as next speaker and began to answer Alisha's request in the meantime (line 22). Thus, in contrast with Alisha's previous repair, where she retained the floor by splitting her turn over several e-turns, here, by the time Alisha's e-turn was sent, it proved redundant to the conversation.

In addition to the use of an apology to signify a self-initiated self-repair, is the use of the asterisk (*). While the asterisk is a familiar symbol indicating ungrammaticality in linguistics and language textbooks, the asterisk has a somewhat opposite use in online communication. Rather than indicating the ungrammaticality of the following sentence, it instead indicates recognition of the ungrammaticality of the preceding sentence, and signifies that a correction follows. Research on L1 monolingual CMC suggests that the convention of using an asterisk to indicate the correction of spelling errors in particular is quite common (cf. Jacobs, 2004). In Extract 5.4, Eri can be seen using the asterisk to indicate her correction of 実は (*jitsuwa* typed 'jitsuha', the truth is) to 実話 (*jitsuwa* typed 'jitsuwa', true story), a convention that Alisha used in correcting her own English typing mistake later in the conversation.

Extract 5.4 Example of Eri's self-initiated self-repair

30. erri says:

実はもふくまれてるよ。

(It also includes the truth is.)
31. erri says:

ごめん、＊実話

(Sorry, * true story)

It should be noted that it is likely participants may have engaged in self-initiated self-repair other than the examples given above; however, in most cases, participants are able to revise their utterances before sending, as outlined previously.

Other-initiated self-repair

The next type of repair involved initiation by an other. On occasion, one participant produced a turn that, although did not contain an error, was problematic to their (NNS) interlocutor's understanding, and this was indicated in the next turn, where the NNS would initiate repair. One way in which repair in such situations was initiated was by requesting clarification. Lucas made such a request when Hisayo used the word *yabai* to describe the fact that the mobile phone she was using to chat was losing power. After receiving Hisayo's explanation, which actually describes the sense of the word (as opposed to a literal translation), Lucas signalled his understanding, and their conversation continued, drawing to a close as Hisayo's mobile phone lost power.

Extract 5.5 Other-initiated self-repair in Hisayo and Lucas' chat

6/11/2007	9:16:46 PM	Hisaa	chotto yabai!!! (uh oh!!!)
6/11/2007	9:17:34 PM	Lucas	what is yabai¿
6/11/2007	9:24:55 PM	Hisaa	it means that bad things happen suddenly!
6/11/2007	9:25:28 PM	Lucas	aaahh... wakarimashita (aaahh... understood)
6/11/2007	9:25:34 PM	Hisaa	my cellphone's battery has lost!!!!!
6/11/2007	9:26:21 PM	Hisaa	Gomen nasai... (I'm sorry...)
6/11/2007	9:26:46 PM	Lucas	uh oh
6/11/2007	9:26:54 PM	Lucas	ok then... i will talk to you later

Notes: As this conversation occurred before Lucas learned to type in Japanese, it was carried out in romanisation.

Requests for clarification occurred not only in relatively fast-paced chat communication. When Alisha encountered the unfamiliar phrase *'shooganai ne'* (inevitable, can't be helped) in an email from Noriko sent on 21 April 2007 at 1:02 AM, she asked in a post-script to her reply later that day at 11:46 PM, 'P.S What is "shooganai ne"¿' In her next email, almost a month later on 16 May 2007 at 1:48 PM, Noriko, Alisha's former tutor, provided her with not only an explanation, but an example of use. A portion of her reply is found in Extract 5.6.

Extract 5.6 Other-initiated self-repair in Alisha and Noriko's email

> P.S What is 'shooganai ne'¿

"Shooganai" means "cannot be helped" literally. So, for example...

A: Kanji wa muzukashii ne.
   (A: Characters are difficult aren't they.)
B: Un, demo benkyoo shinai to ikenai ne. quiz ga arukara ne.
   (B: Yeah, but you have to study. Because there's the quiz.)
A: Sooda ne. Shooganai ne. . .
   (A: You're right. It can't be helped. . .)

Hope this "HELPS"!

Notes: The email system used by Alisha's university was unable to handle Japanese fonts at the time of this message, so both participants used romanisation.

It is interesting to note that Noriko embedded Alisha's question in her reply, making use of a right-pointing angle bracket or 'greater-than' symbol (>). This symbol is commonly used in computing to delimit text, or, in the case of email, to designate text forwarded from the previous email (Crystal, 2004a). What is noteworthy above is the use of quoting, indicated by this symbol, to give the 'illusion of adjacency'. As previously mentioned, Herring (2003) has observed that despite the commonly disrupted turn-taking of chat in particular, the use of quoting in CMC can create the illusion of adjacency by incorporating and juxtaposing turns or portions of turns within a single message (or e-turn). This appears to be equally applicable to emails. Although almost a month passed between the problem source and the outcome, and a large number of topics intervened (relaxation, work, public transport, postal addresses, university assessment, measles, and *kabuki* theatre), Alisha and Noriko's skilful reorganisation of their communication, using textual aids to embed Noriko's problem-source turn in Alisha's repair initiation, which was then embedded in the repair by Noriko, allowed for the relevance of Alisha's repair initiation to be re-established.

Self-initiated other-repair
Occasionally, participants invited repair from their interlocutors. For example, realising that she did not know the correct characters for her former teacher's surname (which employed rather unusual characters), Ellise requested assistance. In reply to a comment Sae Nakagawa had left on her blog, Ellise greeted her former teacher by name, using the Japanese title 「先生」 (*sensei*, teacher). However, rather than risk using the incorrect characters, Ellise opted to write Nakagawa in the phonetic *katakana* script with an apology and pained expression in parentheses.

Extract 5.7 Example of self-initiated other-repair in a comment on Elli's Mixi blog

Elli 2008年01月02日 18:25

～

ナカガワ先生ありがとうございます！（ごめんなさい。。。「なかがわ」の漢字が知りません＞＿＜）来年もM大学で教えますか？

(~Thank you very much Nakagawa-*sensei*! (Sorry… I don't know the characters for '*Nakagawa*' >＿<) Will you teach at M university next year too⌣)

Sae later replied to Ellise's implicit request for help, providing her with the correct characters,「漢字は那珂川だよ。（難しい漢字でしょ？）」(The characters are 那珂川. (They are difficult characters, aren't they⌣)). It is important to note here that Sae, like many other SNS users, made use of only her first name on Mixi for privacy reasons. Thus, it was not possible for Ellise to simply copy Sae's surname from her profile or posts. However, as Sae was her former teacher, Ellise also felt it would be inappropriate to use her first name, although their relationship was now mediated primarily through the informal, first-name-basis channel of Mixi.

Other-initiated other-repair

An example of a mistype that became the subject of other-initiated other-repair (and in this case, uptake) is apparent on Kaylene's Mixi blog. Having posted a picture of herself on her blog on 21 May 2008 with her leg in a cast, Kaylene went on to describe how she had broken her ankle. However, owing to the omission of a single keystroke, rather than writing「骨折」(*kossetsu*, fracture) with a double *s*, Kaylene mistakenly typed「古拙」*kosetsu*, archaic) with a single *s*, resulting in a different character conversion. Thus, she said in one line of her blog,「自転車の事故で足首を古拙したんだ。」(I archaiced my ankle in a bicycle accident). Chikae responded to this blog with the comment extracted below, which is followed by Kaylene's response.

Extract 5.8 Example of other-initiated self-repair in the comments on Kaylene's Mixi blog

チカ 2008 年 05 月 21 日 22:11

えぇ！？骨折したの？？

(Eh!⌣ You fractured it⌣⌣)

足悪いとほんと～に不便だよね 🐌

(It's really~ inconvenient when your leg's bad, isn't it)

…

kay 2008年05月22日 01:03

>チカちゃん、

(> Chika-chan)

はい、骨折した。

(Yes, I fractured it.)

>_<;古拙って、変なタイプミスになちゃったね。ハハ！

(>_<; Archaic was a funny typo, wasn't it. Haha!)

Not only did Kaylene notice Chikae's implicit correction in her comment on 21 May 2008, select the correct form in her reply on 22 May 2008, and address Chikae's correction in her reply, but Kaylene also went back and edited her original blog to display the correct characters. In doing so, Kaylene effectively reformulated her language use for any other readers of her blog.

In another example of other-initiated other-repair, Hisayo provided Lucas with guidance in deciding how to write his name in Japanese at the beginning of his formal study. As previously depicted in Chapter 2, in Lucas' first email typed directly in Japanese script and characters, he wrote his name as 「ラーカス」 (*Rākasu*, Lacas). In her reply, Hisayo suggested he use 「ルーカス」 (*Rūkasu*, Lucas) instead, saying 'I think "*ルーカス*" is better than "*ラーカス*" (>U<)/'. After receiving her advice, Lucas used *Rūkasu*, as per her suggestion, in all of his communication with her from that point forward, adopting this spelling in his university assignments as well.

Complex repair

As mentioned above, repair does not always occur within three or four turns. Some potential causes for delay include participants not understanding their interlocutors' requests, misinterpreting their understandings, or formulating unreliable or unsatisfactory repairs. One example in which all of these issues occurred was in a chat conversation between Lucas and Hisayo, described below. Theirs is an important example, as it demonstrates that even chat users who may otherwise be deft negotiators of meaning and form may encounter difficulties. However, Swain (2006) argues that more complex negotiation sequences provide means for learners to further reflect on form, and secondly, to articulate and transform thinking into 'artifactual' form. This is in keeping with Sealey and Carter's (2004) claims that writing (and CMC) can enable the construction of texts that can lead to the contemplation of those same texts.

In their conversation on 4 April 2007, Lucas stated that he was finding learning the *katakana* script difficult. However, he did not understand

Hisayo's reply at 12:56:15 PM 「ひらがなとにてるから、かんたんにおぼえられるとおもった」 (since it's similar to the *hiragana* script, I thought you would remember it easily). This problem-source e-turn contained the most challenging language Lucas had been exposed to so far in his chat communication with Hisayo. Not only is it significantly longer than any other utterance he or Hisayo had composed so far in Japanese, but the sentence also contained the *–te* form of a verb, and the informal plain verb ending *–ta*, neither of which it appears Lucas had been exposed to before, either through his communication with Hisayo, or in his formal education.

Extract 5.9 Complex repair in Lucas and Hisayo's chat

4/04/2007	12:54:19 PM	Rukasu: pianoob	かたかなはむずかしです (*katakana* is *difficult)
4/04/2007	12:56:15 PM	Hisayo	ひらがなとにてるから、かんたんにおぼえれるとおもった (I thought katakana would be easy for you to remember because it is similar to hiragana)
4/04/2007	12:58:44 PM	Rukasu: pianoob	あのん。。。 (Umn...)
4/04/2007	12:59:28 PM	Rukasu: pianoob	hiragana to niterukara, kantan ni o he ereru to o matta (repetition of Hisayo's utterance above at 12:56:15 – should be *hiragana to niteru kara, kantan ni oboereru to omotta*)
4/04/2007	1:00:06 PM	Hisayo	yes! do you understand¿
4/04/2007	1:00:21 PM	Rukasu: pianoob	すみませがちょっと。。。 (sorry, not really...)
4/04/2007	1:01:54 PM	Hisayo	I thought it was easy to memorize katakana
4/04/2007	1:02:39 PM	Hisayo	because they are similar to hiragana!
4/04/2007	1:03:56 PM	Rukasu: pianoob	a little bit similar

Lucas signified his lack of understanding by saying 「あのん。。。」 'umn...' at 12:58:44 PM, attempting to initiate repair, but when Hisayo did not come forth with an explanation almost one minute later Lucas decided to try a different tactic, retyping her phrase out in romanisation. His repetition of Hisayo's phrase at 12:59:28 PM shows that not only did he have difficulty reading the individual segments of the *hiragana* script (e.g. mistaking *bo* for *he*), but that he also had difficulty comprehending the phrase and determining word boundaries (*oboereru*, which Lucas segmented as *o he ereru*, would normally be written as a single verb). Despite these errors, Hisayo responds excitedly, 'yes! do you understand¿', giving the impression that Lucas' romanisation is correct. In spite of Hisayo's apparent belief that they have reached an outcome, Lucas responded that he still did not understand. Eventually, six minutes (and six turns spread out over eight e-turns) after she first uttered the problem-source statement, Hisayo provided Lucas with an English translation of her sentence in two parts at 1:01:54 PM and 1:02:39 PM, a positive outcome, and their conversation continued smoothly.

It is important also to note the error at 12:54:19 PM above, where Lucas writes むずかしい (*muzukashī*, difficult) without the long *ī* sound, 「むずかし」. This had been corrected by Hisayo in an earlier conversation on 1 April 2007, when Lucas typed 「にほんごわむずかしです」 (Japanese is difficult). Importantly, this utterance contained two errors – again the missing long vowel, and, in addition, the incorrect use of the symbol わ (*wa*) instead of the particle (with the same pronunciation in this case) は (*wa*, typed as 'ha'). Hisayo corrected him 「にほんごはむずかしいです」; however, it appears that Lucas only noted the correction of the particle. Three days later, in the chat excerpted above, Lucas managed to use the particle は correctly in 「かたかなはむずかしです」 (*katakana* is difficult), but made the same spelling mistake. Later in the conversation, Lucas consistently used は correctly, yet he continued to make the same mistake with other words with a long vowel sound, like すばらしい (*subarashī*, excellent), but did not receive any further explicit correction. Despite these continued errors, this example does show Lucas' noting and uptake of Hisayo's correction of his particle use, and suggests that perhaps two corrections in the one e-turn, without appropriate visual signalling such as those strategies given in Table 5.4, was too many to take in.

A similar example occurred in Alisha and Eri's chat conversation, where Alisha did not understand the word 「わり」 (*wari*, more than a little) in Eri's line 58 utterance in Extract 5.10.

Extract 5.10 Complex repair in Alisha and Eri's chat

58. erri says:

そうだろうね、わりと演劇でやってるよ。

(That's right, it's often made into a play.)
59. Alisha says:

いっぱい

(Many)
60. Alisha says:

6

61. erri says:

多くない？

(Isn't that a lot?)
62. Alisha says:

わり？

(Often?)
63. erri says:

わり？

(Often?)
64. Alisha says:

「そうだろうね、わりと演劇でやってるよ。」のわりというはなに？

(What does often mean in 'That's right, it's often made into a play.'?)
65. erri says:

ああ、ごめん　ごめん。its like "Frequently"

(Ah, sorry sorry. It's like 'Frequently')
66. Alisha says:

You mean that it is often made into a tv drama? Or that manga are often made into tv drama?

67. erri says:

it is often made into the play.

As can be seen in the extract, after Eri's utterance in line 58, Alisha composed two e-turns related to another topic, which Eri then responded to. It was not until line 61 that Alisha attempted to initiate repair, in order to find out the meaning of 「わり」, but by this stage, after the intervening thread, Eri appeared uncertain as to the relevance of Alisha's utterance, and responded in kind, 「わり？」 in line 63. Alisha then recreated the context, copying the whole of Eri's original utterance and enclosing it in Japanese quotation marks, and encoded a more explicit reference to Eri's utterance in her reformulated question 「のわりというのはなに？」 (what does *wari* mean in-?) in line 64. Doing so allowed Alisha to reconstruct the conversation in order to give the illusion of adjacency between Eri's utterance and her question, by omitting the intervening turns on an unrelated topic.

After apologising, in line 65, rather than giving a direct translation, Eri describes the sense of *wari*, stating that it is 'like "Frequently"'. In line 66, Alisha moves on to clarify what Eri's original utterance at line 58 was actually referring to – the specific *manga* they were discussing, *Lady Oscar*, or *manga* in general. Eri answers her, stating that she was referring to *Lady Oscar*, and, in doing so, implicitly corrects Alisha's assumption that 「演劇」 (*engeki*, play) means television dramas. In this case, it took nine turns over 10 e-turns to reach the outcome, and five e-turns simply to reach the initiation stage alone, including the intervening thread.

Recasts

Although rare, some participants sought formal assistance with their CMC language use in the form of corrective feedback and peer editing on a primarily linguistic level, in addition to engaging in repair where necessary. As outlined in Chapter 1, corrective feedback such as recasts and peer editing is viewed as influential in a range of perspectives including the Interaction Hypothesis and Sociocultural Theory. Empirical research in a variety of settings by Mackey (1999), Han (2002), and McDonough and Mackey (2006), among others, have confirmed the importance of recasts for learner uptake, and the issue of feedback and editing in a computer-mediated environment within a language course has also been taken up by Matsumura and Hann (2004).

In the present study, participants appear to have invited linguistic feedback from others, which usually took the form of recasts, by commenting on their lack of proficiency and asking explicitly for correction. While the existence of such requests and the reciprocation in the form of recasts is not unusual in itself, the issue highlighted here is that all of the episodes below occurred in public forums. Facebook and Mixi were both used to give and receive such feedback, perhaps demonstrating the impact of what boyd and Heer (2006) term the 'public-yet-private' nature of SNS walls, in an SLA context. Kouper (2010) also found that advice exchange and problem solving are common types of social interaction in an online community on LiveJournal, so participants' use of public online spaces for linguistic problem solving and giving language advice may not be all that unusual.

Lucas and Hisayo were one such pair who frequently provided each other with feedback in the form of recasts on Facebook. Their requests were sometimes explicit; for example, in Hisayo's request to Lucas, 'Hi! I've been better than before!(←is that English correct?!)'. Lucas' response is given in Extract 5.11.

Extract 5.11 Lucas' recast of Hisayo's text

<u>Lucas Ma</u> wrote
at 11:26pm on November 5th, 2007

Yo Hisayo-san. 'I've been better than before!' is not wrong but I think, 'I've been better before' is used more. My English isn't very good anymore because I study Chinese and Japanese now.

Other times, a less explicit invitation was made; for example, in Lucas' request at the end of one of his wall comments, 'P.S. If there are any mistakes, please correct me. ぼくの日本語はよくない！' (My Japanese is not good!). A portion of Hisayo's reply is given given in Extract 5.12.

Extract 5.12 Hisayo's recast of Lucas' text

<u>Hisayo Maeda (Japan)</u> wrote
at 10:27am on March 5th, 2008
…
ok! i'll correct ur 日本語!
　　　　　　　　(Japanese!)
アルバイトがありますよ is more natural ですね;D
(I got a part time job is more natural isn't it; D)
きっさてんではたらきます is better(*୨(ｴ)•)ﾉ
(I work at a café is better better (*୨(ｴ)•)ﾉ)
Lucas の日本語は上手だよ!!!!!!!!!!!!!!!!!!!!!!!!
(Your Japanese is good Lucas!!!!!!!!!!!!!!!!!!!!!!!!)

A number of softening strategies are evident in each of Lucas and Hisayo's corrections. Lucas says that Hisayo's utterance 'is not wrong but I think, "I've been better before" is used more'. After making this correction, he depreciates his own English proficiency by stating 'My English isn't very good anymore.' Similarly, Hisayo uses phrases such as 'is more natural' and 'is better', making use of the sentence-final particle ね (*ne*), which indicates a request for agreement about shared knowledge, to further soften her correction, a winking smile, and a friendly bear text art, and ends by praising Lucas' Japanese. In addition to linguistic softening strategies, available in face-to-face communication, participants also have the use of emoticons and text art, like the smile and bear, at their disposal.

Finally, another example can be found in a series of comments following Kaylene's lengthy blog on Mixi about her car on 27 November 2007, which eventually turned to her Japanese ability. Ruriko praised Kaylene's Japanese in her first comment, 「kaylee日本語本当に上手！！！」 ('kaylee your Japanese is really good!!!'), a compliment which Kaylene then denied in her later reply, 「う〜うん、日本語まだまだ。日記を書くのはすごい時間かかるが、練習でよくなるかな。」 ('Uh-uh, my Japanese has a long way to go. Writing blogs takes a really long time, but maybe it will improve with practice'). Chikae responded by praising her Japanese also, 「めちゃ日本語うまくなってる〜 😄 漢字完璧ね！」 (Your Japanese has gotten really good〜 your characters are perfect!), and it is only after this further praise that Chikae gave some explicit feedback. One of her numerous corrections is given in Extract 5.13.

Extract 5.13 Chikae's recast of Kaylene's text

先日、運転していた時に、煙はエンジンから出してきた。

(Yesterday, when I was driving, smoke out of the engine.)

→煙がエンジンから出てきた。

(→ smoke came out of the engine.)

Chikae produced a large volume of recasts (a list of 10 in total) like the one above related to Kaylene's blog, using the arrow → suggesting transformation towards the corrected form to indicate repair. Although there is little evidence of softening strategies in the text of these corrections, it is important to note that like Lucas and Hisayo, Chikae made sure to employ appropriate softening strategies in her comment as a whole. She began by showing empathy to Kaylene's situation, stating how frightening the experience would have been, and then, as mentioned above, remarks how good Kaylene's Japanese has become. Her final preamble, before the lengthy list of corrections, was 「下記ちょっと私なりに直してみた。参考にしてね！」 (I tried correcting the below text to be a little more how I would write. Please refer to it!).

Such extensive use of softening strategies was not found in any more private forms of communication (such as emails or closed chat conversations) like those discussed below; however, more research would need to be performed to discover if this is a common pattern exclusive to 'public' forums such as SNS like Mixi. Future research could also further address participants' choice of such public forums as a place to give and receive feedback, as it is possible that the writer may desire the corrections that are made to be public, in order to facilitate others' reading.

Peer editing

Before he went to Japan, Jacob's online communication in Japanese was mostly with Kō and Kō's colleagues. As the content was mostly work-related,

Jacob regularly asked one of the other staff in the *manga* and cultural centre where he worked to proofread his drafts. He said that he did so because Kō and his colleagues were 'bigwigs at a university in Japan, so I want to make sure I'm presenting myself clearly'. Jacob reported that he would normally write to Kō 'in Japanese, after I'd had it checked by a native here at the centre, either Gen or Danny, who works in the general office'. Jacob stated that he would 'print it out and just get them to mark it, or, if they're near the computer screen, I'll just show it to them. They'll just highlight all my particles and change everything!' Despite saying that he was confident while composing his emails, Jacob stated seeing these changes 'shattered' him. When neither Gen nor Danny were available and a prompt reply was necessary, Jacob sometimes preferred to write in English, rather than attempt an email in Japanese on his own. He reported 'I figured they would have people who spoke English there. If it was something I could say in Japanese, I'd write in Japanese, but if it was organising things, I thought it was better if their end translated it'. In addition to making use of his daily face-to-face contacts for assistance in proofreading, Jacob also asked them questions on language use, specifically relating to any new words or phrases he had noticed in his email correspondence with Kō. For example, Jacob asked Gen about Kō's use of the word *taihen* (terribly) previously mentioned.

One pair who engaged in mutual editing and proofreading of one another's emails was Lucas and Hisayo. Extract 5.14 depicts a part of an email from Hisayo to Lucas, which Lucas subsequently pasted into a Word document, corrected, and sent back to her as an attachment.

Extract 5.14 Hisayo's email – Edited by Lucas

Hi Lucas!
Thank you for your birthday message(@・ω・@)╱ I've been(turned) 21st years (old)... I can't believe that, because it's old for me...lol And I worked on my bday. Usually, we celebrate with our family or friends. We also eat a "birthday cake". It's (the) same to(as) Australian style, isn't it⸮
I don't need to use the internet with wii⸮!⸮ じゃあ、I'll try it ♪♪
(Well)
And I'll go to US and work in a Japanese company, but I must (be able to) speak in English.:Plol
Didn't you know about my arubaito⸮ I work in/(at) a convenience store for once a week. And I've started new job that(where) I teach English to junior high school and high school students!!!
...

Lucas' changes to the email are obvious in the conventions that he has used, highlighting and strike-throughs for deletions, and text in parentheses for additions. A total of seven editing episodes can be identified in Lucas' changes to Hisayo's email text. Hisayo would also regularly edit Lucas' emails. Yet Lucas went one step further, justifying and elaborating on his changes to Hisayo's text under the heading 'EXPLANATION' included after the original email:

Extract 5.15 Lucas' explanations of corrections to Hisayo's email

Your English is a lot better than when I first met you. There are very few grammar mistakes, and they are only very small. People will still understand what you are saying, but these corrections will make it clearer and more accurate.

1. "Been" implies that you were 21 years old before your birthday yesterday. "turned" is similar to なります and we usually say somebody "turns 21 years old" when it's their 21st birthday

2. "21st" and "21 years old" are used differently. It's hard to explain, but you can use "21st" the way I used just before, where "21st" comes before a noun.

3. We usually say "_____is the same as_____". It's similar to "___は___と同じ"

4. There is nothing wrong with "but I must speak in English". I just think it sounds better the way I corrected it because when you go to USA, it implies that you will be speaking English anyway. "I must be able to speak English" fits your situation better because you are learning to English and still facing some trouble.

5. "in a convenience store" is still correct and is the same as "at a convenience store". There's nothing wrong with it, I just want you to know that you can use "at" as well.

6. "Once a week" is not a duration, so you don't use "for". Not sure but this is same as 毎週一回, yes? If you said "six hours a/per week", then you have to say "I work in/at a convenience store for 6 hours a week".

7. "that I teach" sounds awkward, so I put "where" instead. "where" is a very strange word because you usually use that the same way you use どこ, but it works in some other sentences. You might want to ask your English teacher about the word "where" and how I used it.

In this way, Lucas explained his identification of deviations to Hisayo, employing softening strategies such as beginning by complimenting her improved English, downplaying the seriousness of the deviations, and assuring Hisayo of the comprehensibility of her original message, in the preliminary paragraph. These strategies are continually employed throughout Lucas' explanations, through the use of softeners such as 'we usually'. He also suggests that Hisayo seek the guidance of an expert – her English teacher.

In Marriott's (2003) study of peer editing in academic contact situations, the variability of academic discourse style was highlighted by the fact that for the editor various alternatives were sometimes possible. The same appears to be true of more informal email discourse, as is shown in this case, where in points 4 and 5 in Extract 5.15, Lucas emphasises that there is 'nothing wrong' with Hisayo's phrasing, and that it is 'still correct', but wants to point out an alternative to her anyway. This has important implications for the form that noticing and evaluation takes, and further research is needed to determine to what extent the variability of informal Internet discourse is recognised by participants.

Hisayo's corrections to one of Lucas' emails are shown in Extract 5.16. Like Lucas, Hisayo employed a wide variety of editing functions afforded by Word, in her case, using red text (presented in bold here) to indicate changes, (including placing the word 「いらない」 (*iranai*, unnecessary) in brackets next to text that should be deleted), red wavy lines and a question mark to indicate words she was uncertain of, and boxes around portions of the text that she recommended moving or reorganising.

Extract 5.16 Lucas' email – Edited by Hisayo

中国語の試験はよかったです！まじめに勉強していた！一(いらない)百パーセントをたまった！

(My Chinese exam was good! I was studying hard! I <u>filled</u> **a (unnecessary)** one hundred percent!)

でも日本語の試験のせいせきはわかりません。

(But I do not know my result for my Japanese exam.)

Wiiはインタネットを使わなくてもいいですよ！(ˆ‿ˆ)　私もお金をためなければならないから、

(You don't have to use the Internet for Wii! (ˆ‿ˆ) I also have to save money so,)

六月に一つゲームのソフトを買うんです。このゲームは「大乱闘スマッシュブラザーズX」

(In June I will buy a video game. The game is 'Super Smash Bros Brawl'.)

です。オーストラリアにまだふうきます？、6月26日までふうきます！それは 一日 前に 私の

(It is <u>still release?</u> in Australia, <u>it will release</u> until 26th of June! That is
in one day my)

誕生日の1日前にを(いらない)ふうきますよ！ヤッター！

(birthday one day before **to (unnecessary)** <u>release</u>! Yay-!)

久代さんの「internship program」はどこへしますか？何をしますか？

(Where will you to do 'internship program'? What will you do?)

えっ？今、アルバイトがありますか？私はしりませんでした。どんなアルバイト
をしたいですか？

(Hey? Now, you have a part-time job? I didn't know. What part-time job
do you want to do?)

お金をためなくてはいけませんから、がんばってくださいね

(You have to save money, so good luck)

This case is of particular interest, as Lucas submitted the same text as part
of the email project for his coursework, and hence received feedback from two
sources: his teacher and Hisayo. Over the same stretch of text, 13 editing
episodes were identifiable in both Hisayo's and the teacher's corrections,
although they differed slightly. Despite their similarity, Lucas perceived
Hisayo's edited version of his text as containing more feedback, although he
felt that both his teacher and Hisayo made similar kinds of corrections. The
main difference between Hisayo and Lucas' teacher's corrections, however, is
that Hisayo's corrections show evidence of considering the email in the context of their overall conversation, and thus she makes corrections based not
only on linguistic accuracy, but also structure. Furthermore, Hisayo's change
to the sentence「それは私の誕生日の1日前にふうきますよ！」(It will be released
one day before my birthday!) reflects her background knowledge about Lucas.
If corrected on a purely grammatical level, the resulting sentence would imply
that the game was released on Lucas' birthday, which was one day prior. In
reality, Lucas was talking about a game due to be released the day before his
upcoming birthday, and Hisayo's change reflects her knowledge of the fact
that his birthday had not yet passed.

Although Lucas received Hisayo's corrections prior to the submission date
of his email project, he decided not to incorporate her suggestions into his
submission, as he perceived it as cheating, saying, 'I didn't want to change it,
I wanted to keep the original, so it would be fair and all ... I had a choice of
whether or not to change it, and decided not to'. However, Lucas said laugh-
ingly that after receiving the Word document containing the corrections
shown above, 'I noticed how stupid my email was'. He reported that although
he had been 'expecting heaps of mistakes', his reaction to Hisayo's feedback

was 'damn, I should have done this, I should have done that', as 'she pointed out some pretty obvious ones, or ones that sounded awkward'. Despite these reactions, at the time of our last interview Lucas was eagerly awaiting Hisayo's promised explanations of her corrections – something that he had not received from his teacher. He said that their continued peer editing partnership had evolved 'naturally'; 'she did ask in one of her emails, could you please correct my English?' Of Hisayo's response in kind, Lucas said, 'I assume because I helped her out, she's returning the favour'. When asked if Hisayo's feedback was useful, Lucas responded emphatically; 'hell yeah!' He said, 'otherwise, I'd be sitting there, not knowing I'd made all these stupid mistakes, and I'd do them again, and I'm glad she helped out … I won't make the same mistakes again, and there were ways I could phrase things better'.

While Lucas' opportunity to get feedback from both his teacher and Hisayo in this case was unusual, other participants made use of CMC to receive feedback on their class-related work also. Zac's posting of his translations online in order to obtain feedback from his blog audience in addition to the corrections given by his teacher is one such example. Alisha also asked for assistance with selecting topics for her essays and oral presentations in Japanese on her blog and in emails, as detailed earlier. It appears that there are clear benefits in having the opportunity to receive different types of feedback from a number of sources. The opportunities for language acquisition described in this chapter are summarised below.

Discussion

This chapter has examined the use of a variety of contextual resources in CMC use, both material and cultural, completing the examination of how participants of a variety of backgrounds are 'differently resourced' in various social settings and situated CMC activities. Sealey and Carter's (2004) approach states that contextual resources are differentially available to individuals on the basis of the distribution of material goods. In the present study, participants made use of a number of resources, including books, dictionaries, word processors, plugins, websites, and mobile phone applications, to facilitate their communication. The use of multiple resources was common, and online dictionaries in particular were a popular resource. Importantly, use of these resources appears to be influenced by participants' psychobiographical trajectories, the social settings in which their communication was located, and the situated activity at hand.

Participants' psychobiographical experiences and membership of various institutional groups (such as going to Japan on exchange, or undertaking a specific course at university) gave them access to different skills and knowledge about different resources. In Chapter 2, contact with NSs of Japanese was found to afford participants opportunities to learn about which CMC tools had social currency. The present chapter revealed that the effective use of certain dictionaries and other resources could be attributable to explicit instruction in a classroom setting. The social settings (in particular, domains) of various communicative activities also afforded and constrained participants' use of resources in certain ways. The social setting of SNSs like Mixi and Facebook, or blogs such as Ameba, for example, were found to provide ample opportunities for participants to draw on the contextual resource of language produced by others, making use of NSs' and other NNSs' blogs and comments as models for their own L2 use. Finally, the ways in which participants actively constructed their situated CMC activity also provided opportunities for the use of contextual resources. The use of text-based CMC was found to afford dictionary use by providing participants with relative privacy, which the social setting of face-to-face situations was found to lack. This was especially evident in Oscar's case, who was mocked for using an electronic dictionary in a face-to-face setting. Computer-based dictionaries, in particular, were found to have two distinct affordances. Firstly, ease of access, as attention need not be drawn away from the computer screen, and secondly, allowing the use of copy-and-paste from the window of interaction to and from a resource. This is particularly important for learners who are required to grapple with complex characters, as is the case for the learners of Japanese in the current study.

In terms of cultural resources, as stated in Chapter 1, Sealey and Carter (2004) describe language as pre-eminent. Indeed, participants were found to draw upon the linguistic capital of their partners as live NS 'experts' to obtain feedback, and some even engaged in peer editing. Repair was found to be quite infrequent, as may be expected in informal settings, where self-correction is preferred (Schegloff et al., 1977), but what repair did occur was afforded by a variety of linguistic, visual, repetition, and combined strategies, as identified above. Complex repair, facilitated by the specific affordances of text-based CMC was also found, in which participants co-construct repair over a large number of turns. The repair strategies identified in the present chapter were found to make the subject of repair salient even after the topic had changed, significantly aiding in undertaking delayed repair and restoring relevance in unprecedented ways. Clearly, this finding has implications reaching beyond SLA or L2 CMC alone. Some participants were also found to engage in more formal linguistic feedback, drawing on a wide repertoire of resources afforded by the computer, such as font and formatting options in order to signal corrections. The significance of these findings in relation to those of previous chapters will be discussed in the following chapter.

6   Conclusion

In contrast to previous studies which have typically focused on learner interaction in set tasks given as part of the formal language classroom curricula, the current study has examined language learners' natural interaction in social settings outside the classroom, providing valuable insight into the nature of this communication, and the benefits that can be gained from such interaction. In order to achieve this, the CMC use of 12 Australian learners of Japanese, with 18 of their Japanese contacts was analysed, coupled with data from a series of interviews with both participants. The study has examined both features of language use and opportunities for L2 use and acquisition in CMC, focusing on learners' online L2 relationships, the ways in which learners are using CMC in their L2, and how this communication presents opportunities for language acquisition.

Online Interaction with Native Speakers: Implications

At the beginning of this book, three main questions were posed. The first asked how learners establish and maintain the relationships in which they use an L2 online, the second, about the nature of learners' CMC, and the combinations in which they use CMC in their L2, and the third asked how the use of CMC and other resources may provide opportunities for SLA. These three questions have been addressed in Chapters 3, 4, and 5 respectively.

Chapters 2, 3, 4, and 5 presented the major findings of the current study, according to the domains identified in Layder's (1993) model, set out in Chapter 1. Participants' *psychobiographies* were outlined in Chapter 2, while Chapter 3, drawing on this background, focused on the *social setting* of participants' interaction. Language use in the *situated activity* of CMC was analysed in Chapter 4, which concluded with a pair of case studies examining participants' interactions from these three perspectives, considering how psychobiographies, social setting, and situated activity influence one another. Then, Chapter 5 described the rich opportunities for language acquisition in situated CMC activity by exploring the use of *contextual resources*. The present chapter will provide a synthesis of the major findings presented throughout the preceding chapters, in order to demonstrate the implications for learners, teachers, and researchers.

Participating in Domains and Virtual Communities

One of the key findings of the current study based on a consideration of the social setting of participants' CMC use is the identification of language-specific 'domains'. This finding is grounded not only in the analytical coding of the interaction data collected, but also in interviews with participants, and was particularly related to interaction spaces aimed at groups such as SNSs and websites or forums, rather than typically one-on-one interaction channels such as private email. Thus, in this respect it appears that large-scale networks or 'domains' are a macro phenomenon, although influenced and continuously sustained by micro-level interaction.

The domain in which any given interaction is perceived as being situated was found to affect participants' situated activity in terms of language choice, and use of contextual resources. A sense of being immersed in someone else's space had both positive and negative effects regarding opportunities for language acquisition, as summed up in Alisha's comments. She stated that her internet environment gave her an opportunity to be surrounded by the language, but also made her feel that she would always be a Japanese as a second language speaker. Positive effects included Alisha's sense of virtual immersion or perception of joining a 'virtual community', and greater exposure to Japanese. Lucas' browsing of wall messages and the popular culture-related activities of various participants demonstrates the access to contextual resources that virtual communities may afford. Some of the negative effects documented include those mentioned by Hyacinth in Chapter 3, such as intolerance towards other languages or ethnic groups, which made participation in one particular domain, WebKare, uncomfortable or untenable for her. However, the Australian participants were also found to create their own Japanese-specific spaces and identities via their SNS profiles, of which they had ownership, with social networking profiles constituting an important site for the ongoing construction of identities. In this way, participants exercised their agency to become the masters of their own micro-'domains', drawing on contextual resources from a variety of macro-'domains', demonstrating the influence of experiences in social settings on participants' own construction of their psychobiographies. Being an L2 learner was found to be an important identity for many participants in their online interactions, as evidenced in their foregrounding of this aspect in their profiles. Furthermore, their identification of themselves as 'foreigners' online is further evidence of their perception of domains such as Mixi as 'Japanese domains', and themselves as outsiders, a perception that challenges previous notions of the web as a placeless space.

Being a part of a 'virtual community', in particular, gaining access to an authentic audience, was the most important source of motivation for language production identified in the present study, as highlighted in Chapter 5. A sense of being heard and understood appeared to increase participants' sense of achievement, and increase the likelihood of their continued engagement in L2 use online. A feeling of pride and achievement at having composed a lengthy text in the target language was also found, and cited as important by several participants, but does not appear to be as good an indicator of future participation as receiving encouragement (either explicitly from NS or NNS peers, or in the form of comments or rewards such as *peta*). This suggests that Blood's (2002) observations with respect to the importance of an authentic audience in a monolingual first-language blog environment holds true in L2 settings also.

Entering CMC Networks and Maintaining Relationships

The present study also makes a major contribution towards an understanding of how participants become engaged in CMC use in their L2, and how their relationships are maintained online. Three main avenues for gaining access to CMC in an L2 were identified, consisting of education, international exchange, and established CMC network paths, all of which were bound to participants' psychobiographical trajectories, and the social settings, including institutions such as universities and language-related programmes, in which they participated. Key events, like in-country exchange or local immersion through groups or clubs, were found to dramatically increase participants' opportunities for contact with NSs online, and influence their patterns of use; again, demonstrating the influence of macro-level structures on micro-level interaction, and the importance of time or 'history' as the temporal dimension through which all other elements in Layder's (1993) model move. The case studies of Lucas and Kaylene presented in

Chapter 4 in particular highlight the effects of key events on participants' language and medium choice, CMC networks, and frequency of use.

One of the first ways several participants were introduced to L2 use online was found to be via their formal Japanese language education programmes, often through communication with other NNSs or their teacher. International exchange was found to be one of the key triggers for initiating relationships that were maintained mostly (if not exclusively) online after one partner returned to their home country. Exchange programmes as an organisational structure were also found to foster communication with NSs in a number of ways, including meeting people through hosting, or through going on exchange. Vitally, it was found that access to communication with one's same-age peers, often facilitated by exchange programmes, was important in participants' discovery of other forms of CMC. It has long been recognised in monolingual settings that peer pressure constitutes a driving force in the selection of CMC mediums, particularly SNSs, and this was found to be the case in L2 settings also, demonstrating the influence of interpersonal relationships in sustaining macro-level social structures. Without face-to-face contact with NS peers, it may be difficult for learners to recognise which SNSs are the most popular among their age group, or suitable for their interests. However, success in finding NSs with whom to communicate or collaborate is possible without any face-to-face contact. Seeking Japanese contacts through one's established online community was also found to be a valuable strategy for some participants, for example, Noah, who simply walked up to an avatar he saw 'speaking' Japanese in the WoW in-game environment and, eventually, was invited to join that player's Japanese guild, or Tokio, who sought Genna as an Australian friend through MySpace.

As use of the Internet increases, the current study predicts that seeking out contacts via established CMC networks will become more common. Previously, students of a foreign language who did not go on exchange appear to have had little opportunity to establish links with NS peers. The present research found that for Alisha and Jacob, who were 23 and 24 years of age at the time of the interviews, the relatively rare use of the Internet in Japan during their high school years meant that neither had the opportunity to communicate with NSs via CMC until they started university in 2003 in Australia. As reported in Chapter 5, Alisha commented 'in Japan, they didn't have Internet in houses, so most of my friends who came over to start off with didn't have email addresses, let alone the Internet'. Noah and Genna, however, although only slightly younger, at 21 and 18 years of age respectively, were already members of networks that allowed them easy access to an online Japanese community when they began Japanese study.

Alisha's comment above points to the importance of having an email address to participate in almost any form of CMC. Email addresses were found to function as a 'passport' to both the online world (for relationships that start out in face-to-face settings) and the offline world (for those that start out online). While forms of anonymous CMC do exist, all of the interaction data collected in the present study took place via mediums that require an email address for registration. In this way, email addresses were found to function as a key or passport to the rest of the online world.

Having an email address provides access to these tools, which in turn may provide access to communication with NSs online. However, for some tools, such as Mixi, additional 'keys' to participation are required, including an invitation and a Japanese mobile phone account, as documented in Chapter 3. Such requirements represent one of the ways in which interpersonal communication is constrained by the regulations of large organisations, such as the companies that run SNSs. However, conversely, the sites set up by (mostly) foreigners in Japan to facilitate the membership of those outside, or Zac's sister-in-law's subversion of the system by aiding him in setting up a Mixi account and receiving notifications to her mobile phone on his behalf, are examples of individuals exercising the power of their own agency.

Through swapping email addresses or display names in face-to-face settings, as mentioned by a number of participants, learners can maintain relationships formed face-to-face in an online setting. However, as mentioned above, relationships may progress in the opposite direction also. That is, people who meet online may then decide to meet face-to-face, and, often, this too is facilitated by email. Those who meet on an SNS may swap email addresses in a private message on the site, allowing them to engage in chat or other communication outside of the domain in which their relationship started. This allows for an external, private exchange of messages in order to organise a meeting in person, as was the case for Genna and Tokio. In both scenarios the email address or display name was found to function as a passport between an individual's online and offline persona. Giving out your email address in a face-to-face situation allows your interlocutor to not only contact you but to look you up on a variety of sites and networks, while giving your email address out on an SNS allows for the initiation of private communication via other means, and the possibility of an eventual face-to-face meeting. As Genna's case demonstrates, SNSs like MySpace may provide opportunities to gain contacts; however, some caution is warranted in communicating with previously unknown interlocutors, as was seen in the case of Hyacinth outlined in Chapter 3.

Asking questions to show interest in one's interlocutor was also reported to help maintain communication, although the pacing of questions may be important. Echoing Hanna and de Nooy's (2003) findings on French, it appears that equipping students with the ability to ask questions is crucial.

Code/Orthographic-switching and Turn-taking

The distinction between and analysis of code and orthographic switching represents another of the current study's major contributions to an understanding of bilingual language use online. This finding is of particular importance for interactions in which languages that employ two different character sets are utilised.

Code-switching was prevalent in participants' CMC use, occurring in 70% of the conversations collected for the present study. As previously mentioned, language choice was found to be influenced by the 'domain' in which interaction took place, with participants' use of English and Japanese on Facebook and Mixi corresponding with their identification of these modes as English and Japanese domains respectively. Language choice was also found to be affected by interpersonal relationships, both in terms of participants' relative status, and their respective motivations. Overall, participants' language choice and use of paralinguistic features tended to converge, suggesting that social CMC use is similar to traditional modes of social communication in terms of how interlocutors express closeness, and accommodate each others' preferred styles.

Although accounting for around only 3% of the total e-turns collected, translation was a strategy utilised by several participants, often in an attempt to avoid misunderstanding, either when one participant was unsure whether or not they had clearly expressed themselves in their L2, or when there was a risk of encoding problems which might render their Japanese unreadable on their interlocutor's computer. Translation was also used in several 'bridging blogs' (cf. Herring et al., 2007b) for the enjoyment of translation itself, in order to provide bilingual content for the purposes of reaching a wider audience, or to get feedback on translation assignments for class.

As previously mentioned, a major finding of the present study was the identification of patterns in both code and orthographic switching in CMC where languages employing different character sets are involved. The extra step of switching the input method when changing between Japanese and English was found to affect participants' structure of code-switching, in terms of where in a conversation switches took place. As Huang (2004), writing on Chinese–English communication, argues, code-switching where an orthographic switch is also required should be thought of as a conscious choice. Two types of code-switching were identified, namely inter and intra e-turn switching. In fast-paced conversations, such as those mediated by chat, inter e-turn switching appeared to be preferred, especially by NNSs of Japanese, and others unfamiliar with typing in Japanese, or using a Western keyboard. Based on this analysis, it was theorised that, when orthographic switching is employed with a code-switch, it may be easier for users to switch language between e-turns, rather than attempting to change the input method in the middle of composing an e-turn. In this manner, the technological constraints of IME use were found to affect participants' situated activity. Switching languages and orthographies during an e-turn takes time, and may render one's contribution irrelevant to the conversation if it takes too long to type. Another possible reason posed for the prevalence of code-switching at the e-turn boundary, rather than within it, was that participants often use new e-turns to signal new topics or replies to different threads, and, in some cases, these new turns may trigger a discourse-related switch in language, as was the case in Kaylene and Ruriko's conversation, where overlapping threads of conversation were maintained in two different languages simultaneously. In fact, making use of two different languages appears to have aided participants in distinguishing between concurrent threads, demonstrating that, contrary to some previous characterisations of the structure of CMC conversations, participants employ sophisticated methods of organisation.

Avoidance of code and orthographic switching was also examined. While participants appear to prefer reading *kana* and characters rather than romanised Japanese, technical constraints in some cases made this impossible. In this way, the contextual resources that participants had access to were found to greatly influence their situated CMC activity in terms of language choice or frequency of code-switching. Even when the option to use the Japanese IME was available to participants, avoidance of orthographic switching appears common, particularly in the case of brief borrowings or tag-switching, because, as Genna explained, it is faster to continue typing in English letters. Thus, technology-related factors were also found to influence switching choices, in addition to personal and discourse-related factors.

Providing students with explicit instruction on the different ways to switch orthographies and opportunities to practice typing in the target language appear important in order for learners to feel comfortable in switching between languages. While accuracy is often emphasised in formal educational environments and assessment, typing speed appears crucial in fast-paced CMC.

Acquisition Opportunities in CMC

CMC was found to provide not only chances for language use, but also rich opportunities for language acquisition through the use of a variety of contextual resources, and participation in authentic situated communication. Gaining an audience, accessing real-world materials, and the chance to apply classroom learning in an authentic communicative situation were some of the main benefits of CMC identified that aid in broadening opportunities for language use.

The unprecedented access to candid communication between NS peers that online communication affords was one of the major findings of the current study. Applying boyd and Heer's (2006) concept of 'public yet private' to the L2 realm, evidence of L2 use and acquisition on the basis of models from their NS contacts was uncovered in Chapter 5. In addition to the use of NS peers' communication as a model, a range of other contextual resources were identified.

A number of resources, including books, websites, plugins and mobile phone applications, that participants used to facilitate their communication, were identified and categorised in Chapter 5. Evidence of participants retaining knowledge in the form of vocabulary looked up in the context of an online conversation was also presented. On average, the Australian participants used 2.33 resources each, suggesting that use of multiple resources is not at all uncommon. Online dictionaries were the most commonly used.

Computer-based dictionaries, including online dictionaries, were found to have two distinct advantages over their non-computer-based electronic and printed counterparts. First is the ease with which one can access the resource, as attention need not be switched from the computer screen to a separate object. Moreover, there is also the ability to copy-and-paste from the window in which an interaction is taking place to a dictionary, translator, or glossary, and vice versa, which means a reduction in the possibility of errors, and greater ease in the reading of languages such as Japanese that employ many complex characters. Online resources constitute a very important facility to allow learners to read characters with previously unprecedented ease, facilitating the use of authentic materials much earlier than conventionally thought possible. Such resources have truly revolutionised the learning and use of Japanese as an L2, and are deserving of further scholarly attention. This is especially true given the influence that formal instruction was shown to have on students' out-of-classroom resource selection and use in Chapter 5. This influence in part answers Sealey and Carter's (2004: 197) question of how people are 'differently resourced', demonstrating that educational institutions can equip students with the necessary tools to participate more fully in the situated activity of CMC interaction.

One other important resource was the interlocutor as a live NS 'expert' on the language in question. Participants were found to make use of their partners to ask questions about cultural matters and aspects of language use, and some engaged in formal tutor/tutee relationships, providing support and encouragement, or even peer editing and feedback activities, correcting drafts and providing explanations.

Repair was found to be quite infrequent, in contrast with previous studies conducted in other (formal educational) contexts, but spread across a range of public and private mediums. Linguistic, visual, repetition, and combined types of strategies to explicitly signal repair in electronic discourse were identified. Furthermore, a kind of complex repair was also identified, in which participants co-construct repair after the fourth position. While repair normally occurs within three to four turns in oral language, where cognitive memory is limited and unaided by a written record, the repair strategies identified in Chapter 5 were found to make the subject of repair salient even after the topic had changed, and significantly aid in undertaking repair later in the conversation. This finding has important implications for our understanding of CMC in general.

Some participants were also found to engage in more formal types of linguistic feedback and editing, for primarily language learning (as opposed to communicative) purposes. Like repair strategies, both the Australian and Japanese participants who engaged in peer editing and feedback were found to develop and draw on a wide repertoire of editing strategies, explored in Chapter 5.

Thus, participation in bilingual or L2 CMC and engagement in reading, watching, or listening to authentic materials in L2 domains and virtual communities were found to lead to numerous opportunities for language acquisition, facilitated by a number of different kinds of resources, including reference material, one's interlocutor, and past and present interactions.

The importance of 'lurking' behaviours, including reading, listening, and writing, for providing opportunities for language acquisition and cultural learning was also highlighted in Chapter 3. Engagement in 'lurking' activities may be linked to a participant's psychobiography, as was evidenced in the case of Hyacinth. Participants may choose to engage in such activities because of negative experiences in L2 domains, such as those described on WebKare above, or because of insecurities about their L2 competency. However, 'lurking' still provides numerous opportunities for development, and even seemingly 'passive' activities, such as online shopping, were found to involve sophisticated strategies for the consumption and processing of L2 data.

A Relational View of L2 CMC Use

The analyses over the previous four chapters of the four domains identified by Layder (1993) demonstrate the ways in which they are interconnected. As Layder states, history is the temporal dimension which flows through all four domains, and, in the present study, patterns of socialisation into language learning, CMC use, and use of the L2 were identified which straddle all four domains. Taking a top-down macro to micro view, access to contextual resources in the form of knowledge about dictionaries and retrieval of language models was found to influence the social settings in which participants took part, by facilitating greater access to particular L2 'domains' for NNSs. These social settings, in turn, were found to influence situated activity in CMC, with language choice, access to NSs, and other factors in individual social activity affected by the linguistic or cultural 'domain' in which it took place. This situated activity was then found to influence the self, as participants consciously maintained and adjusted their online identities and amassed a variety of different experiences.

The interconnectedness of these four domains was found to flow in the opposite direction, from the bottom up, micro to macro, also. The self, in terms of participants' interests and experiences, developed over time, and their individual power, in the form of agency, was found to affect the situated activities in which they engaged. Participants maintained contact with those who shared similar interests and were members of the same groups. They found a number of ways to construct their online identities, often depicting themselves as NNSs, experts in English, and interested in Japanese culture. This kind of online identity projection may affect the kinds of interlocutors users are likely to attract and, thus, the situated activities in which they are likely to engage. Experiences such as going on exchange or joining a conversation group were also clearly linked to an increase in NS contacts and exposure to new forms of CMC, thus furthering participants' opportunities to expand their L2 networks online and take part in L2 'domains'. Interests in specific cultural items, such as books or games, were also found to create diverse opportunities for increasing one's network and opportunities to utilise the target language. In turn, the situated activity of CMC also affected the use of contextual resources, with participants finding the freedom to draw on a variety of different resources behind the relative privacy of the computer screen. Participants were found to be resourced differently, on the basis of information provided by educational organisations and access to linguistic models provided by websites, SNSs, and other forums which archive and make publically available user messages.

Theoretical and Methodological Implications

This book has also developed several important innovations for the analysis of electronic discourse more generally, including the establishment of three levels of analysis, and the application and expansion of a social realist approach to explain the dynamic nature of electronic discourse.

The complex structure of CMC

The present study made use of three levels of units of analysis, namely the e-turn at the micro-level, turn at the meso-level, and conversation at the macro-level. The use of the e-turn as the most basic unit of analysis was instrumental in the identification of inter- and intra- e-turn code-switching, as defined in Chapter 4. The analysis of repair moves identified by Schegloff (1992) in an online setting was also considerably facilitated by the use of the e-turn as a unit of analysis. Yet while Thorne's (1999) 'e-turn' functions well as a clear-cut minimal unit, it was found to be insufficient as a unit of analysis to investigate turn management. E-turns which relate to one another are not necessarily adjacent, as e-turns relating to other conversational strands or threads may intervene. Thus, Tudini's (2003) definition of 'turn' was made use of as a second level of analysis. As in oral conversation, where overlap, false starts, hesitations, interruptions, and minimal responses which do not constitute turn occur, a turn in CMC is not as precisely delimited as the e-turn. Because adjacency pairs may be interrupted and topic threads intertwined, it is necessary to closely examine the various management strategies identified in Chapters 4 and 5 that participants make use of in order to organise e-turns into turns. Finally, the term 'conversation' was proposed for use as a top-level unit of analysis, to refer not only to the more conventional chat and VoIP conversations, but also to conversations via email, SNSs, and so on. Six criteria for the identification of a conversation are outlined in Chapter 4. The addition of this third tier allows the researcher to investigate not only the individuals' turn management and construction, but how participants work together to co-construct conversation. Thus, the introduction of the conversation as a level of analysis complements the identification of turns and e-turns in

CMC, as pioneered by Thorne (1999) and Tudini (2003), and completes the model for the analysis of CMC outlined in the current volume. This model presents a much more sophisticated view of CMC use, which was earlier characterised by researchers and the public alike as haphazard and unstructured (as documented by Crystal, 2006, 2011).

The emergent nature of CMC

Finally, it has been argued throughout this book that electronic discourse should be viewed as emergent from speaking, writing, human behaviour, and the influence of technology, in harmony with the social realist approach. Such a model allows for more flexible conceptualisations of online language, based on actual use rather than considering interaction as 'spoken-like' or 'written-like' on the basis of the medium it occurred through alone. The previous chapters demonstrated a need for such a model given that participants' descriptions of their own use was often at odds with traditional categorisations of CMC, such as Genna referring to her emailing as 'chatting' (despite its usual characterisation as 'written'), and Noah's use of Mixi in a 'synchronous' fashion (despite it falling into the conventional 'asynchronous' category). Furthermore, individual interactions, or even different segments of an interaction, can vary as to their 'spoken-like' or 'written-like' nature, and 'synchronous' or 'asynchronous' qualities, which none of the previous models, explored in Chapter 4, readily account for. The view of CMC use proposed in this volume avoids the reductionism necessarily involved when claiming that a certain medium 'is' synchronous or asynchronous, spoken or written. Thus, by defining units of analysis for the investigation of CMC, and developing the social realist approach to explain more fully the dynamic nature of electronic discourse, this volume offers a blueprint for future research on naturalistic CMC in a variety of settings.

References

Agar, M.H. (1996) *The Professional Stranger*. London: Academic Press.

Aitsiselmi, F. (1999) Second language acquisition through email interaction. *ReCALL* 11 (2), 4–11.

Androutsopoulos, J. (2006a) Introduction: Sociolinguistics and computer-mediated communication. *Journal of Sociolinguistics* 10 (4), 419–438.

Androutsopoulos, J. (2006b) Multilingualism, diaspora, and the internet: Codes and identities on German-based diaspora websites. *Journal of Sociolinguistics* 10 (4), 520–547.

Androutsopoulos, J. (2008) Potentials and limitations of discourse-centred online ethnography. *Language@Internet* 5. Online at http://www.languageatinternet.de

Androutsopoulos, J. and Beißwenger, M. (2008) Introduction: Data and methods in computer-mediated discourse analysis. *Language@Internet* 5. Online at http://www.languageatinternet.de/articles/2008/1609

Antaki, C., Ardévol, E., Núñez, F. and Vayreda, A. (2005) 'For she who knows who she is': Managing accountability in online forum messages. *Journal of Computer-Mediated Communication* 11 (1), Article 6. Online at http://jcmc.indiana.edu/vol11/issue1/antaki.html

Archer, M. (2000) *Being Human: The Problem of Agency*. Cambridge: Cambridge University Press.

Atkinson, P., Coffey, A. and Delamont, S. (2003) *Key Themes in Qualitative Research*. Oxford: AltaMira Press.

Auer, P. (1984) *Bilingual Conversation*. Amsterdam: Benjamins.

Auer, P. (1995) The pragmatics of code-switching: A sequential approach. In L. Milroy and P. Muysken (eds) *One Speaker, Two Languages: Cross-disciplinary Perspectives on Code-switching* (pp. 115–135). Cambridge: Cambridge University Press.

Auer, P. (1998) Introduction: Bilingual conversation revisited. In P. Auer (ed.) *Code-switching in Conversation: Language, Interaction and Identity*. London: Routledge.

Babbie, E. (2004) *The Practice of Social Research* (10th edn). Belmont, CA: Thomson/Wadsworth Publishing.

Baralt, M. (2008) Lexical acquisition, awareness, and self-assessment through computer-mediated interaction: The effects of modality and dyad type. Paper presented at the Towards Adaptive CALL: Natural Language Processing for Diagnostic Language Assessment, 21–22 September. Iowa State University.

Baron, N.S. (1998) Letters by phone or speech by other means: The linguistics of email. *Language & Communication* 18 (2), 133–170.

Baron, N.S. (2000) *Alphabet to Email: How Written English Evolved and Where It's Heading.* London: Routledge.

Baron, N.S. (2001) Why email looks like speech: Proofreading, pedagogy, and public face. In J. Aitchison and D. Lewis (eds) *New Media Language* (pp. 102–113). London: Routledge.

Baron, N.S. (2004) See you online: Gender issues in college student use of instant messaging. *Journal of Language and Social Psychology* 23, 397–423.

Basharina, O.K. (2007) An activity theory perspective on student-reported contradictions in intercultural telecollaboration. *Language Learning & Technology* 11 (2), 83–103.

Bazeley, P. (2007) *Qualitative Data Analysis with NVivo.* Los Angeles: Sage Publications.

Beauvois, M.H. (1998) E-talk: Computer-assisted classroom discussion – Attitudes and motivation. In J. Swaffar, S. Romano, P. Markley and K. Arens (eds) *Language Learning Online: Towards Best Practice* (pp. 99 –120). Austin, TX: Labyrinth Publications, The Daedalus Group Inc.

Beißwenger, M. (2008) Situated chat analysis as a window to the user's perspective: Aspects of temporal and sequential organization. *Language@Internet* 5. Online at http://www.languageatinternet.de/articles/2008/1532/beiss.pdf/

Belz, J.A. (2002) Social dimensions of telecollaborative foreign language study. *Language Learning & Technology* 6 (1), 60–81.

Belz, J.A. (2003) Linguistic perspectives on the development of intercultural competence in telecollaboration. *Language Learning & Technology* 7 (2), 68–99.

Belz, J.A. (2004) Telecollaborative language study: A personal overview of praxis and research. Paper presented at the National Foreign Language Resource Centre Symposium: Distance Education, Distributed Learning, and Language Instruction, 27–30 July, Honolulu. Online at http://nflrc.hawaii.edu/NetWorks/NW44/index.htm

Belz, J.A. and Müller-Hartmann, A. (2003) Teachers as intercultural learners: Negotiating German–American telecollaboration along the institutional fault line. *The Modern Language Journal* 87 (i), 71–89.

Belz, J.A. and Reinhardt, J. (2004) Aspects of advanced foreign language proficiency: Internet-mediated German language play. *International Journal of Applied Linguistics* 14 (3), 324–362.

Bertacco, M. and Deponte, A. (2005) Email as a speed-facilitating device: A contribution to the reduced-cues perspective on communication. *Journal of Computer-Mediated Communication* 10 (3), Article 2. Online at http://jcmc.indiana.edu/vol10/issue3/bertacco.html

Biesenbach-Lucas, S., Meloni, C. and Waesenforth, D. (2000) Use of cohesive features in ESL students' email and word-processed texts: A comparative study. *Computer Assisted Language Learning* 13 (3), 221–237.

Biesenbach-Lucas, S. and Waesenforth, D. (2001) E-mail and word processing in the ESL classroom: How the medium affects the message. *Language Learning & Technology* 5 (1), 135–165.

Blizzard Entertainment. (2008) World of Warcraft Armory, accessed 13 March 2009. http://www.wowarmory.com/

Block, D. (1995) Social constraints on interviews. *Prospect* 10 (3), 35–48.

Blood, R. (2002) *The Weblog Handbook: Practical Advice On Creating And Maintaining Your BLOG.* Cambridge: Perseus Publishing.

Boissevain, J. (1974) *Friends of Friends.* Oxford: Basil Blackwell.

Bordia, P. (1997) Face-to-face versus computer-mediated communication: A synthesis of the experimental literature. *The Journal of Business Communication* 34 (1), 99–120.

boyd, D.M. (2007a) We googled you: Should Fred hire Mimi despite her online history? *Harvard Business Review* June. Online at http://www.danah.org/papers/HBRJune2007.html

boyd, D.M. (2007b) Why youth (heart) social network sites: The role of networked publics in teenage social life. In D. Buckingham (ed.) *Youth, Identity, and Digital Media* (pp. 119–142). Cambridge, MA: MIT Press.

boyd, D.M. and Ellison, N.B. (2007) Social network sites: Definition, history, and scholarship. *Journal of Computer-Mediated Communication* 13 (1). Online at http://jcmc.indiana.edu/vol13/issue1/boyd.ellison.html

boyd, D.M. and Heer, J. (2006) Profiles as conversation: Networked identity performance on Friendster. Paper presented at the Proceedings of the Hawai'i International Conference on System Sciences (HICSS-39), 4–7 January, Kauai, HI.

Brock, A. (2005) 'A belief in humanity is a belief in colored men': Using culture to span the digital divide. *Journal of Computer-Mediated Communication* 11 (1), Article 17.

Brown, J.D. and Rodgers, T.S. (2002) *Doing Second Language Research*. New York: Oxford University Press.

Burkhalter, B. (1999) Reading race online: Discovering racial identity in Usenet discussions. In M. Smith and P. Kollock (eds) *Communities in Cyberspace* (pp. 60–75). London: Routledge.

Callot, M. and Belmore, N. (1996) Electronic language: A new variety of English. In S.C. Herring (ed.) *Computer-mediated Communication: Linguistic, Social and Cross-cultural Perspective* (pp. 129–146). Amsterdam: John Benjamins.

Canale, M. and Swain, M. (1980) *Approaches to Communicative Competence*. Singapore: SEAMEO Regional Language Centre.

Carooso, J. (2004) Are you 133t? One-time hacker slang now ridiculed by all except those who use it. *Network World*, 17 May, 76.

Carter, B. and Sealey, A. (2000) Language, structure, and agency: What can realist social theory offer to sociolinguistics? *Journal of Sociolinguistics* 4 (1), 3–20.

Carter, B. and Sealey, A. (2004) Researching 'real' language. In B. Carter and C. New (eds) *Making Realism Work: Realist Social Theory and Empirical Research* (pp. 100–120). Milton Park: Routledge.

Carter, B. and Sealey, A. (2009) Reflexivity, realism and the process of casing. In D. Byrne and C.C. Ragin (eds) *The SAGE Handbook of Case-based Methods* (pp. 69–83). London: SAGE Publications.

Caruso, J.B. and Kvavik, R.B. (2005) ECAR study of students and information technology, 2005: Convenience, connection, control, and learning, accessed 2 June 2009. http://www.educause.edu/content.asp?PAGE_ID=8964&bhcp=1

Cassell, J. and Tversky, D. (2005) The language of online intercultural community formation. *Journal of Computer-Mediated Communication* 10 (2), Article 2. Online at http://jcmc.indiana.edu/vol10/issue2/cassell.html

Chapelle, C. (1998) Multimedia CALL: Lessons to be learned from research on instructed SLA. *Language Learning & Technology* 2 (1), 21–39.

Chapelle, C. (2003) *English Language Learning and Technology: Lectures on Applied Linguistics in the Age of Information and Communication Technology*. Amsterdam: John Benjamins.

Cherney, L. (1995) The MUD register: Conversational modes of action in a text-based virtual reality. Unpublished PhD Thesis, Stanford University.

Chun, D. (1998) Using computer-assisted class discussion to facilitate the acquisition of interactive competence. In J. Swaffar, S. Romano, P. Markley and K. Arens (eds) *Language Learning Online: Towards Best Practice* (pp. 57–80). Austin, TX: Labyrinth Publications, The Daedalus Group Inc.

Chung, Y.G., Graves, B., Wesche, M. and Barfurth, M. (2006) Computer-mediated communication in Korean–English chat rooms: Tandem learning in an international languages program. *The Canadian Modern Language Review/La Revue canadienne des langues vivantes* 62 (1), 49–86.

Condon, S.L. and Cech, C.G. (1996) Discourse management strategies in face-to-face and computer-mediated decision making interactions. *The Electronic Journal of Communication/La Revue Electronique de Communication* 6 (3). Online at http://www.cios.org/EJCPUBLIC/006/3/006314.HTML

Coniam, D. and Wong, R. (2004) Internet relay chat as a tool in the autonomous development of ESL learners' English language ability: An exploratory study. *System* 32 (3), 321–335.

Corbin, J. and Strauss, A.L. (2008) *Basics of Qualitative Analysis* (3rd edn). Los Angeles, CA: Sage.

Corneliussen, H.G. and Walker Rettberg, J. (2008) Introduction: 'Orc Professor LFG', or researching in Azeroth. In H.G. Corneliussen and J. Walker Rettberg (eds) *Digital Culture, Play, and Identity: A World of Warcraft® Reader* (pp. 1–16). Cambridge, MA: MIT Press.

Coulthard, M. (1985) *An Introduction to Discourse Analysis*. Essex: Longman.

Crook, C. and Light, P. (2002) Virtual society and the cultural practice of study. In S. Woolgar (ed.) *Virtual Society? Get Real! Technology, Cyberbole, Reality* (pp. 153–175). Oxford: Oxford University Press.

Crystal, D. (2001a) Forum: A linguistic revolution? *Education, Communication & Information* 1 (2), 93–97.

Crystal, D. (2001b) *Language and the Internet*. Cambridge: Cambridge University Press.

Crystal, D. (2004a) *A Glossary of Netspeak and Textspeak*. Edinburgh: Edinburgh University Press.

Crystal, D. (2004b) *The Language Revolution*. Cambridge: Polity Press.

Crystal, D. (2006) *Language and the Internet* (2nd edn). Cambridge: Cambridge University Press.

Crystal, D. (2011) *Internet Linguistics: A Student Guide*. London: Routledge.

Danet, B. and Herring, S.C. (2007) Introduction. In *The Multilingual Internet: Language, Culture, and Communication Online* (pp. 1–39). Oxford: Oxford University Press.

Darhower, M. (2002) Interactional features of synchronous computer-mediated communication in the intermediate L2 class: A sociocultural case study. *CALICO Journal* 19 (2), 249–277.

Davies, A. (2005) Book review: Alison Sealey and Bob Carter. *Applied linguistics as a social science. Journal of Sociolinguistics* 9 (2), 300–303.

de Bakker, G., Sloep, P. and Jochems, W. (2007) Students and instant messaging: A survey of current use and demands for higher education. *ALT-J Research in Learning Technology* 15 (2), 143–153.

de la Fuente, M.J. (2003) Is SLA interactionist theory relevant to CALL? A study on the effects of computer-mediated interaction in L2 vocabulary acquisition. *Computer Assisted Language Learning* 16 (1), 47–81.

de Nooy, J. and Hanna, B.E. (2009) *Learning Language and Culture via Public Internet Discussion Forums*. New York: Palgrave Macmillian.

December, J. (1993) Characteristics of oral culture in discourse on the net. Paper presented at the Twelfth Annual Penn State Conference on Rhetoric and Composition, 8 July, Pennsylvania. Online at http://www.december.com/john/papers/pscrc93.txt

Dias, J. (2007) Networking . . . netplaying: From a New York minute to a Mixi second. *The JALT CALL Journal* 3 (3), 124.

Dimmick, J., Kline, S. and Stafford, L. (2000) The gratification niches of personal e-mail and the telephone. *Communication Research* 27 (2), 227–249.

Donath, J. and Boyd, D.M. (2004) Public displays of connection. *BT Technology Journal* 22 (4), 71–82.

Dörnyei, Z. (2007) Qualitative data collection. In Z. Dörnyei (ed.) *Research Methods in Applied Linguistics* (pp. 101–124). Oxford: Oxford University Press.

Dowdall, C. (2006) Dissonance between the digitally created words of school and home. *Literacy* 40 (3), 153–163.

Drezner, D.W. and Farrell, H. (2004) Web of influence. Online at http://www.foreign-policy.com

du Bartell, D. (1995) Discourse features of computer-mediated communication: 'Spoken-like' and 'written-like'. In B. Warvik, S.K. Tanskanen and R. Hiltunen (eds) *Organization in Discourse* (pp. 231–241). Turku: University of Turku.

du Bois, J.W. (1991) Transcription design principles for spoken language research. *Pragmatics* 1, 71–106.

Dürscheid, C. (2004) Netzsprache – ein neuer Mythos. *Internetbasierte Kommunikation Special Issue of Osnabrücker Beiträe zur Sprachtheorie* 68, 141–157.

Dwyer, C. (2007) Digital relationships in the 'Myspace' generation: Results from a qualitative study. Paper presented at the Fortieth Hawaii International Conference on System Sciences, 3–6 January. Los Alamitos, CA.

Ellis, R. (1999) *Learning a Second Language through Interaction*. Amsterdam: John Benjamins.

Ellis, R. (2007) Developments in SLA research. Paper presented at the AAAL Conference – Language Learning Celebrates 30 years of AAAL, 21–24 April, Costa Mesa, California. Online at http://www.aaal.org/download/ellis.pdf

Ellis, R. (2009) *The Study of Second Language Acquisition* (2nd edn). Oxford: Oxford University Press.

Ellison, N.B., Steinfield, C. and Lampe, C. (2007) The benefits of Facebook 'friends': Social capital and college students' use of online social network sites. *Journal of Computer-Mediated Communication* 12 (4), Article 1. Online at http://jcmc.indiana.edu/vol12/issue4/ellison.html

ETS. (2011) Benchmark your score. Online at http://www.ea.toeic.eu/toeic/ea/benchmark-your-score/

Faiola, A. and Matei, S.A. (2005) Cultural cognitive style and web design: Beyond a behavioral inquiry into computer-mediated communication. *Journal of Computer-Mediated Communication* 11 (1), Article 18. Retrieved from http://jcmc.indiana.edu/vol11/issue1/faiola.html

Fan, S.K. (2002) フォローアップ・インタビュー [Follow-up interview]. In J.V. Neustupny and S. Miyazaki (eds) 言語研究の方法 *[Techniques for Language Research]* (pp. 87–95). Tōkyō: Kuroshio Shuppan.

Ferrara, K., Bruner, H. and Whittemore, G. (1991) Interactive written discourse as an emergent register. *Written Communication* 8 (1), 8–34.

Firth, A. and Wagner, J. (1997) On discourse, communication, and (some) fundamental concepts in SLA research. *The Modern Language Journal* 81 (iii), 285–300.

Florez-Estrada, N. (1995) Some effects of native–non-native communication via computer email interaction on the development of foreign writing proficiency. Unpublished PhD Thesis, University of Pittsburgh.

Foster, P. and Ohta, A.S. (2005) Negotiation for meaning and peer assistance in second language classrooms. *Applied Linguistics* 26, 402–430.

Foster, P. and Skehan, P. (1996) The influence of planning on performance in task-based learning. *Studies in Second Language Acquisition* 18 (3), 299–324.

Freiermuth, M.R. and Jarrel, D. (2006) Willingness to communicate: Can online chat help? *International Journal of Applied Linguistics* 16 (2), 189–212.

Gass, S.M. and Mackey, A. (2000) *Stimulated Recall Methodology in Second Language Research*. Mahwah, NJ: Lawrence Erlbaum Associates.

Gee, J.P. (2000) Identity as an analytic lens for research in education. *Review of Research in Education* 25, 99–125.

Georgakopoulou, A. and Goutsos, D. (2004) *Discourse Analysis – An Introduction* (2nd edn). Edinburgh: Edinburgh University Press.

Giles, H., Coupland, N. and Coupland, J. (1991) Accommodation theory: Communication, context and consequence. In H. Giles, J. Coupland and N. Coupland (eds) *Contexts of Accommodation: Developments in Applied Sociolinguistics* (pp. 1–68). Cambridge: Cambridge University Press.

Gilmore, A. (2004) A comparison of textbook and authentic interactions. *ELT Journal* 58 (4), 363–374.

Glaser, B.G. and Strauss, A.L. (1967) *The Discovery of Grounded Theory: Strategies for Qualitative Research*. New York: Aldine.

Goody, J. (1986) *The Logic of Writing and the Organization of Society*. Cambridge: Cambridge University Press.

Gottlieb, N. (1993) Written Japanese and the word processor. *Japan Forum* 5 (1), 115–131.

Gray, R. and Stockwell, G. (1998) Using computer-mediated communication for language and culture acquisition. *On-CALL* 12 (3), 2–9.

Greenfield, P.M. and Subrahmanyam, K. (2003) Online discourse in a teen chatroom: New codes and new modes of coherence in a visual medium. *Applied Developmental Psychology* 24, 713–738.

Greenwood, J.D. (1994) *Realism, Identity and Emotion: Reclaiming Social Psychology*. London: Sage.

Grice, H.P. (1975) Logic and conversation. In P. Cole and J. Morgan (eds) *Speech Act: Syntax and Semantics* (Vol. 3, pp. 41–48). New York: Academic Press.

Grinter, R.E. and Palen, L. (2002) Instant messaging in teen life. Paper presented at the CSCW'02, 16–20 November, New Orleans, LA, USA.

Hacking, I. (1997) Taking bad arguments seriously. *London Review of Books* 19 (16), 14–16.

Hada, T. (2006) ギャル文字を読めますか?[Can you read 'gyaru-moji'?]. 言語 *[Language]* 35 (3), 68–69.

Hale, C. and Scanlon, J. (1999) *Wired Style: Principles of English Usage in the Digital Age*. New York: Broadway Books.

Halliday, M.A.K. (1978) *Language as Social Semiotic*. London: Edward Arnold.

Halliday, M.A.K. (1989) *Spoken and Written Language*. Oxford: Oxford University Press.

Han, Z. (2002) A study of the impact of recasts on tense consistency in L2 output. *TESOL Quarterly* 36, 543–572.

Handel, M. and Herbsleb, J.D. (2002) What is chat doing in the workplace? Paper presented at the CSCW'02, 16–20 November, New Orleans, LA, USA.

Hanna, B.E. and de Nooy, J. (2003) A funny thing happened on the way to the forum: Electronic discussion and foreign language learning. *Language Learning & Technology* 7 (1), 71–85.

Hargittai, E. (2007) Whose space? Differences among users and non-users of social network sites. *Journal of Computer-Mediated Communication* 13 (1), Article 14. Online at http://jcmc.indiana.edu/vol13/issue1/hargittai.html

Hashimoto, T. (2006) Factors that affect negotiation of meaning in computer-mediated language learning. Unpublished Masters Thesis, Melbourne University.

Hashimoto, Y. (2001) ケイタイメールの利用実態と使われ方－インターネットによるEメール利用との比較を中心に－[Cell phone usage rates and uses – A focus on comparing email use using the internet]. 日本語学 *[Japanese Linguistics]* 20 (9), 23–31.

Herbsleb, J.D., Atkins, D.L., Boyer, D.G., Handel, M. and Finholt, T.A. (2002) Introducing instant messaging and chat in the workplace. Paper presented at the CHI 2002, 20–25 April, Minneapolis, MN, USA.

Herring, S.C. (1996a) Posting in a different voice: Gender and ethics in computer-mediated communication. In C. Ess (ed.) *Philosophical Perspectives on Computer-mediated Communication* (pp. 115–145). Albany: SUNY Press.

Herring, S.C. (ed.) (1996b) *Computer-mediated Communication: Linguistic, Social and Cross-cultural Perspectives. Pragmatics and Beyond.* Philadelphia, PA: Benjamins.

Herring, S.C. (1999) Interactional coherence in CMC. Paper presented at the Proceedings of the 32nd Hawai'i International Conference on System Sciences (HICSS-32), 5–8 January, Hawaii.

Herring, S.C. (2003) Computer-mediated discourse. In D. Tannen, D. Schiffin and H. Hamilton (eds) *Handbook of Discourse Analysis* (pp. 612–634). Oxford: Blackwell.

Herring, S.C. (2004) Computer-mediated discourse analysis: An approach to researching online behavior. In S.A. Barab, R. Kling and J. Gray (eds) *Designing for Virtual Communities in the Service of Learning* (pp. 338–376). Cambridge: Cambridge University Press.

Herring, S.C., Scheidt, L.A., Kouper, I. and Wright, E. (2007a) Longitudinal content analysis of blogs: 2003–2004. In M. Tremayne (ed.) *Blogging, Citizenship, and the Future of Media* (pp. 3–20). London: Routledge.

Herring, S.C., Paolillo, J.C., Ramos-Veilba, I., Kouper, I., Wright, E., Stoerger, S., Scheidt, L.A. and Clark, B. (2007b) Language networks on LiveJournal. Paper presented at the Fortieth Hawaii Conference on System Sciences, 3–6 January, Los Alamitos.

Hewling, A. (2005) Culture in the online class: Using message analysis to look beyond nationality-based frames of reference. *Journal of Computer-Mediated Communication* 11 (1), Article 16.

Huang, L-j.D. (2004) Code-switching and language use in emails: A case study of a network of Chinese-English bilinguals in Taiwan. Unpublished PhD Thesis, University of Melbourne.

Inagaki, A. (2006) What about blogs? – The potential of a web-based activity for foreign language learning. Unpublished Masters Thesis, Monash University, Melbourne.

Ioannou-Georgiou, S. (1999) *Synchronous Computer Mediated Communication CALL & the Learning Community* (pp. 195–208). Exeter: Elm Bank Publications.

Issacs, E., Walendowski, A., Whittaker, S., Schiano, D.J. and Kamm, C. (2002) The character, functions and styles of instant messaging in the workplace. Paper presented at the CSCW'02, 16–20 November, New Orleans, LA, USA.

Itakura, H. and Nakajima, S. (2001) IT時代における日本語教育：香港・鹿児島間の電子メール双方向型プロジェクトワークの試み [Teaching Japanese education for the era of IT: Research findings from an e-mail project between Hong-Kong and Kagoshima]. 世界の日本語教育 *[Current Report on Japanese-Language Education Around the Globe]* 6, 227–240.

Jacobs, G.E. (2004) Complicating contexts: Issues of methodology in researching the language and literacies of instant messaging. *Reading Research Quarterly* 39 (4), 394–406.

Jepson, K. (2005) Conversations – and negotiated interaction – in text and voice chat rooms. *Language, Learning and Technology* 9 (3), 79–98.

Johnson, M.E. and Brine, J.W. (1999) Design and development of CALL courses in Japan. *CALICO Journal* 17 (2), 251–268.

Jones, R., Lou, J., Yeung, L., Leung, V., Lai, I., Man, C. and Woo, B. (2001) Beyond the screen: A participatory study of computer mediated communication among Hong Kong youth. Paper presented at the Annual Meeting of the American Anthropological Association, Washington.

Jones, S., Millermaier, S., Goya-Martinez, M. and Schuler, J. (2008) Whose space is MySpace? A content analysis of MySpace profiles. *First Monday*. Online at http://www.uic.edu/htbin/cgiwrap/bin/ojs/index.php/fm/article/viewArticle/2202/2024

Kano, Y. (2004) 二双方向ビデオ会議システムとインターネットフォーラムを利用した従来のクラスを超えた日本語コース：日本人大学生との交流の友効 (友好) 利用 [Going beyond the classroom with videoconferencing and internet discussion forum: Effective use of peer editing from Japanese college students]. 世界の日本語教育 *[Current Report on Japanese-Language Education Around the Globe]* 7 (3月), 239–256.

Katsuno, H. and Yano, C. (2007) *Kaomoji* and expressivity in a Japanese housewives' chat room. In B. Danet and S.C. Herring (eds) *The Multilingual Internet: Language, Culture, and Communication Online* (pp. 278–300). Oxford: Oxford University Press.

Kawaura, Y. (2001) iモード的ケータイの意味 [The meaning of i-mode cell phones]. 日本語学 *[Japanese Linguistics]* 20 (9), 72–81.

Kelle, U. (2004) Computer-assisted qualitative data analysis. In C. Seale, G. Gobo, J.F. Gubrium and D. Silverman (eds) *Qualitative Research Practice* (pp. 473–489). London: Sage.

Kennedy, G.E., Judd, T.S., Churchward, A. and Gray, K. (2008) First year students' experiences with technology: Are they really digital natives? *Australasian Journal of Educational Technology* 24 (1), 108–122.

Kern, R.G. (1995) Restructuring classroom interaction with networked computers: Effects on quantity and characteristics of language production. *The Modern Language Journal* 79 (iv), 457–476.

Kimura, T. (2001) インターネットとiモード系携帯電話の狭間 —PACS (ポスト高度消費社会) としての情報ネットワーク社会へ—[The edge of internet and i-mode cell phones – Towards a PACS information network society]. 日本語学 *[Japanese Linguistics]* 20 (9), 54–71.

Kitade, K. (2000) L2 learners' discourse and SLA theories in CMC: Collaborative interaction in internet chat. *Computer Assisted Language Learning* 13 (2), 143–166.

Knobel, M. and Lankshear, C. (2004) Planning pedagogy for i-mode: From flogging to blogging via wi-fi. *English in Australia* 139, 78–102.

Ko, K.-K. (1996) Structural characteristics of computer-mediated language: A comparative analysis of InterChange discourse. *The Electronic Journal of Communication/La Revue Electronique de Communication* 6 (3). Online at http://www.cios.org/EJCPUBLIC/006/3/006315.html

Kock, N. (2008) E-collaboration and e-commerce in virtual worlds: The potential of Second Life and World of Warcraft. *International Journal of e-Collaboration* 4 (3), 1–13.

Köszegi, S., Vetschera, R. and Kersten, G.E. (2004) National cultural differences in the use and perception of internet-based NSS – Does high or low context matter? *International Negotiation* 9, 79–109.

Kötter, M. (2003) Negotiation of meaning and codeswitching in online tandems. *Language Learning & Technology* 7 (2), 145–172.

Kouper, I. (2010) The pragmatics of peer advice in a LiveJournal community. *Language@ Internet* 7, Article 1. Online at http://www.languageatinternet.de

Koyama, S. (2007) *J Bridge*. Tokyo: Bonjinsha.

Krashen, S.D. (1982) *Principles and Practice in Second Language Acquisition*. Oxford: Pergamon.

Kraut, R., Mukhopadhyay, T., Szczypula, J., Kiesler, S. and Scherlis, B. (1999) Information and communication: Alternative uses of the internet in households. *Information System Research* 10, 287–303.

Kurata, N. (2008) Opportunities for second language learning and use in foreign language learners' social networks. Unpublished PhD, Monash University, Melbourne.

Labov, W. (1997) Some further steps in narrative analysis. *The Journal of Narrative and Life History* 7, 395–415.

Lam, W.S.E. (2000) L2 literacy and the design of the self: A case study of a teenager writing on the internet. *TESOL Quarterly* 34 (3), 457–482.

Lam, W.S.E. (2004) Second language socialization in a bilingual chat room: Global and local considerations. *Language, Learning and Technology* 8 (3), 44–66.

Lam, W.S.E. (2006) Re-envisioning language, literacy, and the immigrant subject in new mediascapes. *Pedagogies: An International Journal* 1 (3), 171–195.

Lampe, C., Ellison, N.B. and Steinfield, C. (2006) A Face(book) in the crowd: Social searching vs. social browsing. Paper presented at the CSCW-2006, 4–8 November, New York.

Lantz, A. (2001) Meetings in a distributed group of experts: Comparing face-to-face, chat, and collaborative virtual environments. *Behaviour and Information Technology* 20 (2), 111–117.

Larson, P. (2003) Rethinking Japanese language pedagogy. *ADFL Bulletin* 34 (3), 18–20.

Lave, J. and Wenger, E. (1991) *Situated Learning: Legitimate Peripheral Participation*. Cambridge: Cambridge University Press.

Layder, D. (1993) *New Strategies in Social Research*. Cambridge: Polity Press.

Layder, D. (1997) *Modern Social Theory: Key Debates and New Directions*. London: UCL Press.

Leander, K.M. and McKim, K.K. (2003) Tracing the everyday 'sitings' of adolescents on the internet: A strategic adaptation of ethnography across online and offline spaces. *Education, Communication & Information* 3 (2), 211–240.

Lee, K.M. (2007) Linguistic features of email and ICQ instant messaging in Hong Kong. In B. Danet and S.C. Herring (eds) *The Multilingual Internet: Language, Culture, and Communication Online* (pp. 184–208). New York: Oxford University Press.

Lee, W.-N. and Choi, S.M. (2005) The role of horizontal and vertical individualism and collectivism in online consumers' response toward persuasive communication on the web. *Journal of Computer-Mediated Communication* 11 (1), Article 15. Online at http://jcmc.indiana.edu/vol11/issue1/wnlee.html

Leung, L. (2005) *Virtual Ethnicity: Race, Resistance and the Worldwide Web*. Aldershot: Ashgate.

Levy, M. and Stockwell, G. (2006) *CALL Dimensions: Options and Issues in Computer Assisted Language Learning*. Mahwah, NJ: Lawrence Erlbaum Associates.

Li, T. (2006) 日本語教育を活かすためのリソース・リテラシー[Resource literacy to take advantage of Japanese education]. 海外研修事業編 *[Overseas Studies Project Compilation]* 11. Online at http://hdl.handle.net/10083/720

Liddicoat, A. (1997) Interaction, social structure, and second language use: A response to Firth and Wagner. *The Modern Language Journal* 81 (iii), 313–317.

Liddicoat, A. (2004) The projectability of turn constructional units and the role of prediction in listening. *Discourse Studies* 6 (4), 449–469.

Liddicoat, A. (2007) *An Introduction to Conversation Analysis*. London: Continuum.

Liebscher, G. and Dailey-O'Cain, J. (2005) Learner code-switching in the content-based foreign language classroom. *The Modern Language Journal* 89 (ii), 234–247.

Linker, M. (2001) Epistemic relativism and socially responsible realism: Why Sokal is not an ally in the science wars. *Social Epistemology* 15 (1), 59–70.

Lofland, J., Snow, D., Anderson, L. and Lofland, L.H. (2006) *Analysing Social Settings: A Guide to Qualitative Observation and Analysis*. Toronto: Thomson.

Long, M.H. (1983) Native speaker/non-native speaker conversation and the negotiation of comprehensible input. *Applied Linguistics* 4, 126–141.

Long, M.H. (1996) The role of the linguistic environment in second language acquisition. In W. Ritchie and T. Bhatia (eds) *Handbook of Second Language Acquisition* (pp. 413–468). New York: Academic Press.

Long, M.H. (2007) *Problems in SLA*. Mahwah, NJ: Erlbaum.

Mackey, A. (1999) Input, interaction and second language development: An empirical study of question formation in ESL. *Studies in Second Language Acquisition* 21, 557–587.

Mackey, A., Gass, S.M. and McDonough, K. (2000) How do learners perceive interactional feedback. *Studies in Second Language Acquisition* 22, 471–497.

Mann, C. and Steward, F. (2000) *Internet Communication and Qualitative Research: A Handbook for Researching Online*. Thousand Oaks, CA: Sage Publications.

Mar, J. (2000) Online ontime: The language of internet relay chat. In D. Gibbs and K.L. Krause (eds) *Cyberlines: Languages and Cultures of the Internet* (pp. 151–167). Albert Park: James Nicholas Publishers.

Marriott, H. (2003) Peer editing in academic contact situations. In S. Miyazaki and H. Marriott (eds) 接触場面と日本語教育：ネウストプニーのインパクト *[Contact Situations and Japanese Language Education: Neustupny's Impact]* (pp. 113–141). Tokyo: Meiji Shoin.

Mason, B. (1999) Issues in virtual ethnography in ethnographic studies in real and virtual environments. Paper presented at the Ethnographic Studies in Real and Virtual Environments: Inhabited Information Spaces and Connected Communities Conference. Proceedings of Esprit i3 Workshop on Ethnographic Studies, 24–26 January, Edinburgh: Queen Margaret College.

Matsumoto-Sturt, Y. (2003) 日本語学習者によるワープロの誤用漢字は「同音漢字の誤変換」なのか—非漢字圏日本語学習者の誤用表記分析 [Analysis of orthographic errors in Japanese word processing by English learners of Japanese: Are they all 'homophone' kanji errors?]. 日本語教育 *[Journal of Japanese Language Teaching]* 118, 17–16.

Matsumura, S. and Hann, G. (2004) Computer anxiety and students' preferred feedback methods in EFL writing. *The Modern Language Journal* 88 (3), 403–415.

McCarthy, M. (1991) *Discourse Analysis for Language Teachers*. Cambridge: Cambridge University Press.

McDonough, K. and Mackey, A. (2006) Responses to recasts: Repetitions, primed production, and linguistic development. *Language Learning* 56, 693–720.

McVeigh, B. (2003) Individualization, individuality, interiority and the internet: Japanese university students and email. In N. Gottlieb (ed.) *Japanese Cybercultures* (pp. 19–33). London: Routledge.

Mehnert, U. (1998) The effects of different lengths of time for planning on second language performance. *Studies in Second Language Acquisition* 20, 52–83.

Miles, M.B. and Huberman, A.M. (1994) *Qualitative Data Analysis: An Expanded Sourcebook*. Thousand Oaks, CA: Sage.

Miller, D. and Slater, D. (2000) *The Internet: An Ethnographic Approach*. Oxford: Berg.

Miyake, K. (2001) ポケベルからケイタイ・メールへ―歴史的変遷とその必然性 [From pager to cell phone – Historical transition and necessity]. 日本語学 *[Japanese Linguistics]* 20 (9), 6–21.

Morris, M., Nadler, J., Kurtzberg, T. and Thompson, L. (2002) Schmooze or lose: Social friction and lubrication in email negotiations. *Group Dynamics* 6 (1), 89–100.

Murase, T. and Inoue, K. (2003) 携帯電話のメール利用とその効果　～男女差の検討～ [Effects of e-mail communciation with mobile phone – From male and female perspectives]. 横浜国立大学大学院教育研究科教育相談・支援総合センター紀要 *[Yokohama National University Graduate School of Education Studies Educational Consultation/Support Centre Bulletin]* 3, 97–119.

Murray, D.E. (1991) The composing process for computer conversation. *Written Communication* 8 (1), 35–55.

Murray, D.E. (2000) Protean communication: The language of computer-mediated communication. *TESOL Quarterly* 34 (3), 397–421.

Murray, D.E. (2005) Technologies for second language literacy. *Annual Review of Applied Linguistics* 25, 188–201.

Neuage, T. (2004) Conversation analysis of chatroom talk. Unpublished PhD thesis, University of South Australia, Adelaide.

Neustupný, J.V. (1990) The follow-up interview. *Japanese Studies Association of Australia* 10 (2), 31–33.

Neustupný, J.V. (2002) データはどう集めるか [How do you collect data?]. In J.V. Neustupný and S. Miyazaki (eds) 言語研究の方法 *[Techniques for Language Research]* (Vol. 15–34) (pp. 15–33). Tōkyō: Kuroshio Shuppan.

Neustupný, J.V. and Miyazaki, S. (2002) 言語研究の方法 *[Techniques for Language Research]*. Tōkyō: Kuroshio Shuppan.

Newmeyer, F.J. (2002) Uniformitarian assumptions and language evolution research. In A. Wray (ed.) *The Transition to Language* (pp. 359–375). Oxford: Oxford University Press.

Nguyen, H.T. and Kellogg, G. (2005) Emergent identities in on-line discussions for second language learning. *The Canadian Modern Language Review/La Revue canadienne des langues vivantes* 62 (1), 111–136.

Nishimura, M. (1992) Language choice and in-group identity among Canadian Niseis. *Journal of Asian Pacific Communication* 3 (2), 97–113.

Nishimura, M. (1997) *Japanese/English Code-switching: Syntax and Pragmatics*. New York: Peter Lang Publishing.

Nishimura, Y. (2007) Linguistic innovations and interactional features in Japanese BBS communication. In B. Danet and S.C. Herring (eds) *The Multilingual Internet: Language, Culture and Communication* (pp. 163–183). Oxford: Oxford University Press.

Nojima, H. (1996) 電子メディア時代の人間関係 [Human relations in the age of electronic media]. 日本語学 *[Japanese Linguistics]* 15 (特集　電子社会のコミュニケーション) (Special Issue Electronic Society Communication), 57–66.

Nojima, H. (2001) 携帯端末としての次世代携帯電話 [Next-generation mobile phones and handheld units]. 日本語学 *[Japanese Linguistics]* 20 (9), 82–91.

Nonnecke, B. and Preece, J. (2000) *Lurker Demographics: Counting the Silent. Paper Presented at the CHI 2000.* The Hague: ACM.

Nonnecke, B. and Preece, J. (2003) Silent participants: Getting to know lurkers better. In D. Fisher and C. Lueg (eds) *From Usenet to Co Webs: Interacting with Social Information Spaces* (pp. 110–132). London: Springer.

Norrick, N. (1991) On the organization of corrective exchanges in conversation. *Journal of Pragmatics* 16 (1), 59–83.

Nowak, K.L. and Rauh, C. (2005) The influence of the avatar on online perceptions of anthropomorphism, androgyny, credibility, homophily, and attraction. *Journal of Computer-mediated Communication* 11 (1), Article 8.

Nunan, D. (1992) *Research Methods in Language Learning.* Cambridge: Cambridge University Press.

O'Dowd, R. (2003) Understanding the 'other side': Intercultural learning in a Spanish–English e-mail exchange. *Language Learning & Technology* 7 (2), 118–144.

O'Dowd, R. (2007) Evaluating the outcomes of online intercultural exchange. *ELT Journal* 61 (2), 144–152.

O'Neil, J. and Martin, D. (2003) Text chat in action. Paper presented at the GROUP'03, 9–12 November, Sanibel Island, FL, USA.

O'Rourke, B. (2008) The other C in CMC: What alternative data sources can tell us about text-based synchronous computer mediated communication and language learning. *Computer Assisted Language Learning* 21 (3), 227–251.

Ogino, T. (1996) 電子メールの光と影 [The light and shadows of electronic mail]. 日本語学 *[Japanese Linguistics]* 15 (特集　電子社会のコミュニケーション) [(Special Issue Electronic Society Communication)], 4–11.

Ohm, U. (2007) What role do digital media play in autonomous learning? Reflections on moral philosophy and education, with special reference to the educational value of digital media. *Electronic Journal of Foreign Language Teaching* 4 (1), 140–148.

Okamoto, N. (1998) しゃべる--チャットのコミュニケーション空間(インターネット社会) [Speaking – The communication space of chat (internet society)]. 現代のエスプリ *[Modern Esprit]* 370, 127–137.

Oliver, B. (2005) Australian university students' use of and attitudes towards mobile learning technologies. Paper presented at the IADIS International Conference: Mobile Learning 2005, 28–30 June, Qawra, Malta.

Oliver, B. and Goerke, V. (2007) Australian undergraduates' use and ownership of emerging technologies: Implications and opportunities for creating engaging learning experiences for the net generation. *Australasian Journal of Educational Technology* 23 (2), 171–186.

Ong, W.J. (1982) *Orality and Literacy: The Technologizing of the World.* London: Methuen.

Onishi, N. (2008) Mobile phone novels ring up big sales, but critics fear for Japanese literature. *The Age*, 23 January.

Orita, A. (1999) インターネット上の自己表現とエンパワーメント：「名も無き個人」のつながりと事例分析 [Self-expression and empowerment on the internet: Relationships and case studies of 'individuals without names']. Unpublished Masters Thesis, Keiō University, Tōkyō.

Orlikowski, W.J. and Yates, J. (1994) Genre repertoire: The structuring of communicative practices in organizations. *Administrative Science Quarterly* 39, 541–547.

Ōta, I. (2001) パソコン・メールとケイタイ・メール―「メールの型」からの分析― [PC mail and cell phone mail – Analysis from 'type of mail'). 日本語学 *[Japanese Linguistics]* 20 (9), 44–53.

Ōtawa, N. (2007) 第V部　ニューメディアと若者（2）　―インターネットのコミュニケーション空間　解説 [Chapter V new media and young people (2) – Communication space on the internet commentary]. In A. Kitada and N. Ōtawa (eds) 子どもとニューメディア *[Children and New Media]* (pp. 329–332). Tokyo: Tokyo Tosho Center.

Paolillo, J.C. (1996) Language choice on Soc.Culture.Punjab. *The Electronic Journal of Communication/La Revue Electronique de Communication* 6 (3). Online at http://www.cios.org/EJCPUBLIC/006/3/006312.html

Pasfield-Neofitou, S.E. (2006) Intercultural internet chat between learners of Japanese and English in informal contexts. Unpublished Honours Thesis, Monash University, Melbourne.

Pasfield-Neofitou, S.E. (2007a) Intercultural internet chat and language learning: A sociocultural theory perspective. *Learning and Sociocultural Theory: Exploring Modern Vygotskian Perspectives* 1 (1), 145–162.

Pasfield-Neofitou, S.E. (2007b) Intercultural Japanese–English internet chat and resources for language learning [異文化間の日英チャットと言語学習資源]. Paper presented at the CASTEL-J, 3–5 August, Hawaii.

Pasfield-Neofitou, S.E. (2007c). Japanese–English chat interactions: Language use in internet chat [日英チャットでの相互作用：インターネットチャットにおける言語使用]. Paper presented at the CASTEL-J, 3–5 August, Hawaii.

Pasfield-Neofitou, S.E. (2007d) Textual features of intercultural internet chat between learners of Japanese and English. *CALL-EJ Online* 9 (1). Online at http://www.tell.is.ritsumei.ac.jp/calleonline/journal/9-1/pasfield-neofitou.html

Pasfield-Neofitou, S.E. (2008) Creative applications of social networking for the language learning class. *The International Journal of Learning* 14 (12), 235–240.

Pasfield-Neofitou, S.E. (2009a) Learners' Participation in Informal Japanese–English internet chat. *New Voices* 3, 43–63.

Pasfield-Neofitou, S.E. (2009b) Paper, electronic, or online? Different dictionaries for different activities. *Babel* 43 (2), 12–18.

Pasfield-Neofitou, S.E. (2011) Second language learners' experiences of virtual community and foreignness. *Language Learning & Technology* 15 (2), 92–198.

Pasfield-Neofitou, S.E., Morofushi, M. and Spence-Brown, R. (2009) 実社会への架け橋：初級者に対するSNSを利用した日本語教育 [A bridge to the real world: Japanese language education using an SNS for beginner students]. In C. Thompson-Kinoshita (ed.) 学習者主体の日本語教育：オーストラリアの実践研究 *[New Pedagogies for Learner Agency: Japanese Language Education Research and Practice in Australia]* (pp. 143–160). Tokyo: CoCo Publishing.

Pawson, R. (1989) *A Measure for Measures: A Manifesto for Empirical Sociology.* London: Routledge.

Pe'na, J. and Hancock, J. (2006) An analysis of socioemotional and task communication in online multiplayer video games. *Communication Research* 33 (1), 92–109.

Potter, J. (2000) Responses to Carter and Sealey: Realism and sociolinguistics. *Journal of Sociolinguistics* 4 (1), 21–24.

Prensky, M. (2001) Digital natives, digital immigrants. *On the Horizon* 9 (5), 1–2.

Rampton, B. (1997) *Crossing: Language and Ethnicity among Adolescents.* Harlow: Longman.

Richards, L. (2005) *Handling Qualitative Data: A Practical Guide.* London: Sage Publications.

Ridings, C., Gefen, D. and Arinze, B. (2006) Psychological barriers: Lurker and poster motivation and behavior in online communities. *Communications of the Association for Information Systems* 18, Article 16.

Romiszowski, A. and Mason, R. (2004) Computer-mediated communication. In D.H. Jonassen (ed.) *Handbook of Research on Educational Communications and Technology* (2nd edn, pp. 397–432). Mahwah, NJ: Lawrence Erlbaum Associates.

Sachs, R. and Suh, B-R. (2007) Textually enhanced recasts, learner awareness, and L2 outcomes in synchronous computer-mediated interaction. In A. Mackey (ed.) *Conversational Interaction in Second Language Acquisition: A Collection of Empirical Studies* (pp. 72–93). Oxford: Oxford University Press.

Sacks, H., Schegloff, E.A. and Jefferson, G. (1974) A simplest systematics for the organization of turn-taking for conversation. *Language* 50 (4, Part 1), 696–735.

Sawa, K. (2000) Mobile phones silence chatty students. *Mainichi Daily News*, 22 October, 12.

Schegloff, E.A. (1992) Repair after next turn: The last structurally provided defense of intersubjectivity in conversation. *American Journal of Sociology* 97, 1295–1345.

Schegloff, E.A. (1997) Whose text? Whose context? *Discourse and Society* 8, 165–187.

Schegloff, E.A. (2000) When 'others' initiate repair. *Applied Linguistics* 21 (2), 205–243.

Schegloff, E.A., Jefferson, G. and Sacks, H. (1977) The preference for self correction in the organization of repair in conversation. *Language* 53, 361–382.

Schegloff, E.A., Koshik, I., Jacoby, S. and Olsher, D. (2002) Conversation analysis and applied linguistics. *Annual Review of Applied Linguistics* 22, 3–31.

Schegloff, E.A. and Sacks, H. (1973) Opening up closings. *Semiotica* 8, 289–327.

Schwienhorst, K. (2002) Evaluating tandem language learning in the MOO: Discourse repair strategies in a bilingual internet project. *Computer Assisted Language Learning* 15 (2), 135–145.

Sealey, A. (2007) Linguistic ethnography in realist perspective. *Journal of Sociolinguistics* 11 (5), 641–660.

Sealey, A. and Carter, B. (2001) Social categories and sociolinguistics: Applying a realist approach. *International Journal of the Sociology of Language* 152, 1–19.

Sealey, A. and Carter, B. (2004) *Applied Linguistics as a Social Science*. London: Continuum.

Seedhouse, P. (2005) Conversation analysis as research methodology. In K. Richards and P. Seedhouse (eds) *Applying Conversation Analysis* (pp. 251–266). New York: Palgrave Macmillan.

Selfe, C. and Meyer, P.R. (1991) Testing claims for on-line conferences. *Written Communication* 8 (2), 163–192.

Seliger, H.W. (1983) The language learner as linguist: Of metaphors and realities. *Applied Linguistics* 4, 179–191.

Sfard, A. (1998) On two metaphors for learning and the dangers of choosing just one. *Educational Researchers* 27, 4–13.

Shekary, M. and Tahririan, M.H. (2006) Negotiation of meaning and noticing in text-based online chat. *The Modern Language Journal* 90 (iv), 557–573.

Shibanai, Y. (2007) 私論と輿論の変換装置 －「ネット世論」の行方 [The transformation of personal opinion and public opinion – The future of 'mainstream opinion on the net']. In A. Kitada and N. Ōtawa (eds) 子どもとニューメディア [*Children and New Media*] (pp. 346–363). Tokyo: Tokyo Tosho Center.

Skehan, P. and Foster, P. (2005) Strategic and on-line planning: The influence of surprise information and task time on second language performance. In R. Ellis (ed.) *Planning and Task Performance in a Second Language* (pp. 193–261). Amsterdam: John Benjamins.

Smith, B. (2003) Computer-mediated negotiated interaction: An expanded model. *The Modern Language Journal* 87 (1), 38–57.

Smith, B. (2004) Computer-mediated negotiated interaction and lexical acquisition. *Studies in Second Language Acquisition* 26, 365–398.

Smith, B. (2008) Methodological hurdles in capturing CMC data: The case of the missing self-repair. *Language Learning & Technology* 12 (1), 85–103.

Steiner, P. (1993) On the internet, nobody knows you're a dog. *The New Yorker* 69 (LXIX) (20), 5 July, 61.

STEP. (2011) Level comparison, accessed 12 June 2011. http://stepeiken.org/grade_2

Stockwell, G. (2003) Effects of topic threads on sustainability of email interactions between native speakers and nonnative speakers. *ReCALL* 15 (1), 37–50.

Stockwell, G. (2004) Communication breakdown in asynchronous computer-mediated communication (CMC). *Australian Language & Literacy Matters* 1 (3), 7–10.

Stockwell, G. and Harrington, M.W. (2003) The incidental development of L2 proficiency in NS–NNS email interactions. *CALICO Journal* 20 (2), 337–259.

Stockwell, G. and Levy, M. (2001) Sustainability of e-mail interactions between native speakers and nonnative speakers. *Computer Assisted Language Learning* 14 (5), 419–442.

Stockwell, G. and Stockwell, E.S. (2003) Using email for enhanced cultural awareness. *Australian Language Matters* 11 (1), 3–4.

Stone, B. (2007) Facebook expands into MySpace's territory. *The New York Times*, 25 May. Online at http://www.nytimes.com/2007/05/25/technology/25social.html?_r=1

Strong, G. (2007) Has txt kild the ritn word? *The Age*, 2 October.

Sugimoto, T. and Levin, J.A. (2000) Multiple literacies and multimedia: A comparison of Japanese and American uses of the internet. In G.E. Hawisher and C.L. Selfe (eds) *Global Literacies and the World-Wide Web* (pp. 133–156). New York: Routledge.

Sullivan, M. (2007) Is Facebook the new MySpace? *PCWorld*. Online at http://www.pcworld.com/article/134635/is_facebook_the_new_myspace.html

Sundén, J. (2003) *Material Virtualities: Approaching Online Textual Embodiment*. New York: Peter Lang.

Swain, M. (1985) Communicative competence: Some roles of comprehensible input and comprehensible output in its development. In S.M. Gass and C.M. Madden (eds) *Input in Second Language Acquisition* (pp. 235–253). Rowley: Newbury House.

Swain, M. (2000) The output hypothesis and beyond: Mediating acquisition through collaborative dialogue. In J. Lantolf (ed.) *Sociocultural Perspectives on Second Language Learning* (pp. 97–114). Oxford: Oxford University Press.

Swain, M. (2006) Languaging, agency, and collaboration in advanced second language proficiency. In H. Byrnes (ed.) *Advanced Language Learning: The Contribution of Halliday and Vygotsky* (pp. 95–108). London: Continuum.

Takahashi, E. (2007) 佐世保事件におけるマスメディア報道とインターネット 一間メディア性から立ち現れるマスメディア [Reporting of the Sasebo incident in the mass media and internet – Mass media emerging from intermediality]. In A. Kitada and N. Ōtawa (eds) 子どもとニューメディア [*Children and New Media*] (pp. 333–345). Tokyo: Tokyo Tosho Center.

Takahashi, T. (2008) Mobile phones and social networking sites. Paper presented at the Media, Communication and Humanity 2008 Media@lse Fifth Anniversary Conference, 21–23 September, London.

Tanaka, Y. (2001) 大学生のケイタイメイル・コミュニケーション [University students' cell phone mail/communication]. 日本語学 [*Japanese Linguistics*] 20 (9), 32–43.

Tannen, D., Schiffrin, D. and Hamilton, H. (eds) (2003) *The Handbook of Discourse Analysis*. Oxford: Blackwell Publishing.

Tavakoli, P. and Skehan, P. (2005) Strategic planning, task structure, and performance testing. In R. Ellis (ed.) *Planning and Task-performance in a Second Language* (pp. 239–277). Amsterdam: John Benjamins.

Taylor, P. (1992) Social epistemic rhetoric and social discourse. In G. Hawisher and P. LeBlanc (eds) *Re-imagining Computers and Composition* (pp. 131–148). Portsmouth: Boynton/Cook.

Tella, S. (1992) *Talking Shop via E-mail: A Thematic and Linguistic Analysis of Electronic Mail Communication*. Helsinki: University of Helsinki.

Thorne, S.L. (1999) An activity theoretical analysis of foreign language electronic discourse. Unpublished PhD Thesis, University of California, Berkeley.

Thorne, S.L. (2000) Beyond bounded activity systems: Heterogeneous cultures in instructional uses of persistent conversation. Paper presented at the proceedings of the Thirty-Third Hawaii International Conference on Systems Science, 7–10 January.

Thorne, S.L. (2003) Artifacts and cultures-of-use in intercultural communication. *Language, Learning and Technology* 7 (2), 38–67.

Thorne, S.L. (2008) Transcultural communication in open internet environments and massively multiplayer online games. In S.S. Magnan (ed.) *Mediating Discourse Online* (pp. 305–327). Amsterdam: Benjamins.

Thorne, S.L., Black, R.W. and Sykes, J.M. (2009) Second language use, socialization, and learning in internet interest communities and online gaming. *The Modern Language Journal* 93, 802–821.

Tohsaku, Y.-H. (2006) *Yookoso!: Continuing with Contemporary Japanese: Media Edition* (3rd edn). New York: McGraw-Hill.

Tokaji, A. (1997) コンピュータ上でのコミュニケーションにみられる情緒表現に関する研究 ―情緒表出記号の使用方法について― [A study of emotional expressions in computer-mediated communication – The way of using emotion expressive marks –]. 広島県立大学紀要 *[The Bulletin of Hiroshima Prefectural University]* 8 (2), 125–139.

Torii-Williams, E. (2004) Incorporating the use of e-mail into a Japanese language program. 世界の日本語教育 *[Current Report on Japanese-Language Education Around the Globe]* 7 (3月), 227–237.

Toshima, N. (1998) 演じる--オンラインゲームの中の私（インターネット社会) [Performing – Me in online games (internet society)]. 現代のエスプリ *[Modern Esprit]* 370, 177–187.

Toyoda, E. and Harrison, R. (2002) Categorization of text chat communication between learners and native speakers of Japanese. *Language Learning & Technology* 6 (1), 82–99.

Tudini, V. (2003) Using native speakers in chat. *Language, Learning and Technology* 7 (3), 141–163.

Tudini, V. (2007) Negotiation and intercultural learning in Italian native speaker chat rooms. *The Modern Language Journal* 91 (iv), 577–601.

Turkle, S. (1995) *Life on the Screen: Identity in the Age of the Internet*. New York: Longman.

Underwood, J. (1987) Correo: Electronic mail as communicative practice. *Hispania* 70, 413–414.

Utz, S. (2010) Show me your friends and I will tell you what type of person you are: How one's profile, number of friends, and type of friends influence impression formation on social network sites. *Journal of Computer-Mediated Communication* 15, 314–335.

van Lier, L. (1996) *Interaction in the Language Curriculum: Awareness, Autonomy, & Authenticity*. New York: Longman.

VEC. (2011) TOEFL equivalency table, accessed 12 June 2011. http://secure.vec.bc.ca/toefl-equivalency-table.cfm

Walther, J.B., Van Der Heide, B., Kim, S-Y., Westerman, D. and Tong, S.T. (2008) The role of friends' appearance and behaviour on evaluations of individuals on Facebook: Are we known by the company we keep? *Human Communication Research* 34, 28–49.

Warschauer, M. and Kern, R. (eds) (2000) *Network-based Language Teaching: Concepts and Practice*. Cambridge: Cambridge University Press.

Weininger, M.J. and Shield, L. (2004) Promoting oral production in a written channel: An investigation of learner language in MOO. *Computer Assisted Language Learning* 16 (4), 329–349.

Wendel, J. (1997) *Planning and Second Language Narrative Production.* Tokyo: Temple University.

Werry, C. (1996) Linguistic and interactional features of internet relay chat. In S. Herring (ed.) *Computer-mediated Communication: Linguistic, Social and Cross-cultural Perspectives* (pp. 47–64). Philadelphia, PA: John Benjamins Publishing Company.

Yates, S. (1996) Oral and written aspects of computer conferencing. In S. Herring (ed.) *Computer-mediated Communication: Linguistic, Social and Cross-cultural Perspectives* (pp. 29–46). Philadelphia, PA: John Benjamins Publishing Company.

Yates, S. and Graddol, D. (1996) 'I read this chat is heavy': The discursive construction of identity in CMC. Paper presented at the 5th International Pragmatics Conference, 8 July, Mexico City.

Yonally, D. and Gilfert, S. (1995) Electronic dictionaries in the classroom? Bah, humbug! *The Internet TESL Journal* 1. Online at http://iteslj.org/Articles/Yonally-ElecDict.html

Yoshinari, Y. (1998) 英語教育リソースとしてのインターネット [The internet as an English educational resource]. 獨協大学外国語教育研究 *[Dokkyo University Studies in Foreign Language Teaching]* 17, 305–310.

Yuan, B. and Ellis, R. (2003) The effects of pre-task and on-line planning on fluency, complexity and accuracy in L2 monologic oral production. *Applied Linguistics* 24 (1), 1–27.

Index

For Product Safety Concerns and Information please contact our EU Authorised Representative:

Easy Access System Europe

Mustamäe tee 50

10621 Tallinn

Estonia

gpsr.requests@easproject.com

www.ingramcontent.com/pod-product-compliance
Lightning Source LLC
LaVergne TN
LVHW022306060326
832902LV00020B/3312